Gene — hope that the years
are kind to you + that you enjoy
adding this book to your hobby
library — — —

R. J. Goodet

Catalogue of
GERMAN COINS

Gold, silver and minor coins since 1800
with their valuations

By P. ARNOLD, D. STEINHILBER and H. KUTHMANN

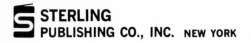
STERLING
PUBLISHING CO., INC.   **NEW YORK**

Oak Tree Press Co., Ltd.
London & Sydney

COIN AND STAMP BOOKS

Copyright © 1972
by PRESIDENT COIN CORP.
4 Warwick Place, Port Washington, N.Y. 11050
Based on "Grosser Deutscher Munzkatalog"
© 1970 by Ernst Battenberg Verlag, Munich, Germany
British edition published by Oak Tree Press Co., Ltd., Nassau, Bahamas
Distributed in Australia by Oak Tree Press Co., Ltd.,
P.O. Box 34, Brickfield Hill, Sydney 2000, N.S.W.
Distributed in the United Kingdom and elsewhere in the British Commonwealth
by Ward Lock Ltd., 116 Baker Street, London W 1
Manufactured in the United States of America
All rights reserved
Library of Congress Catalog Card No.: 72-126855
ISBN 0-8069-6028-0   UK 7061 2268 2
6029-9

CONTENTS

INTRODUCTION

This catalogue contains the coins of all the German states issued from 1800 through the present time. In addition to regular issues, it also records many essay and pattern pieces as well as all of the commemoratives. Emergency coins minted privately or by local communities have not been included. Originally published in a German language edition, this book has been especially designed to make it easy for the collector to locate the coin he is seeking. Every type and nearly every variety is pictured, all are described and valuations are given except for extremely rare coins. Brief historical notes provide background information on the coins and on the issuing states.

The listings are arranged alphabetically according to the names of the issuing states. Within each state the coins are divided according to the reigns of the various rulers. The highest denomination regular coins come first, followed in turn by the next lower denomination. The commemoratives follow in a separate section for each ruler. Each entry has been assigned a catalogue number which is the same in both the German and English language editions. The denomination is followed by an abbreviation which indicates the metallic content according to the following system:

Al (Aluminum)	B (Billon)	Br (Bronze)
Bra (Brass)	C (Copper)	G (Gold)
I (Iron)	N (Nickel)	Z (Zinc)

The inclusive dates of issue follow and in the case of an entry such as "1925-35," it does not necessarily mean that the coin exists with every intervening date. Such a listing does mean that the first and last date are known. The valuations quoted are for very fine to extremely fine specimens of the commonest date. As nearly every coin is clearly illustrated, the inscriptions are repeated in the description only when necessary to differentiate between varieties. When descriptions of coins are omitted, they may be assumed to belong to the last type previously described. The imperial eagle reverses common to the coins of all the issuing states are described as follows:

Type 1: 1871-1873;
Small eagle, date below, small inscription, denomination abbreviated M.

Type 2: 1874-1889:
Small eagle, date at right edge, larger inscription, denomination MARK.

Type 3: 1890-1915;
Large eagle and inscription, date at right, denomination MARK.

The authors of the individual sections are: Dr. Paul Arnold of Dresden—Anhalt, German Democratic Republic, Mecklenburg, Prussia, Reuss, Saxony, Schwarzburg and Stolberg; Dr. Harald Küthman of Munich—Baden, Brunswick, Hannover, Kniphausen, Lauenburg, Lippe, Nassau, Oldenburg, Schaumburg-Lippe, Schleswig-Holstein, Waldeck, Wallmoden and Westphalia; Dr. Dirk Steinhilber of Munich—Bavaria, Berg, Bremen, Danzig, Federal Republic of Germany, Frankfurt, Furstenberg, German Empire including occupation issues, Hamburg, Hesse, Hohenzollern, Isenburg, Leiningen, Lubeck, Prussian Ansbach-Bayreuth, Regensburg, Rheinbund, Saarland, Wurttemberg and Wurzburg. The valuations were provided by Günter Schön. The coats-of-arms were drawn by Dr. Ottfried Neubecker. The adaptation and translation of the text was done by the numismatic staff of Sterling Publishing Company who also wrote the introductory paragraphs. The photographic illustrations, which are all actual size, were mostly taken from plaster casts; in some instances, directly from the coins.

ANHALT

Capital: Dessau

The Anhalt principalities came into being in 1603 when the sons of Joachim Ernst divided their inheritance into five parts. Over the years the lines united, divided and died out. By 1806 when the Holy Roman Empire was abolished, only the duchies of Bernburg, Cothen and Dessau remained. The Cothen line became extinct in 1847 followed by Bernburg in 1863, thus leaving Anhalt a single entity under the Dessau rulers. The Duchy of Anhalt joined the German Empire in 1871 and endured until the abdication of Friedrich II in 1918.

Coins for Anhalt were struck in:
Bernburg
Berlin   Mintmark A (since 1834)

ANHALT-BERNBURG

ALEXIUS FRIEDRICH CHRISTIAN, 1796–1834

Born June 12, 1767, the son of Prince Friedrich Albrecht and his consort, Albertine of Holstein. Alexius was raised to the status of Duke on April 18, 1806. He died March 24, 1834.

1.   1 Ducat (G) 1825. Crowned bear on wall, EX AURO ANHALTINO—"From Anhalt (Harz Mountain) Gold." Rev. Value $450.00

2.   1 Taler (S) 1806, 09. Crowned draped arms. Rev. Value within laurel wreath   62.50

3. 1 Gulden (S) 1806, 08, 09. Crowned
    bear on wall. Rev. Value within
    laurel wreath   20.00

8. 4 Pfennige (C) 1831. As #7 but 4
    PFENNINGE   3.00

4. 1/24 Taler—1 groschen (B) 1822, 23, 27.
    Crowned bear on wall. Rev. Value,
    inscription reads H ANH   3.00

9. 1 Pfennig (C) 1807. Crowned AFC
    monogram. Rev. Value   1.50

5. 1/24 Taler—1 groschen (B) 1831. As #4
    but HZL ANHALT   4.50

10. 1 Pfennig (C) 1808. As #9 but SCHEIDE
    MUNTZ   1.50

6. 1/48 Taler (B) 1807. Crowned arms within
    crossed palms. Rev. Value   5.00

11. 1 Pfennig (C) 1822, 23, 27. As #9 but
    SCHEIDEMUNZE   3.00

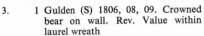

7. 4 Pfennige (C) 1822, 23. Crowned AFC
    monogram. Rev. Value reads 4
    PFENNIGE   2.50

12. 1 Pfennig (C) 1831. As #11 but HZL
    ANHALT   1.50

ALEXANDER CARL, 1834–63

Born March 2, 1805, the son of Duke Alexius Friedrich Christian and his consort, Friderike von Hessen-Kassel. Alexander died August 19, 1863. With his death the Bernburg line became extinct and the lands were united with Dessau.

16.   1 Mining taler (S) 1846, 52, 55. Rev. Crowned bear on wall, EIN THALER XIV EINE FEINE MARK. Edge: GOTT MIT UNS   30.00

13.   1 Double taler—3½ gulden (S) 1840, 45, 55. Head right. Rev. Crowned draped arms with order of Albrecht the Bear. Edge: GOTT MIT UNS—"God With Us"   375.00

17.   2 Mining taler (S) 1861, 62. As #16 but EIN THALER XXX EIN PFUND FEIN. Edge: GOTT SEGNE ANHALT   25.00

14.   1 Taler (S) 1859. Head left. Rev. Crowned arms supported by two bears, order of Albrecht the Bear. Edge: GOTT SEGNE ANHALT—"God Bless Anhalt"   18.50

18.   1/6 Taler (S) 1856. Crowned bear on wall. Rev. Value within laurel wreath and LXXXIV EINE FEINE MARK. Edge: GOTT MIT UNS   7.50

15.   1 Mining taler (S) 1834. Crowned draped arms. Rev. SEGEN DES ANHALT BERGBAUES—"Blessings of the Anhalt Mines." Edge: GOTT MIT UNS   22.50

19.   1/6 Taler (S) 1861, 62. As #18 but CLXXX EIN PFUND FEIN. Edge: GOTT SEGNE ANHALT   6.50

ANHALT-COTHEN

HEINRICH, 1830–47

Born July 30, 1778, the son of Prince Friedrich Erdmann von Cothen-Pless and his consort, Louise Ferdinande von Stolberg-Wernigerode. Heinrich died November 23, 1847. After his death the Cothen lands were united with Dessau.

20.   1 Double taler—3½ gulden (S) 1840. Head left. Rev. Crowned draped arms supported by two bears, order of Albrecht the Bear. Edge: GOTT SEGNE ANHALT   500.00

COMMON COINAGE OF THE LINES OF BERNBURG, COTHEN AND DESSAU

21.   2½ Silbergroschen—1/12 taler (B) 1856–62. Crowned arms. Rev. Value   4.00

22.   1 Groschen—1/24 taler (B) 1839, 40. Crowned arms. Rev. Value   3.00

23.   1 Silbergroschen—1/30 taler (B) 1851–62. Crowned arms. Rev. Value   2.50

24.   6 Pfennige—1/48 taler (B) 1840. Crowned arms. Rev. Value   2.00

25.   3 Pfennige—1/96 taler (C) 1839, 40. Crowned arms. Rev. Value   2.00

26.   3 Pfennige—1/120 taler (C) 1861. Crowned arms. Rev. Value   4.50

27.   1 Pfennig—1/288 taler (C) 1839, 40. Crowned arms. Rev. Value   2.50

28.   1 Pfennig—1/360 taler (C) 1856, 62. Crowned arms. Rev. Value   2.00

ANHALT-DESSAU

LEOPOLD FRIEDRICH, 1817–71

Born October 1, 1794, the son of Prince Friedrich and his consort, Amalie von Hessen-Homburg. Leopold died May 22, 1871.

32.   2½ Silbergroschen—1/12 taler (B) 1864. Crowned arms. Rev. Value   2.50

33.   3 Pfennige—1/120 taler (C) 1864, 67. Crowned arms. Rev. Value   1.50

34.   1 Pfennig—1/360 taler (C) 1864, 67. Crowned arms. Rev. Value   1.25

29.   1 Double taler—3½ gulden (S) 1839, 43, 46. Head left. Rev. Crowned draped arms supported by two bears, order of Albrecht the Bear. Edge: GOTT SEGNE ANHALT   225.00

COMMEMORATIVE ISSUE

30.   1 Taler (S) 1858, 66, 69. Head left. Rev. Crowned arms supported by two bears on ornamental ledge. Edge: GOTT SEGNE ANHALT   25.00

35.   1 Taler (S) 1863. Head left. Rev. Crowned arms within sprays, HERZOGTHUM. Edge: GOTT SEGNE ANHALT   35.00

Commemorates the separation of the Anhalt duchies in 1603 and their reunion in 1863.

31.   1/6 Taler (S) 1865. Head left. Rev. Crowned arms. Edge: GOTT SEGNE ANHALT   5.50

FRIEDRICH I, 1871–1904

Born April 29, 1831, the son of Duke Leopold
Friedrich and his consort, Friederike von Preussen.
Friedrich died January 24, 1904.

36. 20 Mark (G) 1875. Head right with
curly hair, v. ANHALT. Rev. Type 1
eagle. Edge: GOTT MIT UNS   150.00

37. 20 Mark (G) 1896, 1901. Head right
without curls, title VON ANHALT. Rev.
Type 3 eagle. Edge: GOTT MIT UNS   150.00

38. 10 Mark (G) 1896, 1901. Type of #37
but stars and tendrils on edge   200.00

39. 5 Mark (S) 1896. Type of #37 with
edge inscription   475.00

40. 2 Mark (S) 1876. Type of #36 but
reeded edge   225.00

41. 2 Mark (S) 1896. Type of #37 but
reeded edge   100.00

FRIEDRICH II, 1904–18

Born August 19, 1856, the son of Duke Friedrich I
and his consort, Antoinette von Sachsen-Altenburg.
Friedrich died April 21, 1918.

42. 20 Mark (G) 1904. Head left. Rev. Type
3 eagle. Edge: GOTT MIT UNS   125.00

43.   3 Mark (S) 1909, 11. Type of #42   25.00

45.   5 Mark (S) 1914. Conjoined heads of
        Duke and Duchess, dates 1889–1914.
        Rev. Type 3 eagle. Edge: GOTT MIT
        UNS   75.00

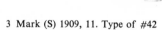

46.   3 Mark (S) 1914. Type of #45   20.00

        The above two coins commemorate
        the 25th wedding anniversary of the
        royal couple.

44.   2 Mark (S) 1904. Type of #42 but
        reeded edge   110.00

BADEN

Capital: Karlsruhe

The title Margrave of Baden was first used in 1112 by Hermann II, son of Berthold the Bearded, the Duke of Carinthia. Over the centuries, the land was divided into various lines, united and divided again. With the extinction of the Baden-Baden line in 1771, however, the properties were united for good under Carl Friedrich of the Baden-Durlach family. By aiding Napoleon, the duke increased the size of his state several-fold. The new lands led to elevations in rank as Baden became an electorate on May 1, 1803, and a grand duchy on July 12, 1806. The grand duchy joined the German Empire in 1871 and endured until the abdication of Friedrich II in 1918.

Coins for Baden were struck in:
Mannheim (1802–26)
Karlsruhe (from 1827)   Mintmark G (since 1872)

ELECTOR CARL FRIEDRICH, 1803–06
(Grand Duke 1806–11)

Born November 22, 1728, son of Prince Friedrich and his consort, Anna Charlotte of Nassau-Dietz-Oranien. Carl Friedrich died June 11, 1811.

ISSUES AS ELECTOR

1.   1 Ducat (S) N.D. (1804). Head with long hair right. Rev. Reclining river god with shield and staff, mountains in background (Essay)

2.   1 Convention taler (S) 1803. Head with long hair right. Rev. Crowned oval arms between palm and olive branches, AD NORMAM CONVENTION— "According to Convention Standard"   300.00

3. 6 Kreuzer (B) 1804. Crowned heart-shaped arms with garland. Rev. Value above two laurel branches 3.00

4. 6 Kreuzer (B) 1804, 05. Crowned many-quartered arms with garland. Rev. As #3 2.50

5. 3 Kreuzer (B) 1803, 05, 06. Type of #3 2.50

6. 1 Kreuzer (C) 1803, 05. Crowned arms with garland. Rev. Value within laurel wreath 2.00

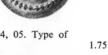

7. ½ Kreuzer (C) 1803, 04, 05. Type of #6 1.75

8. ¼ Kreuzer (C) 1802. Type of #6 2.50

9. 1 Ducat (G) 1807. Head right, with long hair. Rev. Seated river god with shield and staff, mountains in background, AUS RHEINSAND—"From Rhine Sand" 375.00

Struck of gold washed from the Rhine River.

10. 5 Franken (S) 1808. Head of Napoleon I in laurel wreath. Rev. Value within oak wreath. Edge: GOTT BEFESTIGE UNSERN BUND—"God Strengthen our Alliance" (Essay)

11. 1 Convention taler (S) 1809, 10, 11. Bust right with short hair. Rev. Crowned arms between olive and palm branches 55.00

12. 20 Kreuzer (S) 1807. Head right with long hair. Rev. Crowned arms with lion facing left in shield, MARCK 15.00

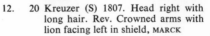

Baden • 17

13.　20 Kreuzer (S) 1808. As #12 but lion facing right in shield and MARK　5.00

21.　1 Kreuzer (C) 1809, 10, 11. As #20 but lion facing right　.75

14.　20 Kreuzer (S) 1809, 10. Head right with short hair. Rev. As #13　4.00

22.　½ Kreuzer (C) 1809, 10. Type of #21　1.00

23.　¼ Kreuzer (C) 1810. Type of #21　Rare

15.　10 Kreuzer (S) 1808. Type of #13　4.00
16.　10 Kreuzer (S) 1809. Type of #14　3.50

CARL LUDWIG FRIEDRICH, 1811–18

Born June 8, 1786, son of Prince Ludwig and his consort, Amalie of Hesse-Darmstadt. Carl Ludwig died December 8, 1818.

24.　1 Kronentaler (S) 1813, 14. Crowned draped arms. Rev. Value within two olive branches　90.00

17.　6 Kreuzer (B) 1807, 08. Crowned arms with lion facing left. Rev. Value above two crossed laurel branches　1.50

18.　6 Kreuzer (B) 1809. As #17 but lion facing right　6.50

19.　3 Kreuzer (B) 1808–11. Crowned arms with lion facing right. Rev. Value above two crossed laurel branches　2.00

20.　1 Kreuzer (C) 1807, 08. Crowned arms, lion facing left. Rev. Value in laurel wreath　2.50

25.　1 Kronentaler (S) 1814–18. As #24 but date between two stars　90.00

26. 6 Kreuzer (B) 1812, 13. Crowned arms with lion, G. H. BADEN. Rev. Value above two crossed olive branches 1.50

35. 1 Kreuzer (C) 1813. As #33 but with G:HERZ:BADEN. Rev. As #34 1.25

27. 6 Kreuzer (B) 1813. As of #26 but G:B: BADEN 1.50

28. 6 Kreuzer (B) 1814–17. Crowned draped arms. Rev. Value 6 KREUTZER in olive wreath 2.50

36. 1 Kreuzer (C) 1813. As #35 but KREUTZER 1.25

29. 6 Kreuzer (B) 1816, 17, 18. As #28 but KREUZER 1.50

30. 3 Kreuzer (B) 1812, 13. As #26 1.50

31. 3 Kreuzer (B) 1813–16. As #28 1.50

37. 1 Kreuzer (C) 1813, 14. Crowned draped arms. Rev. 1 KREUTZER between two olive branches 2.50

38. 1 Kreuzer (C) 1814–17. As #37 but date between stars 1.25

32. 3 Kreuzer (B) 1817, 18. As #31 but KREUZER 2.00

39. 1 Kreuzer (C) 1817. As #38 but KREUZER 1.00

33. 1 Kreuzer (C) 1812. Crowned arms with lion facing right, no legend. Rev. 1 KREUZER in wreath 2.50

34. 1 Kreuzer (C) 1813. As #33. Rev. 1 KREUZER in pearl circle 2.00

40. ½ Kreuzer (C) 1812. Crowned arms with lion in shield. Rev. Value in circle 1.25

41. ½ Kreuzer (C) 1814. Crowned draped arms. Rev. ½ KREUTZER in olive wreath 1.50

42. ½ Kreuzer (C) 1814–17. As #41 but date between two stars 2.50

43. ½ Kreuzer (C) 1817. As #42 but KREUZER 1.50

LUDWIG, 1818–30

Born February 9, 1763, the third son of the first marriage of Grand Duke Carl Friedrich and his consort, Caroline Luise of Hesse-Darmstadt. Ludwig never married and died March 30, 1830.

44. 10 Gulden (G) 1819. Head right with hair combed forward. Designer's initials PH below head. Rev. Crowned shield within two olive branches. Edge: TRAU-SCHAU-WEM—"Trust-Look-To Whom" 250.00

45. 10 Gulden (G) 1821–25. As #44 but no designer's initials 375.00

46. 5 Gulden (G) 1819. Type of #44 .... 125.00

47. 5 Gulden (G) 1821–26. Type of #45 .... 175.00

48. 5 Gulden (G) 1827, 28. As #47 but curled hair 175.00

49. 5 Taler—500 kreuzer (G) 1830. Head right with curled hair combed back. Rev. Crowned shield with House Order between two crossed olive branches 300.00

50. 1 Kronentaler (S) 1819. Crowned draped arms. Rev. Value within two olive branches 75.00

51.   1 Kronentaler (S) 1819. Bust right with
      hair combed forward. Rev. Crowned
      mantled shield   75.00

52.   1 Kronentaler (S) 1819, 20, 21. As #51
      but with DOELL on truncation   50.00

53.   1 Taler—100 kreuzer (S) 1829, 30.
      Type of #49   50.00

54.   2 Gulden (S) 1821–25. Head right.
      Rev. Crowned shield within two
      olive branches. Edge: TRAU-SCHAU-
      WEM   80.00

55.   1 Gulden (S) 1821–25. Type of #54   12.50

56.   1 Gulden (S) 1826. As #55 but curled
      hair combed back   100.00

57.   10 Kreuzer (S) 1829, 30. Head right
      with curled hair combed back. Rev.
      Value within two crossed olive
      branches   7.50

58.   6 Kreuzer (B) 1819. Bust right. Rev.
      Crowned draped arms   2.50

59.   6 Kreuzer (B) 1820. Head right with
      hair combed forward. Rev. As #58   2.50

60.   6 Kreuzer (B) 1820, 21. As #59 but
      crowned shield within two crossed
      olive branches on reverse   2.00

61.　3 Kreuzer (B) 1819, 20. Crowned, draped shield. Rev. Value within two crossed olive branches　2.00

66.　1 Kreuzer (C) 1827–30. Head right with hair combed back. Rev. Type of #64　1.50

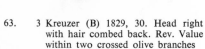

62.　3 Kreuzer (B) 1820–25. As #61 but larger shield, no drape　1.25

67.　½ Kreuzer (C) 1821. Crowned arms. Rev. Value divided, ½ KREUZER within two crossed olive branches　1.25

63.　3 Kreuzer (B) 1829, 30. Head right with hair combed back. Rev. Value within two crossed olive branches　1.25

68.　½ Kreuzer (C) 1822–26. As #67 but value ½ KREUZER　1.00

64.　1 Kreuzer (C) 1820. Crowned, draped arms. Rev. Value within two crossed olive branches　1.50

69.　½ Kreuzer (C) 1828, 29, 30. Head right with hair combed back. Rev. Value within two crossed olive branches　1.00

70.　¼ Kreuzer (C) 1824. Type of #67　1.50

65.　1 Kreuzer (C) 1821–26. As #64 but larger shield, no drape　1.50

71.　1 Pfennig (C) 1822. Crowned shield, G.B.S.M. Rev. Value (Essay)

KARL LEOPOLD FRIEDRICH, 1830–52

Born August 29, 1790, the oldest son of the second marriage of Grand Duke Karl Friedrich and his consort, Luise Caroline, Countess Geyer of Geyersberg. Karl Leopold died April 24, 1852.

72. 1 Ducat (G) 1832–36. Head right with designer's initial D on truncation. Rev. Crowned shield within two crossed olive branches, AUS RHEIN-GOLD—"from Rhine River Gold"   175.00

73. 1 Ducat (G) 1837–42. As #72 but no designer's initial   185.00

74. 1 Ducat (G) 1843–46. As #73 but larger head   200.00

75. 1 Ducat (G) 1847–52. As #74 but still larger head   185.00

76. 1 Ducat (G) 1852. As #75 but star below head   225.00

77. 1 Kronentaler (S) 1830, 31, 32. Head right with DOELL FEC on truncation. Rev. Two crowned griffin on pedestal supporting crowned shield   75.00

78. 1 Kronentaler (S) 1832. As #77 but star under date on reverse   75.00

79. 1 Kronentaler (S) 1832, 33. As #77 but period after BADEN   75.00

80. 1 Kronentaler (S) 1833–37. As #79 but no star under date on reverse   65.00

81. 1 Kronentaler (S) 1834, 36. As #78 but KRONEN-THALER and no star under date   65.00

82. 1 Kronentaler (S) 1836. As #77. Rev. As #81 but KRONEN THALER and 6 in date oversize   65.00

86. 1 Mining kronentaler (S) 1836. Type of #79. Rev. Type of #81   110.00

83. 1 Kronentaler (S) 1832. Head right. Rev. Inscription . . . UND SOPHIE GROSHERZOGIN VON BADEN BESUCHEN DIE MUNZSTAETTE DEN 29 FEBR. 1832. HEIL IHNEN—". . . and Sophie, Grand Duchess of Baden, visit to the mint. Hail to them"   125.00

Commemorates the visit of the Grand Duke and Duchess and their children to the mint.

87. 1 Zollvereins kronentaler (S) 1836. Head right, value below. Rev. Arms of the ten customs union states, inscription "To the Welfare of Your People"   75.00

84. 1 Mining taler (S) 1834. Head right, type of #77. Rev. Crown above crossed hammer and mallet, SEGEN DES BADISCHEN BERGBAUES—"Blessings of the Baden Mines"   100.00

85. 1 Mining kronentaler (S) 1836. Type of #79. Rev. Crowned griffin on flat ledge supporting a shield inscribed GLUCK AUF—"Good Luck" above a crossed mallet and hammer over miner's lamp   110.00

88. 2 Taler—3½ gulden (S) 1841, 42, 43. Head right, with C. VOIGT below. Rev. Value in oak wreath. Edge: CONVENTION VOM 30 IULY 1838   70.00

93. 1 Gulden (S) 1842. Head right. Rev.
As #92 (Essay)

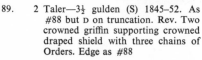

89. 2 Taler—3½ gulden (S) 1845–52. As
#88 but D on truncation. Rev. Two
crowned griffin supporting crowned
draped shield with three chains of
Orders. Edge as #88   75.00

90. 2 Gulden (S) 1845. Type of #89. Rev.
Value, in oak wreath (Essay)

94. 1 Gulden (S) 1842–45. As #92 but
with period after BADEN   15.00

95. 1 Gulden (S) 1845–52. As #94 but
larger head, no period after BADEN   12.50

91. 2 Gulden (S) 1846–52. Type of #89.
Rev. Two crowned griffin supporting
crowned shield on archer's bow, oak
leaves below   27.50

92. 1 Gulden (S) 1837–41. Head right. Rev.
Value within oak wreath   15.00

96. 1 Mining-gulden (S) 1852. Type of
#95. Rev. Type of #85   55.00

Baden • 25

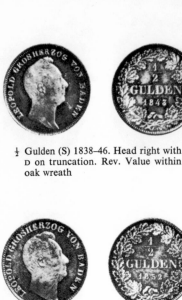

97. ½ Gulden (S) 1838–46. Head right with D on truncation. Rev. Value within oak wreath — 10.00

102. 3 Kreuzer (B) 1832–37. Head right. Rev. Value within two olive branches — 4.00

103. 3 Kreuzer (B) 1841–52. Type of #101 — 1.75

98. ½ Gulden (S) 1846–52. As #97 but larger head, no D — 13.50

104. 1 Kreuzer (C) 1831–37. Head right with D on truncation. Rev. Value within two olive branches — 1.00

105. 1 Kreuzer (C) 1831. As #104 but period after BADEN — .75

 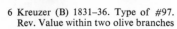

99. 6 Kreuzer (B) 1831–36. Type of #97. Rev. Value within two olive branches — 1.50

106. 1 Kreuzer (C) 1836–46. As #104 but no D — 1.50

100. 6 Kreuzer (B) 1835, 37. As #99 but no D on truncation — 2.00

107. 1 Kreuzer (C) 1845–52. As #106 but period after BADEN and larger head — 1.50

108. ½ Kreuzer (C) 1830, 34, 35. Head right with D on truncation. Rev. Value and star within two olive branches — 1.50

101. 6 Kreuzer (B) 1839–50. Crowned shield supported by two crowned griffin. Rev. Value within two oak branches — 4.00

109. ½ Kreuzer (C) 1842–52. As #108 but no D and larger head. Rev. As #108 but no star — 2.00

FRIEDRICH I, 1852–1907 (Prince Regent, 1852–56)

Born September 9, 1826, the third son of Grand Duke Leopold and his consort, Sophie Wilhelmine of Sweden. Grand Duke 1856–1907, Friedrich died September 28, 1907.

AS PRINCE REGENT FOR LUDWIG (1852–56)

113.   1 Ducat (G) 1854. Head right with moustache. Rev. Crowned shield within two olive branches, AUS RHEINGOLD—"Struck from Rhine River Gold"   400.00

110.   1 Double taler (S) 1844. Type of #88. Rev. Memorial statue, inscription "To His Father Carl Friedrich the Victorious." Edge: CONVENTION VOM 30 IULY 1838   90.00

    Marks the erection of a statue in memory of his father.

111.   1 Hybrid Essay (S) 1844. Reverse of #110 paired with a reverse as #89 but dated 1844. Plain edge (Essay)   —

112.   1 Kreuzer (C) 1844. As #106. Rev. Memorial statue, inscription   30.00

    Marks the erection of a statue in memory of his father.

114.   3½ Gulden—2 taler (S) 1852, 54. Head right with moustache, BALBACH below. Rev. Crowned draped arms supported by two crowned griffin with chains of three Orders. Edge: CONVENTION VOM 30 IULY 1838   100.00

115.   3½ Gulden—2 taler (S) 1855. As #114 but different head and no engraver name   —

123.   1 Vereinstaler (S) 1857–65. Head right with moustache. Rev. Crowned draped arms supported by two crowned griffin with chains of three Orders. Edge: MUNZVERTRAG VOM 24 JANUAR 1857   22.50

116.   2 Gulden (S) 1856. Head right with moustache, C. VOIGT below. Rev. Crowned shield supported by two crowned griffin on archer's bow   100.00

117.   1 Gulden (S) 1856. As #116 but only VOIGT below head. Rev. Value within two oak branches   40.00

118.   1 Gulden (S) 1856. As #117. Rev. Head of Grand Duke Leopold, LEOPOLD GROSHERZOG VON BADEN   40.00

119.   ½ Gulden (S) 1856. Type of #117   25.00

120.   6 Kreuzer (B) 1855, 56. Crowned shield supported by two crowned griffin. Rev. Value within two oak branches   6.50

124.   1 Vereinstaler (S) 1865–71. Head left with short beard. Rev. Type of #123   22.50

121.   3 Kreuzer (B) 1853–56. Type of #120   2.50

122.   1 Kreuzer (C) 1856. Head right with moustache. Rev. Value within two olive branches   2.00

125.   1 Gulden (S) 1856, 59, 60. As #123 but VOIGT below head. Rev. Value within two oak branches   11.50

126. ½ Gulden (S) 1856, 60. Type of #125   9.00

130.   3 Kreuzer (B) 1866–71. Crowned shield supported by two crowned griffin on archer's bow. Rev. Value within two oak branches   4.00

127. ½ Gulden (S) 1860–65. As #125 but without VOIGT   9.00

131.   1 Kreuzer (C) 1856. Head right with moustache. Rev. Value within two olive branches   1.50

128. ½ Gulden (S) 1867, 68, 69. Head left with short beard. Rev. Value within two oak branches   10.00

132.   1 Kreuzer (C) 1859–71. Type of #130   1.50

133.   ½ Kreuzer (C) 1856. Type of #131   1.50

129. ¼ Gulden (S) 1860. Type of #127 (Essay)

134.   ½ Kreuzer (C) 1859–71. Type of #132   1.50

135.   1 Gulden (S) 1857. Type of #125. Rev.
Inscription   125.00

Marks the visit to the mint by the
Grand Duke and Duchess in January,
1857.

138.   1 Gulden (S) 1867. Head left with
short beard. Rev. Value within two
oak branches, inscription   47.50

Marks the second Baden shooting
festival at Karlsruhe in 1867

139.   1 Kreuzer (C) 1868. Crowned shield
supported by two griffin, SCHEIDE-
MUNZE below. Rev. Inscription   25.00

Marks the 50th anniversary cele-
bration of Baden's Constitution on
Aug. 22, 1868.

136.   1 Gulden (S) 1863. Type of #125. Rev.
Baden standing with lance and
shield, fruit at right, a seated griffin
at left, inscription, I. BAD. etc.   50.00

Marks the first Baden shooting festival at Mannheim in 1863.

140.   1 Kreuzer (C) 1871. Type of #139.
Rev. Inscription, star with rays
above, dove below   —

Celebrates the 1871 victory over
France in the Franco-Prussian War.

137.   1 Prize Gulden (S) N.D. Type of #125.
Rev. Inscription "For Diligence and
Morality," between palm fronds,
"Grand Ducal Garrison School"
around outside   —

School premium award of gulden
size.

141.   1 Kreuzer (C) 1871. Type of #140 but
1. KREUZER below shield   15.00

147.   10 Mark (G) 1890–1901. Type of #144   37.50

142.   20 Mark (G) 1872, 73. Head left with full
       beard. Rev. Type 1 eagle. Edge:
       GOTT MIT UNS   45.00

148.   10 Mark (G) 1902–07. Head right with
       long beard. Rev. Type 3 eagle   45.00

143.   20 Mark (G) 1874. As #142 but Type 2
       eagle on reverse   50.00

149.   5 Mark (G) 1877. Type of #143. Plain
       edge   112.50

144.   20 Mark (G) 1894, 95. As #142 but Type
       3 eagle on reverse   45.00

145.   10 Mark (G) 1872, 73. Type of #142.
       Edge: Vines and stars   35.00

146.   10 Mark (G) 1875–88. Type of #143   35.00

150.   5 Mark (S) 1874–88. Head left with
       full beard. Rev. Type 2 eagle. Edge:
       GOTT MIT UNS   37.50

151.   5 Mark (S) 1891–1902. As #150 but
        type 3 eagle   25.00

152.   5 Mark (S) 1902–07. Head right with
        long beard. Rev. Type 3 eagle   20.00

156.   5 Mark (S) 1902. Head right with long
        beard, laurel branch between dates
        1852 and 1902. Rev. Type 3 eagle   42.50

153.   2 Mark (S) 1876–88. Type of #150.
        Reeded edge   32.50

157.   2 Mark (S) 1902. Type of #156   10.00

        The above two coins commemorate
        the 50th anniversary of the reign.

154.   2 Mark (S) 1892–1902. Type of #151   15.00

158.   5 Mark (S) 1906. Conjoined heads to
        right with dates 1856 and 1906. Rev.
        Type 3 eagle   50.00

155.   2 Mark (S) 1902–07. Type of #152   12.50

32 • **Baden**

159.   2 Mark (S) 1906. Type of #158   10.00

        The above two coins commemorate
        the golden wedding anniversary of
        the royal couple.

160.   5 Mark (S) 1907. As #156 but dates
        1826 and 1907 below head   50.00

164.   5 Mark (S) 1908, 13. Type of #163   22.50

161.   2 Mark (S) 1907. Type of #160   12.50
        The above two coins mark the death
        of the Grand Duke.

FRIEDRICH II, 1907–18

Born July 9, 1857, the oldest son of Grand Duke
Friedrich and his consort, Luise of Prussia. Friedrich
II abdicated his throne in 1918 and died August 9,
1928.

165.   3 Mark (S) 1908–15. Type of #163   6.00

162.   20 Mark (G) 1911–14. Head left with
        moustache. Rev. Type 3 eagle. Edge: 55.00
        GOTT MIT UNS

163.   10 Mark (G) 1909–13. Type of #162
        Edge: Vines and stars   60.00

166.   2 Mark (S) 1911, 13. Type of #164   60.00

BAVARIA

Capital: Munich

Bavaria takes its name from the Baiowarii tribe that inhabited the area about A.D. 500. The territory became part of the Frankish kingdom, then the Carolingian empire, passing in 1180 to Otto III of Wittelsbach, an ancestor of the modern rulers of Bavaria. The duchy was given the electoral honor in 1623 and raised to the status of a kingdom in 1806. A new constitution written in 1818 established a constitutional monarchy. A long series of commemorative coins record the important events in Bavaria during this period. The kingdom joined the German Empire in 1871 but retained some special privilege—its own diplomatic corps and its own post and railroad administration. Ludwig III was deposed in 1918.

Coins for Bavaria were struck in:
Mannheim (1802 for the Palatinate)
Hall (1806 for the Tyrol)
Munich   Mintmark D (since 1872)

ELECTOR MAXIMILIAN IV, JOSEPH, 1799–1805 (as King Maximilian I, Joseph, 1806–25)

Born May 27, 1756, son of Count Palatine Friedrich Michael of Birkenfeld-Zweibrucken and his consort, Maria Francesca Dorothea of Pfalz-Sulzbach. Maximilian Joseph died October 13, 1825.

ISSUES AS ELECTOR

2.   1 Ducat (G) 1799–1802. As #1 but inscription reads MAXIM.IOSEPH   125.00

1.   1 Ducat (G) 1799–1802. Head right, inscription reads MAX.IOS. Rev. Crowned arms between palm and laurel branches, PRO DEO ET POPULO—"For God and the People"   125.00

3.   1 Ducat (G) 1804, 05. Bust right. Rev. As #1 but FUR GOTT UND VATERLAND—"For God and the Fatherland"   175.00

4. 1 Convention taler (S) 1799–1802. Head right with C.D. on truncation. Rev. Crowned arms between two palm branches   40.00

6. 1 Convention taler for the Rhine-Palatinate (S) 1802. Head right with B below. Rev. Arms crowned with electoral cap within palm and laurel branches, PAL.RH. below   350.00

7. 1 Convention taler (S) 1802. Uniformed bust right, inscription reads CHUR-FURST IN BAIERN. Rev. Type of #4. Edge: ZEHEN EINE FEINE MARK   25.00

5. 1 Convention taler (S) 1802. As #4 but no C.D. on truncation   25.00

10.   ½ Convention taler (S) 1799–1803. Type
of #4   10.00

8.   1 Convention taler (S) 1803. As #7 but
GOTT UND DAS VATERLAND on reverse
and no inscription on edge   50.00

11.   ½ Convention taler (S) 1803, 04, 05. As
#9 but FUR GOTT UND VATERLAND on
reverse   10.00

9.   1 Convention taler (S) 1803, 04, 05. As
#7 but inscription reads CHURFURST
ZU PFALZ-BAIERN. Rev. As #8, but
crowned arms within palm and laurel
branches. Edge: As #7   42.50

12.   20 Convention kreuzer (S) 1799–1803.
Head right within laurel wreath.
Rev. Type of #4   6.00

13. 20 Convention kreuzer (S) 1804, 05.
Type of #11 6.50

14. 10 Convention kreuzer (S) 1800, 01.
Type of #12 5.50

15. 6 Kreuzer (B) 1799–1803. Head right,
MAX.IOS.P.B.R. etc. Rev. Crowned
arms within two palm branches 3.00

16. 6 Kreuzer (B) 1801, 03, 04. As #15 but
MAX.IOS.H.I.B.C. 3.00

17. 6 Kreuzer (B) 1804, 05. As #15 but
MAX.IOS.C.Z.P.B. and laurel and palm
branches on reverse 3.00

18. 3 Kreuzer (groschen) (B) 1799–1802.
Type of #15 2.00

19. 3 Kreuzer (groschen) (B) 1803, 04.
Type of #16 2.00

20. 3 Kreuzer (groschen) (B) 1804, 05.
Type of #17 2.00

21. 1 Kreuzer (B) 1799–1803. Type of #17.
Rev. Type of #15 1.50

22. 1 Kreuzer (B) 1800–04. As #16, but no
inscription on reverse 1.50

23. 1 Kreuzer for the Rhine-Palatinate (B)
1802. Arms crowned with electoral
cap between R P. Rev. Value in
wreath 6.50

24.	1 Kreuzer (B) 1801, 02. Type of #15	3.00

25.	1 Kreuzer (B) 1803, 04, 05. As #21 but arms between laurel and palm branches on reverse	1.50

26.	2 Pfennig (C) 1799–1805. Arms. Rev. Value	1.50

27.	½ Kreuzer for the Rhine-Palatinate (C) 1802. Arms crowned with electoral cap between R P. Rev. Value in wreath	5.00

30.	1 Prize taler (S) N.D. Type of #9. Rev. LOHN DER ERZIEHER VERWAISTER IUGEND—"Reward for Educating Destitute Youth" within oak wreath. Edge: ZEHEN EINE FEINE MARK (also plain edge)

School premium of taler size.

31.	1 Prize taler (S) N.D. Type of #7. Rev. As #30

28.	1 Pfennig (C) 1799–1805. Arms. Rev. Value	1.25

29.	1 Heller (C) 1799–1805. Arms within diamond. Rev. Value within diamond	1.25

32.	1 Prize taler (S) N.D. As #30. Rev. LOHN FUR DIE ERZIEHUNG VERLASSENER KINDER—"Reward for the Educating of Forsaken Children" around plow, ZUM ACKERBÀU—"For Agriculture"	250.00

33.   ¼ Prize taler (S) N.D. As below #32 but DEN ERZIEHERN on reverse

34.   ½ Prize taler (S) N.D. Bust right, inscription reads CHURFURST ZU PFALZBAIERN. Rev. LOHN DES FLEISSES—"Reward for Diligence" within oak wreath

School premium of half taler size.

35.   ½ Prize taler (S) N.D. Similar to #34 but JOS.LOSCH on truncation of arm

36.   ½ Prize taler (S) N.D. Bust right, J. LOSCH on truncation of arm, inscription reads CHURFURST IN BAIERN. Rev. As #34

37.   1 Ducat (G) 1806. Bust right. Rev. Crowned arms supported by two lions   350.00

38.   1 Ducat (G) 1807–22. Head right. Rev. Type of #37 but different shield   137.50

39.   1 River gold ducat (G) 1821. Head right. Rev. River god in middle, the Frauenkirche in Munich in background, EX AURO ISARAE—"Struck from Isar River Gold"   875.00

40.   1 River gold ducat (G) 1821. As #39. Rev. River god at left, EX AURO OENI—"Struck from Inn River Gold"   700.00

41.   1 River gold ducat (G) 1821. As #39. Rev. River god at right, EX AURO DANUBII—"Struck from Danube River Gold"   700.00

Bavaria • **39**

42. 1 River gold ducat (G) 1821. As #39. Rev. View of Speyer, AVGVSTA NEMETVM, EX AVRO RHENI—"Struck from Rhine River Gold" 550.00

43. 1 Ducat (G) 1823, 24, 25. As #38 but older face 137.50

45. 1 Convention taler (S) 1806. Uniformed bust right, with hair plait. Rev. Crowned arms supported by two facing crowned lions. Edge: ZEHEN EINE FEINE MARK 115.00

44. 1 Krontaler (S) 1809–25. Head right. Rev. Crown above crossed scepter and sword. Edge: BAIERISCHER KRON-THALER 45.00

46. 1 Convention taler (S) 1806. As #45 but lions facing outward 137.50

47.   1 Convention taler (S) 1807. As #45 but small shield in middle of arms has crowned crossed scepter and sword   110.00

49.   1 Convention taler (S) 1822–25. Larger uniformed bust right. Rev. Type of # 47   90.00

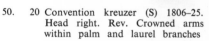

50.   20 Convention kreuzer (S) 1806–25. Head right. Rev. Crowned arms within palm and laurel branches   10.00

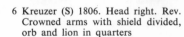

48.   1 Convention taler (S) 1807–22. Uniformed bust right without hair plait. Rev. Type of #47   80.00

51.   6 Kreuzer (S) 1806. Head right. Rev. Crowned arms with shield divided, orb and lion in quarters   10.00

52. 6 Kreuzer (B) 1806–25. As #51 but shield with crown above crossed scepter and sword ... 4.00

57. 1 Pfennig (C) 1806–25. Type of #56 ... 2.50

53. 3 Kreuzer (B) 1807–25. Type of #52 ... 5.50

58. 1 Heller (C) 1806–25. Crowned arms within diamond. Rev. Value within diamond ... 3.00

54. 1 Kreuzer for the Tyrol (C) 1806. Crowned arms between palm and laurel branches with middle shield divided. Rev. Value ... 10.00

55. 1 Kreuzer (B) 1806–25. Type of #52 ... 4.00

56. 2 Pfennig (C) 1806–25. Crowned arms on plain field. Rev. Value ... 3.50

59. 1 Convention taler (S) 1818. Armored, laureate bust right. Rev. Block inscribed CHARTA MAGNA, inscription MAGNUS—"The Mighty Order of the Centuries is Born Anew." Edge: ZEHEN EINE FEINE MARK ... 55.00

Commemorates the granting of the Bavarian constitution in 1818.

62.　½ Prize taler (S) N.D. As #34 but inscription reads KONIG　　125.00

School premium of half taler size.

60.　1 Prize double taler (S) N.D. Type of #48. Rev. Type of #30

School premium of taler size on double-thick planchet.

63.　½ Prize taler (S) N.D. Head right. Rev. Type of #34　　87.50

61.　1 Prize taler (S) N.D. Type of #48. Rev. Type of #32

School premium of taler size.

64.　½ Prize taler (S) N.D. Similar to #63 but different head, lettering and wreath　　87.50

Bavaria　•　43

LUDWIG I KARL AUGUST, 1825–48

Born August 25, 1786, son of Maximilian Joseph and his consort, Wilhelmine Auguste, Princess of Hesse-Darmstadt. Ludwig died February 29, 1868 in Nice.

65. 1 Ducat (G) 1826, 27, 28. Head right, inscription reads LUDWIG. Rev. Crowned arms supported by two lions, GERECHT UND BEHARRLICH— "Righteous and Constant"   175.00

66. 1 Ducat (G) 1828–35. As #65 but inscription reads LUDWIG I   215.00

67. 1 River gold ducat (G) 1830. Head right, LUDOVICUS I. Rev. River god in middle, the Frauenkirche in Munich in background, EX AURO ISARAE— "Struck from Isar River Gold"   750.00

68. 1 River gold ducat (G) 1830. As #67. Rev. River god at left, EX AURO OENI—"Struck from Inn River Gold"   750.00

69. 1 River gold ducat (G) 1830. As #67. Rev. River god at right, EX AURO DANUBII—"Struck from Danube River Gold"   750.00

70. 1 River gold ducat (G) 1830. As #67. Rev. View of Speyer, AUGUSTA NEMETUM, EX AURO RHENI—"Struck from Rhine River Gold"   550.00

71. 1 Ducat (G) 1840–48. Head right, VOIGT below. Rev. As #65, but lions facing outward   150.00

72. 1 River gold ducat (G) 1842, 46. As #67. Rev. As #70, but different inscription   600.00

#73.

73. 3½ Gulden—2 taler (S) 1839, 40, 41.
Head right, C. VOIGT below. Rev.
Value in oak wreath. Edge: CON-
VENTION VOM 30 IULY 1838   87.50

76.   1 Krontaler (S) 1830–37. As #75 but
        LUDWIG I   55.00

74. 3½ Gulden—2 taler (S) 1842–48. As
#73. Rev. Crowned arms sup-
ported by two lions   80.00

77.   2 Gulden (S) 1845–48. Type of #73.
        Rev. Crowned arms supported by
        two lions   30.00

75.   1 Krontaler (S) 1826–29. Head right.
        Rev. Crown in wreath of laurel and
        oak branches. Edge: BAYERISCHER
        KRONTHALER   65.00

78.   1 Gulden (S) 1837–48. Type of #73.
        Rev. Value in oak wreath   20.00

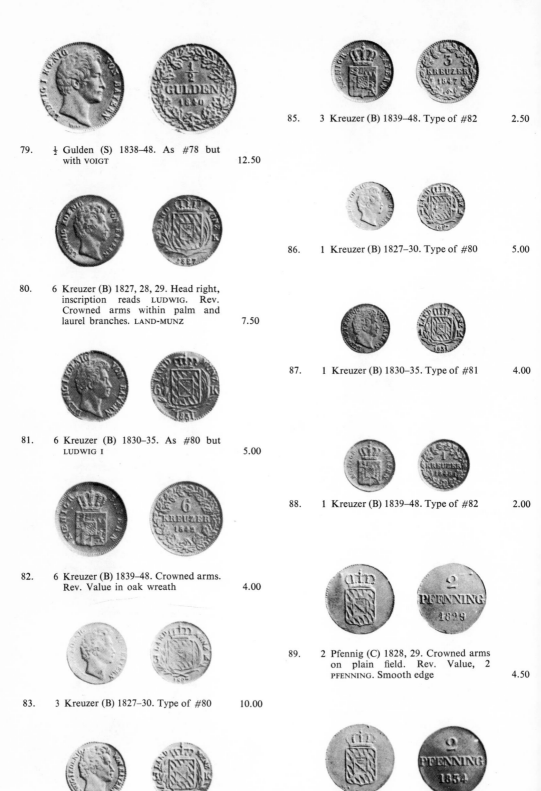

79.   ½ Gulden (S) 1838–48. As #78 but
with VOIGT   12.50

85.   3 Kreuzer (B) 1839–48. Type of #82   2.50

80.   6 Kreuzer (B) 1827, 28, 29. Head right,
inscription reads LUDWIG. Rev.
Crowned arms within palm and
laurel branches. LAND-MUNZ   7.50

86.   1 Kreuzer (B) 1827–30. Type of #80   5.00

87.   1 Kreuzer (B) 1830–35. Type of #81   4.00

81.   6 Kreuzer (B) 1830–35. As #80 but
LUDWIG I   5.00

88.   1 Kreuzer (B) 1839–48. Type of #82   2.00

82.   6 Kreuzer (B) 1839–48. Crowned arms.
Rev. Value in oak wreath   4.00

89.   2 Pfennig (C) 1828, 29. Crowned arms
on plain field. Rev. Value, 2
PFENNING. Smooth edge   4.50

83.   3 Kreuzer (B) 1827–30. Type of #80   10.00

90.   2 Pfennig (C) 1830–35. As #89 but
reeded edge   2.50

84.   3 Kreuzer (B) 1830–36. Type of #81   8.50

91. 2 Pfennig (C) 1839–48. Crowned arms
     within oak wreath. Rev. Value, 2
     PFENNIGE   2.00

92. 1 Pfennig (C) 1828, 29. Type of #89   3.00

93. 1 Pfennig (C) 1830–35. Type of #90   2.50

94. 1 Pfennig (C) 1839–48. Type of #91   2.00

95. 1 Heller (C) 1828, 29. Crowned arms
     within diamond. Rev. Value within
     diamond. Smooth edge   3.00

96. 1 Heller (C) 1830–35. As #95 but
     reeded edge   3.00

97. 1 Heller (C) 1839–48. Type of #91   2.00

COMMEMORATIVE ISSUES

98. 1 Double taler (S) 1837. Head right,
     C. VOIGT below. Rev. Standing figure
     of Moneta encircled by arms of
     Bavaria, Wurttemberg, Hesse, Frank-
     furt, Nassau and Baden, MUNZ-
     VEREINIGUNG SUDTEUTSCHER STAATEN
     —"Monetary Union of South Ger-
     man States." Edge: DREY EINHALB
     GULDEN VII E.F.M.   100.00

     Marks the monetary union of the six
     south German states.

99. 1 Double taler (S) 1838. As #98. Rev.
     Names of ancient districts of Bavaria
     in eight laurel wreaths, inscription in
     middle   DIE   EINTHEILUNG—"The
     divisions of the kingdom restored to
     their historic basis"   115.00

     Marks   the   reapportionment   of
     Bavaria.

100. 1 Double taler (S) 1839. As #98. Rev.
     Equestrian statue,   REITERSAULE—
     "Equestrian Column of Maximi-
     lian I, Elector of Bavaria, Erected by
     King Ludwig I"   100.00

     Marks the erection of memorial
     statue.

101.　1 Double taler (S) 1840. As #98. Rev. Statue on pedestal, standing. STAND-BILD—"Statue of Albrecht Durer Erected at Nuremberg" 140.00

Marks the erection of a memorial statue to the great artist.

104.　1 Double taler (S) 1842. As #98. Rev. Two conjoined portraits to right, MAXIMILIAN—"Maximilian, Crown Prince of Bavaria, and Marie, Crown Princess of Prussia, Married on October 12, 1842" 110.00

Issued in commemoration of the wedding.

102.　1 Double taler (S) 1841. As #98. Rev. Statue on pedestal, STANDBILD— "Statue of Jean Paul Friedrich Richter Erected at Bayreuth" 115.00

Marks the erection of statue in memory of famous German writer.

105.　1 Double taler (S) 1843. As #98. Rev. Statue of Margrave Frederick on pedestal, HUNDERTJAHRIGE—Centenary of the Founding of the Academy of Erlangen by Margrave Frederick of Brandenburg-Bayreuth" 120.00

Commemorates the 100th anniversary of the University.

103.　1 Double taler (S) 1842. As #98. Rev. Temple on terraces, WALHALLA 115.00

Commemorates the completion of a replica of the Parthenon near Regensburg. Called Valhalla (the Nordic resting place of slain heroes), the building was meant to be a memorial to the illustrious men of Germany.

106.　1 Double taler (S) 1844. As #98. Rev. Colonade, FELDHERRNHALLE—"General's Hall" 115.00

Marks the completion of the Temple of Heroes Hall in Munich.

107.　1 Double taler (S) 1845. As #98. Rev.
　　　Statue on pedestal　　　175.00

　　　For the erection of a statue in mem-
　　　ory of Chancellor Baron von
　　　Kreittmayr.

110.　1 Double taler (S) 1847. As #98. Rev.
　　　Statue on pedestal　　　225.00

　　　Marks the erection of a statue in
　　　Wurzburg in memory of Bishop
　　　Julius Echter von Mespelbrunn.

108.　1 Double taler (S) 1845. As #98. Rev.
　　　Bavaria holding two crowned shields
　　　standing in front of oak tree　　130.00

　　　Commemorates the births of two
　　　grandsons.

111.　1 Double taler (S) 1848. As #98. Rev.
　　　King presenting crown to his son
　　　LUDWIG I GIEBT—"Ludwig I gives
　　　the crown to his son Maximilian on
　　　March 20, 1848"　　　350.00

　　　Marks the abdication of the king in
　　　favor of his son.

#112

109.　1 Double taler (S) 1846. As #98. Rev.
　　　Male and female river gods seated
　　　with clasped hands, LUDWIGSCANAL　140.00

　　　For the completion of a canal be-
　　　tween the Danube and Main rivers.

112.   1 Taler (S) 1825. Head right, C. VOIGT below neck. Rev. King in coronation regalia, TRITT—"Assumes the government of the country on October 13, 1825"   140.00

Commemorates the King's coronation.

115.   1 Taler (S) 1826. As #112. Rev. Inscription within laurel wreath   115.00

On the removal of the University from Landshut to Munich.

116.   1 Taler (S) 1827. As #112. Rev. Caduceus between two cornucopias   115.00

Commemorates the signing of the Bavaria-Wurttemberg customs treaty.

113.   1 Taler (S) 1825. Head right (by Stiglmaier). Rev. King in coronation regalia, BESCHWORT—"Oath to Support the Constitution." Edge: ZEHEN EINE FEINE MARK (Essay)

114.   1 Taler (S) 1826. As #112. Rev. Facing heads, DEM VERDIENSTE—"The Crown honors Reichenbach and Fraunhofer"   125.00

Marks the death of two famous scientists.

117.   1 Taler (S) 1827. As #113. Rev. Similar to #116 but date in Roman numerals (Essay)

118.   1 Taler (S) 1827. As #112. Rev. Cross of the Order of Ludwig within laurel and oak branches   125.00

Commemorates the founding of the order to be awarded for faithful service.

121.   1 Taler (S) 1828. As #112. Rev. Head of the Queen on medallion encircled by eight medallions with likenesses of the royal children, SEGEN DES HIMMELS—"Blessings of Heaven"   80.00

Proclaims the blessings of heaven bestowed upon the royal family.

119.   1 Taler (S) 1827. As #112. Rev. Cross of the Order of Therese within two lily branches, inscription reads DIE KOENIGIN   115.00

Commemorates the founding of the Theresien Order by Queen Therese.

122.   1 Taler (S) 1828. As #113. Rev. Similar to #121 but date in Roman numerals (Essay)

120.   1 Taler (S) 1827. As #119 but inscription reads STIFTUNG (Essay)   —

123.   1 Taler (S) 1828. As #112. Rev. Column   115.00

Commemorates the monument erected by Count von Schoenborn on the tenth anniversary of the Constitution.

124. 1 Taler (S) 1829. As #112. Rev. Two cornucopias and caduceus dividing arms 115.00

Celebrates the commercial treaty between the four states of Bavaria, Prussia, Wurttemberg and Hesse.

127. 1 Taler (S) 1832. As #112. Rev. Prince receiving crown from Hellas (Greece) 125.00

On the selection of Prince Otto of Bavaria as the first King of Greece.

125. 1 Taler (S) 1830. As #112. Rev. Seated figure of Bavaria with a dog at her feet, BAYERNS TREUE—"Faithfulness of the Bavarians" 115.00

Commemorates the loyalty of the Bavarians to the Royal Family.

128. 1 Taler (S) 1833. As #112. Rev. Standing female holding caduceus and cornucopia, anchor and prow of ship behind 100.00

Marks the formation of a customs union between Prussia, Saxony, Hesse and Thuringia.

129. 1 Taler (S) 1833. As #112. Rev. Obelisk in Munich, DENKMAL etc.— "Monument for the Thirty Thousand Bavarians Who Died in the Russian War" 125.00

Marks the erection of a memorial obelisk in Munich.

126. 1 Taler (S) 1831. As #112. Rev. Rampant lion with shield inscribed GERECHT UND BEHARRLICH—"Just and Constant" 120.00

Marks the opening of the Legislature.

130.　1 Taler (S) 1834. As #112. Rev. EHRE DEM EHRE GEBUHRT—"Honor to Whom Honor Is Due" around oak wreath, LANDTAG—"Legislature" within　125.00

Issued in tribute to the provincial legislature.

133.　1 Taler (S) 1835. As #112. Rev. Female figure leaning against column　115.00

Marks the establishment of the Bavarian Mortgage Bank.

131.　1 Taler (S) 1834. As #112. Rev. Monument　125.00

Celebrates the erection of a monument at Oberwittelsbach to the devotion of the Bavarians to their ruling house.

134.　1 Taler (S) 1835. As #112. Rev. Monument at Bad Aibling　140.00

Records the erection of a monument by Bavarian women to commemorate the leave-taking of young King Otto of Greece from his mother, Queen Therese of Bavaria.

135.　1 Taler (S) 1835. As #112. Rev. Reclining female with caduceus and laurel wreath in right hand, her left hand resting on winged wheel　125.00

On the construction of the first steam railway in Germany from Nuremberg to Furth.

132.　1 Taler (S) 1835. As #112. Rev. Caduceus between two laurel branches　115.00

On the entry of Baden into the German customs union.

136. 1 Taler (S) 1835. As #112. Rev. Memorial statue on pedestal   100.00

Marks the erection of a monument in Munich to King Maximilian Joseph.

139. 1 Taler (S) 1837. As #112. Rev. Cross of the St. Michael's Order within laurel and oak wreath   137.50

Records the designation of the St. Michael's Order as an Order of Merit.

MAXIMILIAN II JOSEPH, 1848–64

Born November 28, 1811, son of King Ludwig I and his consort, Theresia Charlotte Louise of Sachsen-Altenburg. Maximilian died March 10, 1864.

137. 1 Taler (S) 1835. As #112. Rev. Standing figure of Bavaria, a monk and two boys   115.00

On the occasion of a school being handed over to the Benedictine Order.

140. 1 Krone (G) 1857–64. Head right, VOIGT below. Rev. Value within oak wreath. Edge: GOTT SEGNE BAYERN— "God Bless Bavaria"   1,375.00

141. ½ Krone (G) 1857–64. Type of #140 but C.V. below head   875.00

138. 1 Taler (S) 1836. As #112. Rev. Chapel   115.00

Marks the erection of the Otto Chapel at Kiefersfelden to commemorate Prince Otto's departure from his homeland to become King of Greece.

142. 1 Ducat (G) 1849–56. Head right, inscription KOENIG V. BAYERN. Rev. Crowned arms supported by two lions   137.50

143. 1 Ducat (G) 1850. As #142 but BAVARIAE REX   2,500.00

144. 1 River gold ducat (G) 1850–63. Type
      of #143. Rev. View of Speyer, date
      in Roman numerals, EX AURO RHENI   650.00

145. 1 Mining ducat (G) 1855. Type of
      #142 but AUS DEM BERGBAU BEI
      GOLDKRONACH—"From the Mines of
      Goldkronach" on reverse   1,625.00

147. 2 Vereinstaler (S) 1859, 60. Type of
      #146. Edge: GOTT SEGNE BAYERN   115.00

146. 3½ Gulden—2 taler (S) 1849–56. Head
      right, C. VOIGT below. Rev. Crowned
      arms supported by two lions. Edge:
      CONVENTION VOM 30 IULY 1838   75.00

148. 2 Vereinstaler (S) 1861–64. As #146
      but different hair style   100.00

153. 6 Kreuzer (B) 1849–56. Crowned arms. Rev. Value within oak wreath 3.00

149. 1 Vereinstaler (S) 1857–64. Type of #148 25.00

154. 3 Kreuzer (B) 1849–56. Type of #153 2.50

155. 1 Kreuzer (B) 1849–56. Type of #153 1.75

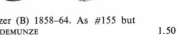

150. 2 Gulden (S) 1848–56. Type of #148 30.00

156. 1 Kreuzer (B) 1858–64. As #155 but SCHEIDEMUNZE 1.50

151. 1 Gulden (S) 1848–64. Head right. Rev. Value within oak wreath 20.00

157. 2 Pfennige (C) 1849, 50. Crowned arms within oak wreath. Rev. Value 1.50

152. ½ Gulden (S) 1848–64. Type of #151 15.00

158. ½ Kreuzer (C) 1851–56. Type of #157 2.00

159. 2 Pfennig (C) 1858–64. As #157 but SCHEIDEMUNZE and 2 PFENNING on reverse 1.50

160. 1 Pfennig (C) 1849–56. Type of #157 1.50

161. 1 Pfennig (C) 1858–64. As #160 but SCHEIDEMUNZE and 1 PFENNING on reverse 1.50

162. 1 Heller (C) 1849–56. Type of #157 2.00

COMMEMORATIVE ISSUES

164. 1 Double taler (S) 1848. As #163. Rev. Statue on pedestal 325.00

Marks the erection of a statue to honor Johann Christoph, knight of Gluck.

165. 1 Double taler (S) 1849. As #163. Rev. Statue on pedestal 325.00

Records a statue in memory of Roland de Latre, called Orlando di Lasso, erected in Munich by King Ludwig I.

163. 1 Double taler (S) 1848. Head right, c. VOIGT below. Rev. Bavaria with lion leaning against a pedestal holding a scroll inscribed VER-FASSUNG—"Constitution" 200.00

Commemorates the new constitution of 1848.

166. 1 Double taler (S) 1854. As #163. Rev. Front view of the Glass Palace in Munich 150.00

For the exhibition of German products in the Glass Palace.

Born August 25, 1845, son of King Maximilian II and his consort, Marie Friederike Franziska Auguste Hedwig, Princess of Prussia. Ludwig II died June 13, 1886.

170.   1 Krone (G) 1864–69. Head right, VOIGT below. Rev. Value within oak wreath. Edge: GOTT SEGNE BAYERN   1,375.00

167.   1 Double taler (S) 1856. As #163. Rev. Monument   225.00

Commemorates the monument to King Maximilian II erected in Lindau by the cities on the South-North railway.

171.   ½ Krone (G) 1864–69. Type of #170   750.00

168.   2 Gulden or "Mariengulden" (S) 1855. Type of #163. Rev. Madonna and child on pedestal, PATRONA BAVARIAE —"Patroness of Bavaria." Edge: ZWEY GULDEN   30.00

On the restoration of the Madonna column in Munich.

169.   1 Mariengulden (S or Z) N.D. Head right. Rev. Madonna column (Essay)   225.00

172.   2 Vereinstaler (S) 1865, 67, 69. Head right, C. VOIGT below. Rev. Crowned arms supported by two lions   875.00

173.　1 Vereinstaler (S) 1864, 65, 66. As
　　　#172 but part in hair　　　25.00

176.　1 Vereinstaler (S) 1866–71. Head right,
　　　C. VOIGT below, LVDOVICVS. Rev.
　　　Madonna and child on throne of
　　　clouds. Edge: XXX EIN PFUND FEIN　17.50

177.　1 Gulden (S) 1864, 65, 66. Head right,
　　　part in hair, C. VOIGT below. Rev.
　　　Value within oak wreath　　　32.50

174.　1 Vereinstaler (S) 1866–71. As #173
　　　but no part in the hair　　　20.00

178.　1 Gulden (S) 1866–71. As #177 but no
　　　part in hair　　　22.50

175.　1 Vereinstaler (S) 1871. Head right, J.
　　　RIES below. Rev. As #172　　200.00

179.　½ Gulden (S) 1864, 65, 66. As #177,
　　　but VOIGT below head　　　15.00

180. ½ Gulden (S) 1866–71. As #178 but
VOIGT below head 17.50

187. 1 Gift ducat (G) N.D. As #186, but C.V.
below. Rev. Crown in laurel wreath 200.00

181. 6 Kreuzer (B) 1866, 67. Crowned arms.
Rev. Value within oak wreath 8.50

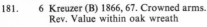

186. 1 Double ducat medal (G) 1869. Head
right, VOIGT below. Rev. Inscription 200.00

On the 200th anniversary of the
King's Lifeguards.

182. 3 Kreuzer (B) 1865–68. Type of #181 5.00

183. 1 Kreuzer (B) 1865–71. Type of #181 1.50

184. 2 Pfennig (C) 1865–71. Crowned arms
within oak wreath. Rev. Value 1.50

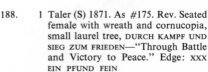

185. 1 Pfennig (C) 1865–71. Type of #184 1.25

188. 1 Taler (S) 1871. As #175. Rev. Seated
female with wreath and cornucopia,
small laurel tree, DURCH KAMPF UND
SIEG ZUM FRIEDEN—"Through Battle
and Victory to Peace." Edge: XXX
EIN PFUND FEIN 17.50

Commemorates the German victory
in the Franco-Prussian war.

189. 20 Mark (G) 1872, 73. Head right (by J. Ries). Rev. Type 1 eagle. Edge: GOTT MIT UNS   40.00

190. 20 Mark (G) 1874–78. As #189 but Type 2 eagle   42.50

191. 10 Mark (G) 1872–73. Type of #189 but edge vines and stars   35.00

192. 10 Mark (G) 1874–81. Type of #191   35.00

193. 5 Mark (G) 1877–78. As #190 but smooth edge   105.00

194. 5 Mark (S) 1874, 75, 76. Head right (by J. Ries). Rev. Type 2 eagle. Edge: GOTT MIT UNS   17.50

195. 2 Mark (S) 1876–83. As #194 but reeded edge   20.00

OTTO, 1886–1913

Born April 24, 1848, second son of King Maximilian II and his consort, Marie Friederike Franziska Auguste Hedwig, Princess of Prussia. Suffering from insanity, Otto was put under a guardian in 1878. On the death of his brother in 1886, Otto succeeded to the throne under the regency of his uncle Luitpold. Luitpold's son Prince Ludwig became regent in 1912. Otto was deposed in 1913 and died October 11, 1916.

196. 20 Mark (G) 1895–1913. Head left (by A. Borsch). Rev. Type 3 eagle   35.00

197. 10 Mark (G) 1888. Type of #196. Rev.
Type 2 eagle   55.00

198. 10 Mark (G) 1890–1900. Type of #196   35.00

199. 10 Mark (G) 1900–12. As #196 but
inscription reads v. BAYERN   35.00

200. 5 Mark (S) 1888. Head left (by A.
Borsch). Rev. Type 2 eagle   175.00

201. 5 Mark (S) 1891–1913. As #200. Rev.
Type 3 eagle   12.00

202. 3 Mark (S) 1908–13. Type of #201   6.50

203. 2 Mark (S) 1888. Type of #200   75.00

204. 2 Mark (S) 1891–1913. Type of #201   6.50

PRINCE-REGENT LUITPOLD, 1886–1912

Born March 12, 1821, third son of King Ludwig I and his consort, Therese. Luitpold served as regent for Otto I from 1886 until 1912. The Prince-Regent died December 12, 1912.

COMMEMORATIVE ISSUES

207. 2 Mark (S) 1911. As #205, but reeded edge   7.50

The above three coins celebrate Luitpold's 90th birthday.

LUDWIG III, 1913–18

Born January 7, 1845, son of Prince-Regent Luitpold and his consort Auguste. Ludwig was deposed in November, 1918, and died October 18, 1921.

208. 20 Mark (G) 1914. Head left (by A. Borsch). Rev. Type 3 eagle   300.00

205. 5 Mark (S) 1911. Head right with 1821 12 MARZ 1911 below. Rev. Type 3 eagle. Edge: GOTT MIT UNS   25.00

206. 3 Mark (S) 1911. Type of #205   10.00

209. 5 Mark (S) 1914. Type of #208   50.00

210.   3 Mark (S) 1914. Type of #208   10.00

211.   2 Mark (S) 1914. Type of #208   20.00

212.   3 Mark (S) 1918. Conjoined heads of
         King Ludwig and Queen Marie
         Therese. Rev. Type 3 eagle   3,750.00

         Marks the golden wedding anniver-
         sary of the royal couple.

BERG

Capital: Dusseldorf

The title Count of Berg dates from 1101. Raised to a duchy during the 14th century, Berg eventually went to Bavaria. In 1806 Napoleon seized the duchy, uniting it with other territories to create the Grand Duchy of Berg for his brother-in-law Joachim Murat. Napoleon made Murat king of Naples in 1808, naming his nephew Ludwig hereditary Grand Duke of Berg. Following Napoleon's defeat, the Congress of Vienna awarded Berg to Prussia.

Coins for Berg were struck in Dusseldorf.

Duchy

MAXIMILIAN JOSEPH, ELECTOR OF BAVARIA, 1799–1806

1.   1 Reichs taler (S) 1802–05. Head right, P.R. below. Rev. Value within two laurel branches   175.00

2.   1 Reichs taler (S) 1805, 06. As #1 but T.S. below   150.00

3.   ½ Reichs taler (S) 1803, 04. As #1 but R below   90.00

4.   III Stuber (S) 1801–06. Crowned MJ monogram within wreath. Rev. Value, R below   22.50

5.   III Stuber (S) 1805, 06. As #4. Rev. Value, s below   11.50

6.   III Stuber (S) 1806. Type of #5 but LANDMÜNZ   13.50

Berg • 65

7.   ½ Stuber (C) 1802, 03, 04. As #4, but
     inscription instead of wreath   22.50

8.   ½ Stuber (C) 1805. As #7 but s below   12.50

10. 1 Cassa taler (S) 1807. Head right.
     Rev. Crowned draped arms with
     Grand Cross of the Legion of
     Honor and two Marshal's batons   450.00

Grand Duchy

GRAND DUKE JOACHIM MURAT, 1806–08

King of Naples 1808–15
Born March 25, 1767, son of an inn-keeper. He became a famous general under Napoleon I. Joachim
was executed by firing squad October 13, 1815.

11. 1 Cassa taler (S) 1807. As #10 but Rev.
     legend begins at right   600.00

9.   1 Reichs taler (S) 1806. Head right.
     Rev. Value within two laurel
     branches   350.00

12. 3 Stuber (S) 1806, 07. Crowned J
     within two laurel branches. Rev.
     Value   9.00

BREMEN
Free City

Originally the seat of a bishopric established by St. Willehad in 787, Bremen was soon elevated to the status of an archbishopric. The city was declared a free imperial town in 1646 by Emperor Ferdinand III. Bremen was annexed by the French during the Napoleonic Wars but was restored to independence by the 1815 Congress of Vienna. Bremen became part of the German Empire in 1871, retaining its right to issue coins.

Coins for Bremen were struck in:
Bremen (until 1859)
Brunswick (1859 only)
Hannover (since 1859)　　　Mintmark B
Hamburg　　　　　　　　　　　J

1.　36 Grote (S) 1840–59. Crowned oval
　　arms supported by two lions. Rev.
　　Value within oak wreath, 15 L. 14 G　18.75

2.　36 Grote (S) 1859, 64. Crowned cor-
　　nered arms supported by two lions.
　　Rev. Type of #1　22.50

3.   12 Grote (S) 1840–46. Crowned arms.
Rev. As #1 but 11 L. 15 G.   3.00

4.   12 Grote (S) 1859, 60. Crowned cor-
nered arms. Rev. Type of #3   6.00

5.   6 Grote (S) 1840. Type of #3   9.00

6.   6 Grote (S) 1857. Type of #3 but rev.
7 L. 16 G.   6.00

7.   6 Grote (S) 1861. As #4 but rev.
7 L. 16 G.   6.00

8.   1 Groten (B) 1840. As #3. Rev. Value
within oak wreath   7.50

9.   ½ Groten (C) 1841. Type of #8   4.50

10.   2½ Schwaren (C) 1802. Key dividing
date. Rev. Value within stars   3.00

11.   2½ Schwaren (C) 1820. Type of #10   3.00

12.   2½ Schwaren (C) 1841–66. As #10, but
no stars   6.50

13.   1 Schwaren (C) 1859. Type of #12   4.50

COMMEMORATIVE ISSUES

14.   1 Gedenktaler (S) 1863. Crowned arms
supported by two lions. Rev. ZUR 50
within oak wreath. Edge: GOTT
MIT UNS   67.50

        Marks the 50th anniversary of the
liberation of Germany.

15.   1 Gedenktaler (S) 1864. Bremer bourse
building with oak leaves and arms
below. Rev. GEDENKTHALER ZUR   70.00

Marks the opening of the new busi-
ness exchange in Bremen.

18.   20 Mark (G) 1906. Crowned arms supported by two lions. Rev. Type 3
eagle. Edge: GOTT MIT UNS   175.00

19.   10 Mark (G) 1907. As #18 but edge
vines and stars   170.00

16.   1 Gedenktaler (S) 1865. As #14. Rev.
ZWEITES DEUTSCHES. Edge: GOTT MIT
UNS   37.50

Marks the second German Shooting
Festival.

20.   5 Mark (S) 1906. Type of #18   75.00

17.   1 Gedenktaler (S) 1871. As #14. Rev.
ZUR ERINNERUNG. Edge: GOTT WAR
MIT UNS—"God Was With Us"   37.50

Commemorates the victory over the
French in 1871.

21.   2 Mark (S) 1904. Type of #18 but
reeded edge   25.00

Bremen • 69

BRUNSWICK (BRAUNSCHWEIG)

Capital: Brunswick

Over the centuries the Brunswick lands were divided among heirs, then reunited as lines died out. By 1735, two main lines had been established—Brunswick-Luneburg-Celle which became electors and kings of Hannover (see separate listing) and Brunswick-Wolfenbuttel. During the Napoleonic Wars, Brunswick was made part of the Kingdom of Westphalia created by Napoleon for his brother Jerome. The duchy was restored by the 1815 Congress of Vienna. Brunswick joined the German Empire in 1871 and was ruled by regents under Prussian control from 1884–1913. Duke Ernst August was forced to abdicate in 1918.

Coins for Brunswick were struck in:
  Brunswick (1813–59)
  Hannover (until 1864)
  Berlin (from 1875)   Mintmark A

FRIEDRICH WILHELM, 1806–15

Born October 9, 1771, the fourth son of Duke Carl Wilhelm Ferdinand and his consort, Auguste, daughter of Friedrich Ludwig, Prince of Wales. Duke Friedrich Wilhelm was killed in the Battle of Quatre Bras against Napoleon, June 16, 1815.

1.   10 Taler (G) 1813, 14. Crowned many
     quartered arms, with garlands. Rev.
     Value, M.C. below   225.00

2.　10 Taler (G) 1814. As #1 but Rev. F.R.　875.00

3.　5 Taler (G) 1814, 15. Type of #2　162.50

4.　1 Ducat (G) 1814. As #1 but Rev. EX AVRO HERCINIA—"Struck from Harz Gold"　400.00

5.　1 Ducat (G) 1815. As #4 but F.R. on reverse　500.00

6.　2½ Taler (G) 1815. Type of #2　312.50

7.　24 Mariengroschen—2/3 taler (S) 1814, 15. Crowned arms with small garlands. Rev. 24 in stars, MARIEN GROSCH　37.50

8.　1/6 Taler (S) 1813, 14. Prancing horse left, M.C. below. Rev. Value　22.50

9.　1/12 Taler (S) 1813, 14. Type of #8　2.00

10.　1/12 Taler (B) 1815. As #8 but no M.C. Rev. F.R. under date　1.75

11.　1 Groschen—1/24 taler (B) 1814, 15. Type of #10　2.00

12.　6 Pfennige (B) 1814. Type of #8. Rev. Value　1.50

13.　6 Pfennige (B) 1814. As #8 but B. instead of BR in legend. Rev. Type of #12　1.50

14.　6 Pfennige (B) 1814, 15. As #8 but F.R. below mound. Rev. Type of #12　2.00

15.　4 Pfennige (C) 1814. Crowned initials, F.R. below. Rev. Value PFENNING (Essay)

Brunswick (Braunschweig) • **71**

16.   2 Pfennige (C) 1814, 15. Type of #15   1.50

17.   2 Pfennige (C) 1815. As #16 but no
      F.R.   1.50

18.   1 Pfennig (C) 1813, 14. Type of #8.
      Rev. Value   1.50

19.   1 Pfennig (C) 1814, 15, 18. As #18 but
      with F.R.   1.50

CARL, 1815–30

Born October 30, 1804, eldest son of Duke Friedrich
Wilhelm and his consort, Marie Elisabeth Wilhelmine
of Baden. He was ousted by revolt in 1823, but the
government was under the regency of King George IV
of England from 1815–26. Carl never married, and
died August 18, 1873.

UNDER THE GUARDIANSHIP OF GEORGE,
PRINCE OF WALES, AS PRINCE-REGENT

20.   10 Taler (G) 1817, 18, 19. Crowned
      arms with garlands. Rev. Value F.R.
      below, inscription with BRVNS   225.00

21.   10 Taler (G) 1822. As #20 but different
      inscription and Rev. C.V.C. instead of
      F.R. below date   400.00

22.   5 Taler (G) 1816–19. Type of #20
      but Rev. BR. instead of BRVNS   137.50

23.   5 Taler (G) 1822, 23. Type of #21 but
      Rev. BR instead of BRVNS   137.50

24.   2½ Taler (G) 1816, 18, 19. Type of #20,
      but Rev. BR. instead of BRVNS   112.50

25.   2½ Taler (G) 1822. Type of #23   125.00

26.   1 Specietaler (S) 1821. Crowned arms
      with garlands. Rev. Value   750.00

27.   24 Mariengroschen—2/3 taler (S) 1815–
      18. Crowned arms with small gar-
      land in field, inscription ends PRINC
      REGENS. Rev. Value with F.R. below
      date   15.00

28.   24 Mariengroschen—2/3 taler (S) 1820.
      As #27 but inscription ends REX
      BRITANNIAR. Rev. M.C. below date   8.00

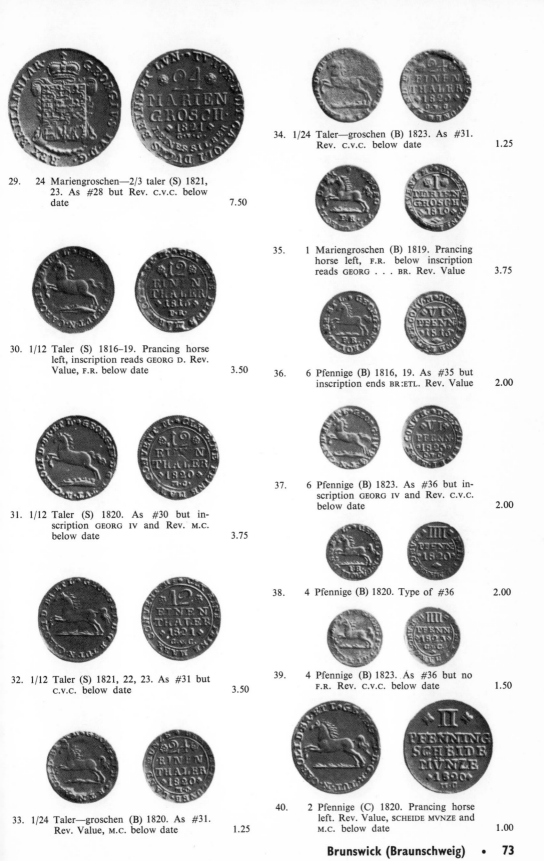

29. 24 Mariengroschen—2/3 taler (S) 1821, 23. As #28 but Rev. C.V.C. below date ... 7.50

30. 1/12 Taler (S) 1816–19. Prancing horse left, inscription reads GEORG D. Rev. Value, F.R. below date ... 3.50

31. 1/12 Taler (S) 1820. As #30 but inscription GEORG IV and Rev. M.C. below date ... 3.75

32. 1/12 Taler (S) 1821, 22, 23. As #31 but C.V.C. below date ... 3.50

33. 1/24 Taler—groschen (B) 1820. As #31. Rev. Value, M.C. below date ... 1.25

34. 1/24 Taler—groschen (B) 1823. As #31. Rev. C.V.C. below date ... 1.25

35. 1 Mariengroschen (B) 1819. Prancing horse left, F.R. below inscription reads GEORG . . . BR. Rev. Value ... 3.75

36. 6 Pfennige (B) 1816, 19. As #35 but inscription ends BR:ETL. Rev. Value ... 2.00

37. 6 Pfennige (B) 1823. As #36 but inscription GEORG IV and Rev. C.V.C. below date ... 2.00

38. 4 Pfennige (B) 1820. Type of #36 ... 2.00

39. 4 Pfennige (B) 1823. As #36 but no F.R. Rev. C.V.C. below date ... 1.50

40. 2 Pfennige (C) 1820. Prancing horse left. Rev. Value, SCHEIDE MVNZE and M.C. below date ... 1.00

41. 2 Pfennige (C) 1823. As #40, but Rev. c.v.c. below date 1.00

42. 1 Pfennig (C) 1816. Prancing horse left, F.R. below, inscription GEORG P.R.T.N. Rev. Value 2.50

43. 1 Pfennig (C) 1816–20. As #42 but inscription reads GEORG T.N. 1.25

44. 1 Pfennig (C) 1818. As #42 but inscription GEORG D.G. 2.00

45. 1 Pfennig (C) 1819. Type of #43 .... 2.00

46. 1 Pfennig (C) 1820. As #42 but no F.R. and inscription reads GEORG.IV. Rev. M.C. below date 2.00

47. 10 Taler (G) 1824–30. Crowned arms with garland. Rev. Value 225.00

48. 10 Taler (G) 1827, 28, 29. Uniformed bust left. Inscription ends LUENEB. Rev. Crowned, draped arms supported by two wildmen 225.00

49. 5 Taler (G) 1824–30. Type of #47 .... 125.00

50. 5 Taler (G) 1825. As #47 but much finer detail (Essay?) 300.00

51. 1 Ducat (G) 1825. Draped, helmeted arms. Rev. Value, AUS HARZGOLD— "Struck from Harz Gold" below ... 375.00

52. 2½ Taler (G) 1825, 28. Type of #47 ... 125.00

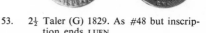

53. 2½ Taler (G) 1829. As #48 but inscription ends LUEN 175.00

54. 24 Mariengroschen—2/3 taler (S) 1823–29. Crowned arms with small garland in field, inscription ZU BRAUNS. Rev. Value — 15.00

58. 1/12 Taler (S) 1825, 26. As #57 but L. instead of LUEN — 2.00

59. 1/24 Taler—groschen (S) 1825. As #57 but inscription ends BR U.LUEN — Rare

55. 24 Mariengroschen—2/3 taler (S) 1824, 25, 28. As #54 but inscription ZU BRAUNSCHW — 7.50

60. 6 Pfennige (S) 1828. As #57 but inscription ends BR U L — 3.75

56. ½ Taler (S) 1829. Uniformed bust left. Rev. Crowned, draped arms with Order of Heinrich the Lion, supported by two wildmen (Essay) — —

61. 2 Pfennige (C) 1824–30. Type of #58. Rev. Value with no inscription — 1.00

57. 1/12 Taler (S) 1823–30. Prancing horse left, inscription ends BRAUNSCHW. U. LUEN. Rev. Value, with inscription and C.V.C. below date — 3.00

62. 1 Pfennig (C) 1823–30. As #59 but with star over horse. Rev. Type of #61 — 1.00

63. 1 Pfennig (C) 1824. Prancing horse left, inscription ends BRAUNSCHW U L. Rev. As #61 — —

WILHELM, 1831–84

Born April 25, 1806, second son of Duke Friedrich Wilhelm and his consort, Marie Elisabeth Wilhelmine of Baden. He was regent from February to April, 1831. Wilhelm never married and he died October 18, 1884.

64.   10 Taler (G) 1831. Prancing horse left. Rev. Value   225.00

65.   10 Taler (G) 1831–34. Crowned arms supported by two wildmen. Rev. Value within two oak branches   225.00

66.   10 Taler (G) 1850. Head right, with B below inscription ends U.L. Rev. Crowned, draped arms   300.00

67.   10 Taler (G) 1853–57. As #66 but inscription ends LUN instead of L   167.50

68.   1 Krone (G) 1857, 58, 59. As #67, but Rev. Value within two oak branches   325.00

69.   5 Taler (G) 1832, 34. As #65, but no oak branches on reverse   200.00

70.   2½ Taler (G) 1832. Type of #69   137.50

71.   2½ Taler (G) 1851. Head right. Rev. Value with B below date   162.50

72.   1 Double taler—3½ gulden (S) 1842–50. Head right, with FRITZ F. at truncation and CVC below. Rev. Crowned, draped arms, ribbon inscribed NEC ASPERA TERRENT—"Nor Do Difficulties Terrify." Edge: CONVENTION VOM 30 JULY 1838   62.50

78. 1 Taler (S) 1839–50. As #77 but smaller head and without FRITZ.F. 17.50

79. 1 Taler (S) 1851. As #78 but B below, inscription ends U.L. 37.50

73. 1 Double taler (S) 1850–55. As #72 but B below head 70.00

74. 1 Double taler—3½ gulden (S) 1849, 50. Head right with full beard, CVC below. Rev. Prancing horse left. Edge: Type of #72 (Essay) —

75. 1 Taler (S) 1837. Head right, with FRITZ on truncation and C.V.C. below. Rev. Crowned arms. Edge: NEC ASPERA TERRENT (Essay) —

76. 1 Taler (S) 1837. As #75 but CVC. Rev. Crowned, draped arms. Edge: As #75 (Essay) —

80. 1 Taler (S) 1853, 54, 55. As #79 but inscription ends LUN 22.50

77. 1 Taler (S) 1837–40. As # 76 but with FRITZ.F. at truncation 20.00

81. 1 Vereinstaler (S) 1859–71. Head right, B below. Rev. Crowned, draped arms. Edge: As #75 20.00

Brunswick (Braunschweig) • **77**

82. 24 Mariengroschen—2/3 taler (S) 1832, 33, 34. Crowned arms supported by two wildmen. Rev. Value   17.50

89. 2 Pfennige (C) 1851–56. Prancing horse left, no inscription. Rev. Value, B under date   1.25

83. 4 Gute Groschen—1/6 taler (S) 1840. Head right. Rev. Value   7.00

84. 1 Guter Groschen—1/24 taler (B) 1846. Prancing horse left, CVC at truncation. Rev. 24 EINEN THALER (Essay)   —

85. 1 Guter Groschen—1/24 taler (B) 1847. As #84. Rev. 1 GUTER GROSCHEN (Essay)   —

90. 2 Pfennige (C) 1859, 60. Prancing horse left, HERZOGTH. BRAUNSCHWEIG. Rev. Value   1.75

86. 1 Groschen—1/30 vereinstaler (B) 1857–60. Prancing horse left. Rev. Value   1.00

91. 1 Pfennig (C) 1831–34. Type of #88 but inscription ends BR.U.LUEN.   1.25

92. 1 Pfennig (C) 1846. Crowned initial. Rev. Value (Essay)   —

93. 1 Pfennig (C) 1846. Prancing horse right. Rev. Value (Essay)   —

87. 1 Halber Groschen—1/60 vereinstaler (B) 1858, 59, 60. Type of #86   2.00

94. 1 Pfennig (C) 1851–56. Type of #89   2.00

95. 1 Pfennig (C) 1854, 56. As #89 but Rev. no B under date   5.50

88. 2 Pfennige (C) 1832, 33, 34. Prancing horse left, inscription ends BRAUNSCHW. U.L. Rev. Value, PFENNING   1.50

96. 1 Pfennig (C) 1859, 60. Type of #90   1.50

97. 1 Double taler (S) 1856. As #73. Rev.
Crowned arms of Brunswick and
Luneburg, ZUR FEIER within two
laurel branches. Edge: 2 TH 3½ G VII
E.F. MARK VEREINSMUNZE   75.00

Commemorates the 25th anniversary
of the reign.

99. 5 Mark (S) 1915. Conjoined heads
right, ERNST AUGUST-VIKTORIA LUISE.
Rev. Type 3 eagle. Edge: GOTT MIT
UNS   450.00

AFTER INCORPORATION INTO THE EMPIRE

98. 20 Mark (G) 1875, 76. Head left. Rev.
Type 2 eagle. Edge: GOTT MIT UNS   137.50

100. 5 Mark (S) 1915. As #99 but U. LUNEB.
added at end of inscription   162.50

ERNST AUGUST, 1913–18

Born November 17, 1887, son of Ernst August Crown
Prince of Hannover, Duke of Cumberland, and his
consort, Thyra, Princess of Denmark. Ernst August
abdicated his throne in 1918, and died January 30,
1953.

#99

101. 3 Mark (S) 1915. Type of #99   300.00

102. 3 Mark (S) 1915. Type of #100   62.50

The above four coins commemorate
the marriage and accession of Ernst
August to the throne.

Brunswick (Braunschweig) • **79**

DANZIG
Free City

Long under Polish influence, Danzig went to Prussia at the second partition of Poland in 1793. Napoleon declared it a free city in 1807 but it was returned to Prussia in 1814. Following Allied occupation during World War I, Danzig was again separated from Germany in 1920 and made a Free City. Again incorporated into Germany in 1939, the city went to Poland after World War II and is now known as Gdansk.

Coins for Danzig were struck in:
Danzig (1808–12)
Berlin (from 1920)
Utrecht (1923)

1807–1814

1. 1 Groschen (C) 1809, 12. Crowned arms supported by two lions. Rev. Value — 8.75

2. 1 Schilling (C) 1808, 12. Crowned arms within date. Rev. Value — 8.75

3. 1/5 Gulden (S) 1808. Crowned arms supported by two lions. Rev. Value within two palm branches (Essay) — —

4. 1/5 Gulden (S) 1809. As #3 but in bow frame. Rev. Value with two crossed branches below (Essay) — —

1920–1939

5. 25 Gulden (G) 1923. Arms between two columns with two standing lions. Rev. Neptune with trident. Edge: NEC TEMERE NEC TIMIDE—"Neither Rashly Nor Timidly" — 650.00

6. 25 Gulden (G) 1930. Arms supported by two lions. Rev. Type of #3. Edge: Type of #5 — 1,850.00

7. 10 Gulden (N) 1935. City Hall, 10. Rev. Arms supported by two lions facing out, NEC TEMERE NEC TIMIDE — 200.00

8.   5 Gulden (S) 1923, 27. Marian Church. Rev. Arms supported by two facing lions. Edge: Type of #5   62.50

9.   5 Gulden (S- C) 1932. As #8, but arms supported by two lions facing out.   100.00

10.   5 Gulden (S–C) 1932. Harbor scene. Rev. and edge as #8   100.00

11.   5 Gulden (N) 1935. Caravel, 5. Rev. Type of #7   100.00

12.   2 Gulden (S) 1923. Caravel, 2. Rev. Arms supported by two facing lions. Edge: As #5   25.00

13.   2 Gulden (S-C) 1932. Caravel. Rev. and edge: Type of #8   50.00

14.   1 Gulden (S) 1923. Type of #12   12.00

15.   1 Gulden (N) 1932. Value in field. Rev. Arms between date   12.50

16.   ½ Gulden (S) 1923, 27. Arms between date, value. Rev. Caravel   11.50

17.   ½ Gulden (N) 1932. Arms. Rev. Value   16.50

18. 10 Pfennig (Z) 1920. Arms. Rev. Oblong
    shield with 10   15.00

19. 10 Pfennig (Z) 1920. As #18. Rev. 10 in
    large numerals   125.00

22. 5 Pfennige (C-N) 1923, 28. As #20,
    but no FREIE STADT   3.00

20. 10 Pfennige (C-N) 1923. 10 PFENNIGE.
    Rev. Arms between date   3.75

23. 5 Pfennig (C) 1932. As #21. Rev.
    Flounder   2.00

24. 2 Pfennig (C) 1923, 26, 37. Value.
    Rev. Arms between date   2.50

21. 10 Pfennig (C) 1932. 10 PFENNIG FREIE
    STADT DANZIG. Rev. Codfish   2.50

25. 1 Pfennig (C) 1923–37. Type of #24   2.00

FRANKFURT
Grand Duchy
Free City

For several centuries the site of the election of the Holy Roman Emperors, Frankfurt am Main was an independent city until 1806 when Napoleon merged it into the Confederation of the Rhine. In 1810, it became the center of the Grand Duchy of Frankfurt which Napoleon created for Carl Theodor von Dalberg. The 1815 Congress of Vienna restored its freedom and the city became the seat of the German Confederation. Frankfurt sided with Austria in the Austro-Prussian War of 1866 and the victorious Prussians incorporated it into the Prussian province of Hesse-Nassau.

Coins for Frankfurt were struck in:
Frankfurt
Darmstadt (1838)

Grand Duchy

CARL THEODOR VON DALBERG, 1810–15

Dalberg was Prince Primate of the Rhenish Confederation and a former elector of Mainz. Napoleon created the Grand Duchy for him in 1810. After Napoleon's defeat, Dalberg was stripped of all possessions and retired to the bishopric of Regensburg.

1.   1 Heller (C) 1810, 12. Crowned arms,
GROSH. FRANKF.-SCHEIDEMUNZ. Rev.
Value   4.00

Free City

1.   1 Ducat (G) 1853, 56. Crowned eagle.
Rev. Value within oak wreath   175.00

2. 3½ Gulden—2 taler (S) 1841–55. Crowned eagle. Rev. Value in oak wreath. Edge: CONVENTION VOM 30 IULY 1838   70.00

3. 3½ Gulden—2 taler (S) 1840–44. View of city. Rev. Type of #2   100.00

4. 2 Vereinstaler (S) 1860–66. Bust right of Franconia. Rev. Crowned eagle. Edge: STARK IM RECHT—"Strength in Right"   45.00

5. 2 Gulden (S) 1845–56. Type of #2   30.00

6. 1 Vereinstaler (S) 1857. Bust right of Franconia with A.V. NORDHEIM at truncation. Large towers in background. Rev. Crowned eagle. Edge: As #4   125.00

7. 1 Vereinstaler (S) 1857, 58. As #6 but an additional roof at left in background   62.50

8. 1 Vereinstaler (S) 1859, 60. Bust right of Franconia, A.V. NORDHEIM at truncation. Rev. and edge: Type of #6   20.00

9. 1 Vereinstaler (S) 1861. As #8 but different hair-knot   67.50

14. 1 Gulden (S) 1862, 63. Crowned eagle with arabesques. Rev. Type of #11   32.50

10. 1 Vereinstaler (S) 1862–65. As #8 but different dress   27.50

15. ½ Gulden (S) 1838, 40, 41. Type of #11   3.75

11. 1 Gulden (S) 1838–41. Crowned eagle. Rev. Value within oak wreath   12.50

16. ½ Gulden (S) 1842–49. Type of #12   3.75

12. 1 Gulden (S) 1842–55. Type of #2. Rev. Type of #11   20.00

17. ½ Gulden (S) 1862. Type of #14   37.50

13. 1 Gulden (S) 1859, 61. As #12 but eagle without arabesques   17.50

18. 6 Kreuzer (S) 1838–46. Type of #11   5.00

Frankfurt • 85

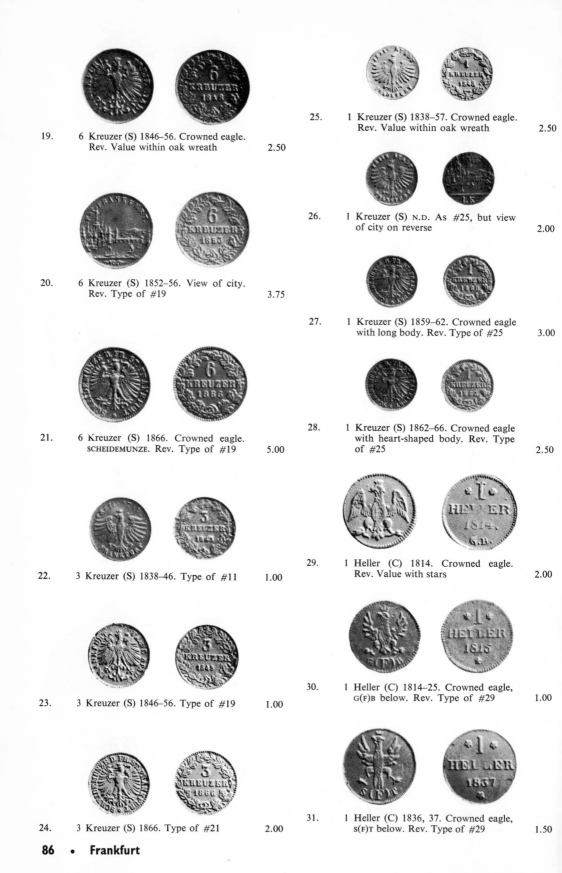

19.   6 Kreuzer (S) 1846–56. Crowned eagle.
Rev. Value within oak wreath   2.50

20.   6 Kreuzer (S) 1852–56. View of city.
Rev. Type of #19   3.75

21.   6 Kreuzer (S) 1866. Crowned eagle.
SCHEIDEMUNZE. Rev. Type of #19   5.00

22.   3 Kreuzer (S) 1838–46. Type of #11   1.00

23.   3 Kreuzer (S) 1846–56. Type of #19   1.00

24.   3 Kreuzer (S) 1866. Type of #21   2.00

25.   1 Kreuzer (S) 1838–57. Crowned eagle.
Rev. Value within oak wreath   2.50

26.   1 Kreuzer (S) N.D. As #25, but view
of city on reverse   2.00

27.   1 Kreuzer (S) 1859–62. Crowned eagle
with long body. Rev. Type of #25   3.00

28.   1 Kreuzer (S) 1862–66. Crowned eagle
with heart-shaped body. Rev. Type
of #25   2.50

29.   1 Heller (C) 1814. Crowned eagle.
Rev. Value with stars   2.00

30.   1 Heller (C) 1814–25. Crowned eagle,
G(F)B below. Rev. Type of #29   1.00

31.   1 Heller (C) 1836, 37. Crowned eagle,
S(F)T below. Rev. Type of #29   1.50

32.   1 Heller (C) 1838. Crowned eagle.
Rev. As #29, but no stars   1.50

33.   1 Heller (C) 1841–52. Type of #32   1.50

34.   1 Heller (C) 1852–58. Type of #19.
Rev. Type of #32   1.50

35.   1 Heller (C) 1859–65. Type of #21.
Rev. Type of #29   2.00

COMMEMORATIVE ISSUES

36.   1 Double taler—3½ gulden (S) 1840.
ZUR V. SACULARFEIER, in field—
EROFFNUNG DER. Rev. Value, VEREINS
MUNZE in oak wreath   350.00

Marks the opening of the new mint
in 1840.

37.   1 Double gulden (S) 1848. Double
eagle, CONSTITUIRENDE VERSAMMLUNG
I.D.F. STADT FRANKFURT 1. MAI 1848.
Rev. Crowned eagle, BERATHUNG U.
GRUNDUNG E. DEUTSCHEN PARLA-
MENTS 31 MARZ 1848. Edge: ZWEY
GULDEN (Essay)   —

38.   1 Double gulden (S) 1848. As #37 but
18.MAI.1848. Edge: ZWEY GULDEN   62.50

The above two coins mark the
establishment of the German Parlia-
ment.

39.   1 Double gulden (S) 1848. As #38.
Rev. ERZHERZOG. Edge: Type of #38   50.00

Commemorates the election of the
Archduke Johann of Austria as
Vicar of the Empire.

40.   1 Double gulden (S) 1849. As #38.
Rev. FRIEDRICH WILHELM. Edge:
Type of #38   500.00

Commemorates the election of
Friedrich Wilhelm IV of Prussia as
Emperor of Germany.

41.   1 Double gulden (S) 1849. Crowned
eagle. Rev. In laurel wreath—ZU
GOTHE's. Edge: Type of #38   62.50

Marks the 100th anniversary of the
birth of Goethe.

42.   1 Double gulden (S) 1855. As #41.
Rev. In laurel wreath—ZUR DRITTEN.
Edge: Type of #38   50.00

Marks the 300th anniversary of re-
ligious freedom.

43.   1 Taler (S) 1859. As #14. Rev. EIN
GEDENKTHALER. Edge: STARK IM
RECHT   55.00

Marks the 100th anniversary of the
birth of Schiller.

44.   1 Taler (S) 1862. As #14. Rev. Standing woman with shield upon which is
double eagle. EIN GEDENKTHALER.
Edge: Type of #43   35.00

Marks the German Shooting Festival.

45.   1 Taler (S) 1863. Crowned eagle. Rev.
View of the city square, FURSTENTAG
ZU. Edge: Type of #43   50.00

Marks the Assembly of Princes.

FURSTENBERG

The principality of Furstenberg in southern Baden dates from the 13th century. Enlarged in 1803 by the secularization of a number of monasteries and convents, Furstenberg itself was mediatized in 1806 with the property divided among Baden, Wurttemberg and Hohenzollern-Sigmaringen.

Coins for Furstenberg were struck in Stuttgart.

KARL JOACHIM, 1796–1804

Born March 31, 1771, son of Prince Joseph Wenzel (1762–83) and his consort, Maria Josepha, Countess of Waldburg. Karl Joachim died May 17, 1804.

4. 10 Kreuzer (S) 1804. Type of #3   40.00

5. 6 Kreuzer (S) 1804. Monogram of cj.
    Rev. Crowned arms between date   37.50

1. 1 Convention taler (S) 1804. Bust right,
    with I.L.W. below truncation. Rev.
    Crowned arms   750.00

2. 20 Kreuzer (S) 1804. Bust right, with w
    below truncation, inscription ends
    PRINC. IN FURSTENBERG. Rev.
    Crowned arms   62.50

6. 3 Kreuzer (S) 1804. Type of #5   25.00

3. 20 Kreuzer (S) 1804. As #2 but in-
    scription ends PRINC FURSTENBERG   62.50

7. 1 Kreuzer (C) 1804. Crowned arms.
    Rev. Value within laurel and palm
    branches   20.00

HAMBURG
Free City

The town of Hamburg traces its origins to the early 9th century. Its alliance with Lubeck in 1241 was the beginning of the Hanseatic League. Occupied by the French during the Napoleonic Wars, Hamburg was restored to its status as a free city in 1815. The city joined the North German Confederation in 1866 and became part of the German Empire in 1871, retaining its right to mint coins.

Coins for Hamburg were struck in:

Hamburg	Mintmark J (after 1874)
Altona (1805, 1842–45)	
Hannover	Mintmark B

5.   1 Ducat (G) 1807. Standing Hammonia, NUMMUS AUREUS HAMBURGENSIS. Rev. Type of #3   125.00

1.   1 Double ducat (G) 1800–05. Oblong tablet, MON. AVR. Rev. Double eagle, D.G. ROM   162.50

2.   1 Double ducat (G) 1806. As #1. Rev. Double eagle D.G.R.   170.00

3.   1 Double ducat (G) 1808, 09, 10. City gate, NVMVS AVREVS HAMBVRGENSIS. Rev. Oblong tablet, 67 AEQV   175.00

6.   1 Ducat (G) 1808, 09, 10. As #3, but square tablet on reverse   100.00

4.   1 Ducat (G) 1800–06. Type of #1   90.00

7.　　1 Ducat (G) 1811–34. Standing knight with lance and shield showing arms of Hamburg, dividing date. Rev. Oblong tablet　　90.00

8.　　1 Ducat (G) 1835–50. Standing knight in armor with sword and shield showing arms of Hamburg, dividing date. Rev. As #7　　90.00

9.　　1 Ducat (G) 1851, 52, 53. As #8 but Rev. 67 between rosettes　　90.00

10.　　1 Ducat (G) 1854–67. As #8, but different shape shield. Rev. Value　　75.00

11.　　1 Ducat (G) 1868–72. Type of #10　　65.00

#12

12.　　1 Double mark—32 schilling (S) 1808. Helmeted arms, H.S.K. below. Rev. Value　　32.50

13.　　1 Double mark—32 schilling (S) 1809. As #12 but different design and smaller planchet　　32.50

14.　　1 Double mark—32 schilling (S) 1809. As #13, but mint mark C.A.J.G. below　　32.50

15. 1 Schilling (B) 1817, 18, 19. Castle with H.S.K. below. Rev. Value — 2.00

16. 1 Schilling (B) 1823–40. Type of #15 — 1.50

17. 1 Schilling (B) 1841. Type of #15 — 1.25

18. 1 Schilling (B) 1846. As #17 but no H.S.K. below — 1.25

19. 1 Schilling (B) 1851. As #18 but Rev. 1 in stars, not rosettes — 1.25

20. 1 Schilling (B) 1855. As #19 but with beaded edge and A below date — 1.50

21. 1 Schilling (B) 1855. As #20 but Rev. without A — 2.00

22. 1 Sechsling (B) 1800, 03. Castle with O.H.K. below. Rev. Value — 1.25

23. 1 Sechsling (B) 1807, 09, 17. Type of #15 — 2.00

24. 1 Sechsling (B) 1823–39. As #23, but different detail — 1.50

25. 1 Sechsling (B) 1841. Type of #15 — 1.65

26. 1 Sechsling (B) 1846. As #25 but no H.S.K. — 2.00

27. 1 Sechsling (B) 1851. Type of #26 but Rev. 1 in stars, not rosettes — 1.50

28. 1 Sechsling (B) 1855. Type of #20 — 2.00

29. 1 Sechsling (B) 1855. As #28, but no A under date — 2.00

30.   1 Dreiling (B) 1800, 03. Type of #22   1.25

31.   1 Dreiling (B) 1807–39. Type of #23   2.00

32.   1 Dreiling (B) 1841. Castle, H.S.K. below. Rev. Value   2.00

33.   1 Dreiling (B) 1846. As #32, but without H.S.K.   1.25

34.   1 Dreiling (B) 1851. As #33 but Rev. 1 in stars   1.50

35.   1 Dreiling (B) 1855. Type of #20. Rev. Value with A   2.00

36.   1 Dreiling (B) 1855. As #35 but Rev. without A   2.00

37.   20 Mark (G) 1875–89. Helmeted arms supported by two lions. Rev. Type 2 eagle. Edge: GOTT MIT UNS   42.50

38.   20 Mark (G) 1893–1913. As #37, but Rev. Type 3 eagle   40.00

39.   10 Mark (G) 1873. Helmeted, rounded arms. Rev. Type 1 eagle   212.50

40.   10 Mark (G) 1874. Helmeted, pointed arms. Rev. Type 2 eagle   170.00

41.   10 Mark (G) 1875–88. Helmeted arms supported by two lions. Rev. Type of #40   42.50

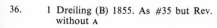

Hamburg • **93**

42.   10 Mark (G) 1890–1913. As #41, but
        Rev. Type 3 eagle   37.50

45.   5 Mark (S) 1891–1913. As #44. Rev.
        Type 3 eagle   17.50

43.   5 Mark (G) 1877. Type of #41   112.50

46.   3 Mark (S) 1908–14. Type of #45   7.50

44.   5 Mark (S) 1875, 76, 88. Helmeted
        arms supported by two lions. Rev.
        Type 2 eagle. Edge: GOTT MIT UNS   30.00

47.   2 Mark (S) 1876–88. As #44, but
        reeded edge   20.00

48.   2 Mark (S) 1892–1914. As #45, but
        reeded edge   12.50

#45

HANNOVER

Capital: Hannover

Hannover came into use as the name of a state in 1692 when Duke Ernst August of Brunswick-Luneburg became an elector of the Holy Roman Empire. He chose to call himself elector of Hannover after his capital city rather than elector of Brunswick as custom dictated. In 1714, Elector Georg Ludwig inherited the throne of Great Britain and from then until 1837 the two realms had a joint ruler. During the Napoleonic wars, Hannover was first occupied by Prussia, then incorporated into the Kingdom of Westphalia which Napoleon created for his brother Jerome. Restored in 1813, Hannover was raised to the status of a kingdom in 1814. The union with Britain was broken in 1837 when Victoria succeeded to that throne. As Salic Law prohibited a woman from ruling in Hannover, the realm passed to Ernst August, the fifth son of George III. Hannover sided with Austria in the Austro-Prussian War of 1866, Prussian troops invaded and the kingdom was annexed as a province to Prussia.

Coins for Hannover were struck in:

Clausthal   Mintmark C (1814–41)
                          A for "Administration" (1832–49)
Hannover   B (1800–78)

GEORGE III, 1760–1820

Born June 4, 1738, son of Friedrich Ludwig, Prince of Wales, and his consort, Auguste, Princess of Sachsen-Gotha. In 1811, his son, August Friedrich, Prince of Wales, took over the regency for his insane father. George III died January 29, 1820.

1.   10 Taler (G) 1813, 14. Prancing horse left, s on ledge, GHH below ledge. Rev. Value   250.00

2.   5 Taler (G) 1813, 14, 15. Crowned, draped arms with Order of the Garter inscribed HONI SOIT QVI MAL Y PENSE—"Evil To Him Who Thinks Evil Of It." Rev. Value, T.W. below date   200.00

3. 5 Taler (G) 1814, 15. Prancing horse left, EX AURO HERCINIAE—"Struck from Harz Gold." Rev. Value — 200.00

4. 2½ Taler (G) 1814. As #1 but no s — 150.00

5. 2/3 Taler—gulden (S) 1813. As #2, but T.W. below arms. Rev. Value (Essay) — —

6. 2/3 Taler (S) 1813, 14. Laureated head right, C below truncation. Rev. Value — 13.75

7. 2/3 Taler (S) 1814. As #6, but M below truncation — 12.50

8. 1 Ducat (G) 1815, 18. Prancing horse left. Rev. Value and EX AURO HERCINIAE—"Struck from Harz Gold" — 200.00

9. 2/3 Taler—16 gute groschen (S) 1820. Prancing horse left with M on ledge, BRITANNIARUM. Rev. Value — 37.50

10. 2/3 Taler—16 gute groschen (S) 1820. As #9 but inscription BRITAN & HANNOV REX — —

11. 1/12 Taler—3 mariengroschen (B) 1814, 15, 16. Prancing horse left with s on ledge. Rev. Value and NACH DEM REICHS FUSS — 2.50

12. 1/12 Taler—3 mariengroschen (B) 1816, 17, 18. Prancing horse left, C.H.H. below ledge. Rev. Value and CONVENTIONS MUNZE — 5.00

13. 1/12 Taler—3 mariengroschen (B) 1819, 20. As #12 but L.A.B. below — 3.00

14. 1/12 Taler—3 mariengroschen (B) 1819. As #12 but L.B. below — 3.00

15. 1/24 Taler (B) 1814. Prancing horse left, date below. Rev. Type of #11 — 2.50

16. 1/24 Taler (B) 1817, 18. Crowned GR monogram. Rev. Value, H below — 1.25

17. 1/36 Taler—mariengroschen (B) 1814. Crowned GR monogram, C below. Rev. Value, NACH DEM REICHS FUSS — 2.50

18 1/36 Taler—mariengroschen (B) 1816, 17, 18. Type of #16 — 2.50

19. ½ Mariengroschen—4 pfennige (B) 1814, 15. Type of #17 — 2.00

20. ½ Mariengroschen—4 pfennige (B) 1815, 16. As #17 but H below — 2.00

21. ½ Mariengroschen—4 pfennige (B) 1816, 17. Crowned GR monogram, CONVENT MUNZE. Rev. Value — 2.00

22. 2 Pfennige (C) 1817, 18. Crowned GR monogram, date below. Rev. Value, PFENNING — 1.75

23. 1 Pfennig (C) 1814. As #22, but H below. Rev. Value — 2.00

24. 1 Pfennig (C) 1814. As #22, but C below — 1.75

25. 1 Pfennig (C) 1814–20. Type of #22 — 1.50

GEORG IV, 1820–30

Born August 12, 1762, son of King George III and his consort, Sophie Charlotte of Mecklenburg-Strelitz. Georg IV died June 26, 1830.

As Prince-Regent for his father from January 10, 1811, to January 29, 1820. Following the death of his father, King George III, he became Regent until 1830.

31. 2/3 Taler—16 gute groschen (S) 1820. Prancing horse left, M on ledge, XX EINE F MARK below, BRITAN &. Rev. Value, CONVENTIONS MUNZE   10.00

26. 10 Taler (G) 1821–30. Laureated head left, in pearl circle. Rev. Value   237.50

32. 2/3 Taler—16 gute groschen (S) 1820. As #31 but XX E F MARK below and Rev. CONV MUNZE FEIN SILBER   9.50

27. 5 Taler (G) 1821–30. Type of #26   112.50

28. 5 Taler (G) 1821. Prancing horse left, with EX AURO HERCIN—"Struck from Harz gold" below, GEORG IV D G BRITANN. Rev. Value   1,000.00

33. 2/3 Taler—16 gute groschen (S) 1820. As #31. Rev. As #32   9.50

29. 1 Ducat (G) 1821, 24, 27. Prancing horse left. Rev. Value, EX AURO HERCINIAE—"Struck from Harz gold"   450.00

34. 2/3 Taler—16 gute groschen (S) 1821. As #32 but Rev. FEIN SILB   8.75

30. 2½ Taler (G) 1821, 27, 30. Type of #26   97.50

35. 2/3 Taler—16 gute groschen (S) 1821. As #32 but inscription ends BRITANN ET. Rev. Value   11.50

36. 2/3 Taler—16 gute groschen (S) 1822. As #35. Rev. Value, FEINES SILB   —

37. 2/3 Taler—16 gute groschen (S) 1822. As #35. Rev. Value, FEINES SILBER   —

38. 2/3 Taler—16 gute groschen (S) 1822–30. Type of #37   6.50

39. 2/3 Taler—16 gute groschen (S) 1822–29. Laureated head left, M at truncation, C below. Rev. Value, N D LEIPZIGER   22.50

40. 2/3 Taler—16 gute groschen (S) 1826, 27, 28. Laureated head left. Rev. Value, 18 STUCK   21.50

41. 1/6 Taler (S) 1821. Prancing horse left, B below ledge. Rev. Value   11.50

42. 1/12 Taler—3 mariengroschen (B) 1820, 21. As #41, but L.B. below. Rev. Value   3.00

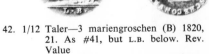

43. 1/12 Taler—3 mariengroschen (B) 1822, 23, 24. Type of #42   2.75

Hannover • 99

44. 1/24 Taler (B) 1826, 27, 28. Crowned GR monogram, IV below, CONVENTIONS MUNZE. Rev. Value   2.00

45. 4 Pfennige (B) 1822–30. As #44 but CONVENT MUNZE   2.50

46. 4 Pfennige (C) 1827. Crowned GR monogram. Rev. Value, C below   3.00

47. 2 Pfennige (C) 1821–30. Type of #46   1.25

48. 2 Pfennige (C) 1826. As #46 but Rev. B below   1.75

49. 1 Pfennig (C) 1821–30. Type of #46   1.75

50.   1 Pfennig (C) 1826–30. Type of #48   1.50

MINTED FOR THE PRINCIPALITY OF OSTFRIESLAND

51.   2 Stuber (B) 1823. Crowned GR monogram, IV below. Rev. Value   10.00

52.   1 Stuber (B) 1823. Type of #51   7.50

53.   ¼ Stuber (C) 1823, 24, 25. Type of #51   2.50

COMMEMORATIVE ISSUE

54.   1 Mining taler (S) 1830. Draped, laureated bust, left. Rev. DIE GRUBE BERGWERKS   300.00

Honors the silver mines of Clausthal.

WILHELM IV, 1830–37

Born August 21, 1765, son of King George III and his consort, Sophie Charlotte of Mecklenburg-Strelitz. As the Duke of Cumberland he succeeded his brother as King of Great Britain and Hannover. Wilhelm IV died June 26, 1837.

55. 10 Taler (G) 1832. Head right, GULIEMUS IV. Rev. Crowned arms, shield inscription NEC ASPERA TERRENT—"Nor Do Difficulties Terrify" 225.00

56. 10 Taler (G) 1833. As #55 but inscription WILHELM IV . . . HANNOV, and Rev. chain of the Order of Welfen on shield 225.00

57. 10 Taler (G) 1835, 36, 37. As #56 but inscription ends HANNOVER with B under truncation. Rev. Different shape of crown and shield 190.00

58. 5 Taler (G) 1835. Type of #57 350.00

59. 1 Ducat (G) 1831. Prancing horse left. Rev. Value, EX AURO HERCINIAE—"Struck from Harz gold" 400.00

60. 2½ Taler (G) 1832, 33, 35. Head right, GULIELM. IV. Rev. Value 137.50

61. 2½ Taler (G) 1836, 37. Head right, B below, WILHELM IV. KOENIG. Rev. Value 125.00

62. 1 Taler (S) 1834. As #61, but WILHELM IV KOENIG. Rev. Crowned arms with chain of the Order of Welfen between oak and laurel branches, inscription begins XIV EINE F.M. 55.00

63. 1 Taler (S) 1834, 35. As #62 but A below. Rev. Value 20.00

64. 1 Taler (S) 1835, 36, 37. As #63. Rev. As #62 but date between FEINES SILBER and inscription begins EIN THALER 21.50

65.　1 Taler (S) 1836. As #62 but different
　　　head. Rev. As #64　　　　　　　　　　20.00

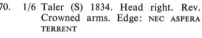

69.　2/3 Taler (S) 1834. As #68 but Rev.
　　　value dividing date　　　　　　　　17.50

66.　2/3 Taler—16 gute groschen (S) 1830–34.
　　　Prancing horse left, with M or L on
　　　ledge. Rev. Value　　　　　　　　　11.50

70.　1/6 Taler (S) 1834. Head right. Rev.
　　　Crowned arms. Edge: NEC ASPERA
　　　TERRENT　　　　　　　　　　　　　6.50

67.　2/3 Taler (S) 1832, 33. Crowned arms,
　　　with ribbon of the Order of the
　　　Garter inscribed HONNI SOIT QUI MAL
　　　Y PENSE. Rev. Value　　　　　　　20.00

71.　1/12 Taler (S) 1834–37. Head right, B
　　　below. Rev. Value, JUSTIRT below　　2.50

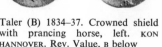

72.　1/24 Taler (B) 1834–37. Crowned shield
　　　with prancing horse, left. KON
　　　HANNOVER. Rev. Value, B below　　2.00

68.　2/3 Taler (S) 1834. Head right, W at
　　　truncation. Rev. Value　　　　　　18.75

73.　1/24 Taler (B) 1835, 36. As #72 but Rev.
　　　A below　　　　　　　　　　　　　2.00

74.   4 Pfennige (C) 1831. Crowned WR monogram, date below. Rev. Value   4.50

79.   2 Pfennige (C) 1837. As #78 but with pearl circle. Rev. PFENNIG, pearl circle   4.50

75.   4 Pfennige (B) 1835, 36, 37. As #72 but KON. HANNOV. Rev. Value   3.75

80.   1 Pfennig (C) 1831–34. Type of #74. Rev. I PFENNIG with A or C below   3.50

76.   2 Pfennige (C) 1831, 33, 34. Type of #74   1.25

81.   1 Pfennig (C) 1832, 34. As #74, but B below on reverse   1.75

82.   1 Pfennig (C) 1834. Type of #77   2.50

77.   2 Pfennige (C) 1834. As #74 but IV below. Rev. Value   1.25

83.   1 Pfennig (C) 1835, 36, 37. Type of #78   3.00

78.   2 Pfennige (C) 1835, 36, 37. Type of #73. Rev. PFENNIGE   1.00

84.   1 Pfennig (C) 1835, 36, 37. Type of #78 but Rev. B below   1.75

85.   2/3 Taler (S) 1833. AUSBEUTE DER GRUBE.
Rev. Type of #67   50.00

86.   2/3 Taler (S) 1834. As #68. Rev. AUS-
BEUTE DER GRUBE   150.00

ERNST AUGUST, 1837–51

Born June 5, 1771, the fifth son of King George III and
his consort, Sophie Charlotte Princess of Mecklenburg-Strelitz. As the Duke of Cumberland, he succeeded his brother Wilhelm IV as King of Hannover
on June 20, 1837. Ernst August died November 18,
1851.

87.   10 Taler (G) 1837, 38. Head right, B
below. Rev. Crowned arms with
heart-shaped shield and Order of
Welfen. Edge: NEC ASPERA TERRENT   300.00

88.   10 Taler (G) 1839. As #87 but s below   212.50

89.   10 Taler (G) 1844. As #87 but BRANDT
F. on truncation with S or B below.
Rev. Crowned arms on cartouche   200.00

90.   10 Taler (G) 1846, 47, 48. Head right, B
below, inscription ends V. HANNOVER.
Rev. Type of #89   200.00

91.   10 Taler (G) 1849, 50, 51. As #90 but
inscription ends VON HANNOVER   180.00

92.   5 Taler (G) 1839. Type of #88   162.50

93.   5 Taler (G) 1845, 46, 48. Head right, в below. Rev. Type of #89   137.50

99.   1 Taler (S) 1838. Head right, w at truncation, A below. Rev. Crowned arms between oak and laurel branches, order chains. Edge: NEC ASPERA TERRENT   21.50

94.   5 Taler (G) 1849, 51. As #93. Rev. Crowned arms with tournament collar   100.00

100.   1 Taler (S) 1838, 39, 40. As #99 but larger head   16.25

95.   5 Taler (G) 1849, 50. As #93, but Rev. inscription ends HARZ GOLD   250.00

101.   1 Taler (S) 1840. As #99, but Rev. without order chain and branches of leaves   16.25

96.   2½ Taler (G) 1839, 40, 43. As #90, but s below. Rev. Value   115.00

102.   1 Taler (S) 1840, 41. As #99, but Rev. crowned arms with tournament collar on cartouche. Edge: Type of #99   17.50

97.   2½ Taler (G) 1845–48. Type of #96   115.00

98.   2½ Taler (G) 1850. As #91 but Rev. date divided above, value below   120.00

103.   1 Taler (S) 1840. As #99 but only s below. Rev. and edge: As #102   17.50

104.   1 Taler (S) 1841. As #103 but BRANDT
F. at truncation   16.50

108.   2/3 Taler (S) 1838, 39. Head right, A
below. Rev. Value. Edge: NEC ASPERA
TERRENT   25.00

105.   1 Taler (S) 1842–49. As #104 but A
below head. Rev. Arms without plain
square shield   15.00

109.   1/6 Taler (S) 1840. Head right, s below.
Rev. Crowned arms on cartouche.
Edge: NEC ASPERA TERRENT   5.00

110.   1/6 Taler (S) 1841. As #109, but shield
with square corners on reverse   3.75

106.   1 Taler (S) 1844–47. As #105 but B
under head   20.00

111.   1/6 Taler (S) 1844, 45, 47. As #110 but
B below   3.50

107.   1 Taler (S) 1848, 49. Head right, B
below, BREHMER F. at truncation.
Rev. Crowned arms. Edge: NEC
ASPERA TERRENT   18.75

112.   1/12 Taler (S) 1838, 39, 40. As #109 but
with B or s below. Rev. Value   3.00

113. 1/12 Taler (S) 1841–44. Head right with s below. Rev. Value   3.00

114. 1/12 Taler (S) 1844–47. As #113 but в below   3.00

115. 1/12 Taler (S) 1848–51. Type of #114   2.50

116. 1/24 Taler (B) 1838–42. Crowned shield with prancing horse, left. Rev. Value with в or s below   2.00

117. 1/24 Taler (B) 1839–46. As #116, but Rev. A below   2.00

118. 1/24 Taler (B) 1845, 46. Prancing horse left, в below. Rev. Value and SCHEIDEMUNZE   2.00

119. 6 Pfennige (B) 1843, 44, 45. Crowned shield with prancing horse, left, s or в below. Rev. Value   1.75

120. 6 Pfennige (B) 1846–51. Type of #118 with pearl circle. Rev. Value, SCHEIDE M   1.50

121. 4 Pfennige (B) 1838–42. As #75, but Rev. в or s below   2.00

122. 2 Pfennige (C) 1837–46. Crowned EAR monogram. Rev. Value, A below   1.50

123 2 Pfennige (C) 1842, 44. As #122, but Rev. s below   5.00

124. 2 Pfennige (C) 1845–51. As #122 but within ring. Rev. в below, within ring   1.25

125. 2 Pfennige (C) 1846–49. As #124, but Rev. A below   1.25

Hannover • **107**

126.   1 Pfennig (C) 1837–46. Type of #122   1.25

127.   1 Pfennig (C) 1838. As #122 but with date below. Rev. Value, SCHEIDE MUNZE   2.00

128.   1 Pfennig (C) 1838–42. Type of #122, but Rev. B or s below   4.50

129.   1 Pfennig (C) 1845–51. Type of #124   3.50

130.   1 Pfennig (C) 1846–49. Type of #125   2.50

COMMEMORATIVE ISSUES

131.   1 Taler (S) 1839. Head right, w at truncation, A below. Rev. GLUCK AUF! CLAUSTHAL IM SEPTEMBER within two laurel branches   25.00

Marks the King's visit to the Clausthal mint.

132.   1 Taler (S) 1843. As #104. Rev. GEORG KRONPRINZ. Smooth edge   187.50

Commemorates the wedding of Crown Prince Georg of Hannover and the Duchess Marie of Sachsen-Altenburg.

133.   1 Taler (S) 1849. As #107, but Rev. HARZ SEGEN over crown   87.50

134.   1 Taler (S) 1850, 51. As #107, but Rev. BERGSEGEN DES HARZES over crown   18.75

135.   1 Pfennig (C) 1839. Type of #122. Rev. In ivy wreath GLUCK AUF!   16.25

Marks the King's visit to the Clausthal mint.

GEORG V, 1851–66

Born May 27, 1819, son of King Ernst August and his consort, Friederike, Princess of Mecklenburg-Strelitz. He was King of Hannover from November 18, 1851, until Hannover was absorbed by Prussia in 1866. George V died June 12, 1878.

141.   ½ Krone (G) 1857–66. Type of #140   250.00

136.   10 Taler (G) 1853–56. Head left, with BREHMER F at truncation, B below. Rev. Crowned arms on cartouche, date below. Edge: NEC ASPERA TERRENT   187.50

137.   5 Taler (G) 1853, 55, 56. Type of #136   115.00

142.   1 Double taler—3½ gulden (S) 1854, 55. As #136. Rev. Crowned arms supported by crowned lion and unicorn, all on band inscribed SUSCIPERE ET FINIRE—"Undertaking and Finishing." Edge: As #136   75.00

138.   5 Taler (G) 1853, 56. As #136, but Rev. HARZ GOLD   200.00

139.   2½ Taler (G) 1853, 55. As #136, but Rev. date above   112.50

140.   1 Krone (G) 1857–66. As #136 but only BREHMER at truncation. Rev. Value within two oak branches   212.50

143.   1 Double taler (S) 1862, 66. Type of #142   55.00

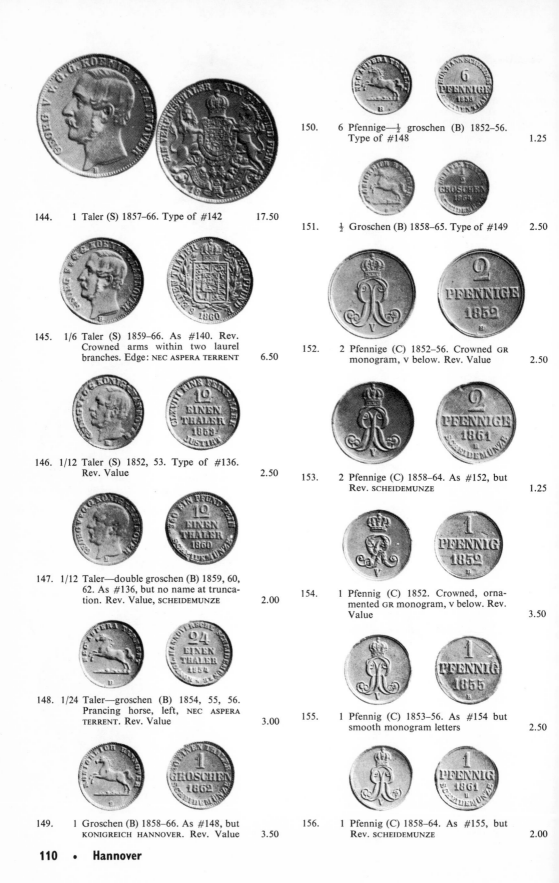

144. 1 Taler (S) 1857–66. Type of #142   17.50

145. 1/6 Taler (S) 1859–66. As #140. Rev.
Crowned arms within two laurel
branches. Edge: NEC ASPERA TERRENT   6.50

146. 1/12 Taler (S) 1852, 53. Type of #136.
Rev. Value   2.50

147. 1/12 Taler—double groschen (B) 1859, 60,
62. As #136, but no name at truncation. Rev. Value, SCHEIDEMUNZE   2.00

148. 1/24 Taler—groschen (B) 1854, 55, 56.
Prancing horse, left, NEC ASPERA
TERRENT. Rev. Value   3.00

149. 1 Groschen (B) 1858–66. As #148, but
KONIGREICH HANNOVER. Rev. Value   3.50

150. 6 Pfennige—½ groschen (B) 1852–56.
Type of #148   1.25

151. ½ Groschen (B) 1858–65. Type of #149   2.50

152. 2 Pfennige (C) 1852–56. Crowned GR
monogram, v below. Rev. Value   2.50

153. 2 Pfennige (C) 1858–64. As #152, but
Rev. SCHEIDEMUNZE   1.25

154. 1 Pfennig (C) 1852. Crowned, orna-
mented GR monogram, v below. Rev.
Value   3.50

155. 1 Pfennig (C) 1853–56. As #154 but
smooth monogram letters   2.50

156. 1 Pfennig (C) 1858–64. As #155, but
Rev. SCHEIDEMUNZE   2.00

160.	1 Taler (S) 1865. (No value or rate of exchange shown on coin.) As #136. Rev. Within two laurel branches DEN SIEGERN. Edge: Type of #157 40.00

Marks the 50th anniversary of the Battle of Waterloo.

157.	1 Double taler (S) 1854. (No value or rate of exchange shown on coin.) As #136. Rev. ERNST AUGUST within two laurel and oak branches. Edge: NEC ASPERA TERRENT 250.00

Marks the visit of the royal family to the mint.

161.	1 Taler (S) 1865. (No value shown on coin.) Type of #136. Rev. Within two oak branches ZUR 50. Edge: 30 EIN PFUND F. EIN THALER 87.50

158.	1 Taler (S) 1852–56. Type of #136. Rev. Type of #134. Edge: Type of #157 25.00

159.	1 Taler (S) 1853. (No value or rate of exchange shown on coin.) As #136. Rev. Within two laurel branches ZUR ERINNERUNG 875.00

Marks the visit of the royal family to the mint.

162.	1 Taler (S) 1865. (No value shown on coin.) Type of #136. Rev. Upstal-boom tree and standing knight with sword and lance, EALA FRYA FRESNA. Edge: Type of #161 100.00

The above two coins mark the 50th anniversary of the union of East Friesia with Hannover.

HESSE

The name Hesse comes from the Hessi tribe that occupied this area in Roman times. The duchies themselves date from the 13th century. The sons of Duke Philip the Magnanimous (died 1567) divided their inheritance into the Cassel and Darmstadt lines plus two others which quickly died out. Hesse-Homburg was created in 1622 for the younger brother of the duke of Hesse-Darmstadt.

HESSE-CASSEL

Capital: Cassel

This branch of the Hesse family is best known as the source of the mercenary soldiers who fought for the British at the time of the American Revolution. The landgraviate was raised to an electorate in 1803 but Napoleon incorporated the lands into the Kingdom of Westphalia that he created for his brother Jerome in 1807. Restored in 1813, the electorate was the scene of internal disorder in the period 1830–52. Hesse-Cassel sided with Austria in the Austro-Prussian War of 1866 which resulted in the victorious Prussians annexing the state.

Coins for Hesse-Cassel were struck in:
Cassel
Clausthal (1807)   Mintmark C

ELECTOR WILHELM I, 1803–21 (As Count Wilhelm IX, 1785–1803)

Born June 3, 1743, son of Friedrich II and his consort Maria, daughter of King George II of Great Britain. Wilhelm I died February 27, 1821.

1.   5 Taler—pistole or Wilhelm d'or (G) 1803, 05, 06. Head right. Rev. Column with electoral cap, flags and arms, reclining lion in front   300.00

2.   5 Taler—pistole or Wilhelm d'or (G) 1814, 15. Head right, WILHELMUS I.D.G. Rev. Crowned arms (1814 considered an essay)   225.00

3.   5 Taler—pistole or Wilhelm d'or (G) 1817, 19. Head right, WILHELMUS I. ELECT. HASS. LANDGR. M.D. FULD. Rev. Crowned arms   225.00

4. 5 Taler—pistole or Wilhelm d'or (G) 1820. Head right, KURF S.L.Z. Rev. Crowned arms   437.50

5. 1 Taler (S) 1819, 20. Head right, KURF. SOUV. Rev. Value within laurel wreath. Edge: KUR HESS: LAND MUNZE   40.00

6. ½ Taler (S) 1819, 20. As #5, but KURF S.L.Z.   8.75

7. 1/6 Taler (S) 1803. Crowned arms within two laurel branches. Rev. Value   3.75

8. 1/6 Taler (S) 1803–07. Type of #7   2.50

9. 1/24 Taler—groschen (S) 1803–07. Crowned lion, left. Rev. Value   1.25

10. 1/24 Taler—groschen (S) 1814–21. Type of #9   1.25

11. 4 Heller (C) 1815–21. Crowned WK monogram. Rev. Value   1.50

12. 2 Heller (C) 1814. WK monogram with elector's cap. Rev. Value   1.25

13. 2 Heller (C) 1816, 18, 20. Type of #11   1.25

14. 1 Heller (C) 1803–14. Type of #12   1.00
15. 1 Heller (C) 1817–20. Type of #11   .75

21. 1/3 Taler (S) 1822–29. As #20, but
S. L. V. HESSEN   2.50

22. 1/6 Taler (S) 1821, 22. Crowned arms
within two laurel branches. Rev.
Value   12.50

16. 1 Convention taler (S) 1813. Head
right, κ on truncation. Rev. Crowned
arms. Edge: EIN CONVENTIONS-
THALER (Essay)   —

ELECTOR WILHELM II, 1821–47

Born July 28, 1777, son of Wilhelm I and his consort,
Wilhelmine Caroline. Wilhelm II died November 20,
1847.

23. 1/6 Taler (S) 1823–31. Type of #21   3.75

24. 1/6 Taler (S) 1831. Bust right, with KURF.
V. HESSEN. Rev. Value within laurel
wreath   5.00

25. 1/24 Taler—groschen (S) 1822. Crowned
lion. Rev. Value   1.65

17. 5 Taler—pistole or Wilhelm d'or (G)
1821, 23. Bust right, with S.L.Z.
HESSEN. Rev. Crowned arms   287.50

18. 5 Taler—pistole or Wilhelm d'or (G)
1823–29. As #17 but S.L.V. HESSEN   300.00

26. 4 Heller (C) 1821–31. Crowned WK
monogram. Rev. Value   1.00

19. 1 Taler (S) 1821, 22. Bust right, with
SOUV. LANDGR. Z. HESSEN. Rev. Value
within laurel wreath. Edge: KUR HESS:
LAND MUNZE   45.00

20. 1 Taler (S) 1821. As #19, but no period
after HESSEN   —

27. 2 Heller (C) 1831, 33. Type of #26   1.00

28.   1 Heller (C) 1822–27. Type of #26   .75

29.   1 Heller (C) 1822–31. Type of #26   .75

COINAGE FOR THE COUNTY OF SCHAUMBURG

30.   1 Guter pfennig (C) 1804–14. Elector's cap over arms dividing w.к. Rev. Value, mint mark F   2.00

31.   1 Guter pfennig (C) 1815. As #30, but design instead of mint mark   2.50

32.   1 Guter pfennig (C) 1816–32. As #31, but crown dividing w.к.   1.75

COINAGE FOR OBER-HESSEN, HANAU AND FULDA

33.   6 Kreuzer (S) 1826, 27, 28. Crowned arms. Rev. Value within rosettes   2.00

34.   6 Kreuzer (S) 1831–34. As #33 but no rosettes on reverse   2.00

35.   1 Kreuzer (C) 1825–35. Type of #33   2.00

36.   ½ Kreuzer (C) 1803, 04. Elector's cap over arms. Rev. Value   1.75

37.   ½ Kreuzer (C) 1824–35. Type of #33 (1835 considered an essay)   1.50

38.   ¼ Kreuzer (C) 1824–35. Type of #33   1.25

39.   3 Kreuzer (C) 1824. Crowned arms. Rev. Value (Essay)   —

ELECTOR WILHELM II (Under Regency of Prince Friedrich Wilhelm, 1831–47)

40.   10 Taler—double pistole (G) 1838, 40, 41. Crowned arms with the chain of the Order of the Golden Lion and with KURPR. U. MITREG. Rev. Value   215.00

45.   2 Taler—3½ gulden (S) 1847. As #43 but KURPRINZ-MITREGENT. Edge: Type of #43   212.50

41.   5 Taler—pistole (G) 1834–45. Type of #40   150.00

42.   5 Taler—pistole (G) 1847. As #40 but KURPR.—MITREG   275.00

46.   1 Taler (S) 1832–42. Crowned arms with chain of the Order of the Golden Lion and with KURPR. U. MITREGENT. Rev. Value. Edge: GOTT BESCHIRME UNS   20.00

47.   1/6 Taler (S) 1833–46. Type of #46   3.75

48.   1/6 Taler (S) 1846, 47. As #46 but KURPR.-MITREG   3.00

43.   2 Taler—3½ gulden (S) 1840–45. Crowned, draped arms with chain of the Order of the Golden Lion and with KURPR. U. MITREGENT. Rev. Value. Edge: GOTT BESCHIRME UNS— "God Protect Us"   37.50

49.   2 Silbergroschen (B) 1842. Crowned arms. Rev. Value, SCHEIDE MUNZE   2.00

44.   2 Taler—3½ gulden (S) 1844, 45. As #43 but larger letters. Edge: Type of #43   45.00

50.   1 Silbergroschen (B) 1841, 45, 47. As #49, but Rev. SCHEIDE-MUNZE   1.50

51. ½ Silbergroschen (B) 1842. Type of #49   1.50

52. 3 Heller (C) 1843–46. Type of #49   .75

53. 2 Heller (C) 1843. Type of #49   2.00

54. 1 Heller (C) 1842. Type of #49   1.25

55. 1 Heller (C) 1843, 45, 47. Type of #49   1.00

COMMEMORATIVE ISSUES

56. ½ Edder-Gold ducat (G) 1835. ACTIEN GOLDWASCHE A.D.EDDER. Rev. BE-GONNEN 1832. BEENDIGT 1835   312.50

Marks the beginning and the ending of Edder gold washing.

57. 3 Heller (C) 1842. Crowned arms. Rev. Value (Essay)   —

58. 2 Heller (C) 1842. Type of #57   —

ELECTOR FRIEDRICH WILHELM I, 1847–66

Born August 20, 1802, son of Wilhelm II and his consort, Friederike Christiane Auguste, Princess of Prussia. Friedrich Wilhelm I died January 6, 1875.

59. 5 Taler—pistole (G) 1851. Head right, with C.P. at truncation. Rev. Crowned many-sectioned arms with chain of the Order of the Golden Lion. Edge: GOTT MIT UNS   500.00

60. 2 Taler—3½ gulden (S) 1851, 54, 55. As #59, but Rev. crowned, draped arms with chain of the Order of the Golden Lion. Edge: Type of #59   75.00

61. 1 Taler (S) 1851, 54, 55. Head right, with C. PFEUFFER F. at truncation. Rev. Crowned arms with chain of the Order of the Golden Lion. Edge: Type of #59   22.50

Hesse-Cassel • 117

65.   2½ Silbergroschen (B) 1852–65. As #59.
        Rev. Value. Smooth edge   2.50

62.   1 Vereinstaler (S) 1858–65. Type of
           #60   25.00

63.   1 Vereinstaler (S) 1858–65. Type of
           #60, but no C.P. at truncation   15.00

66.   1 Silbergroschen (B) 1851–66. Crowned
        arms, HESSEN. Rev. Value. Reeded
        edge   2.00

67.   3 Heller (C) 1848–66. Crowned arms.
        Rev. Value, KURHESSICHE. Reeded
        edge   1.00

64.   1/6 Taler (S) 1851–56. As #59, but
           crowned arms with lion, left, and
           chain of the Order of the Golden
           Lion   4.00

68.   1 Heller (C) 1849–66. Type of #67   1.00

69.   1 Heller (C) 1860. Type of #66. Rev.
        Type of #67 (Essay)   —

HESSE-DARMSTADT

Capital: Darmstadt

Landgrave Ludwig X sided with Napoleon and was elevated to the status of grand duke in 1806. Switching to the Allied side in 1813, Hesse-Darmstadt was awarded additional territories including the cities of Mainz and Worms by the 1815 Congress of Vienna. Hesse-Darmstadt sided with Austria in the Austro-Prussian War of 1866 and was forced to pay heavy penalties to the victorious Prussians including the relinquishment of Hesse-Homburg which it had just acquired. Hesse joined the German Empire in 1871 and endured until the abdication of Grand Duke Ernst Ludwig in 1918.

Coins for Hesse-Darmstadt were struck in:
Darmstadt (until 1882)
Berlin (from 1888)　　　Mintmark A

GRAND DUKE LUDWIG I, 1806–30 (As Count Ludwig X, 1790–1806)

Born June 14, 1753, son of Count Ludwig IX and his consort, Henriette Christiane Karoline Luise of Zweibrucken-Birkenfeld. Ludwig I died April 6, 1830.

70. 　10 Gulden (G) 1826, 27. Head left. Rev. Crowned, draped arms with the Cross of Ludwig's Order, HR around date　　　325.00

71. 　1 Kronentaler (S) 1819. Uniformed bust left, with H. below arm. Rev. As #70, but H.R. above date. Edge: GOTT EHRE VATERLAND—"God, Honor, Fatherland"　　　70.00

74. 20 Kreuzer (S) 1807. As #73 but FRISCH F. at truncation. Rev. Crowned arms dividing date, R.F. below. Reeded edge — 5.00

75. 20 Kreuzer (S) 1807, 08, 09. As #74, but L at truncation — 6.50

72. 1 Kronentaler (S) 1825. Head right. Rev. As #71 but no periods after HR. Edge: Type of #71 — 65.00

76. 20 Kreuzer (S) 1809. Head right. Rev. Type of #74 — 4.00

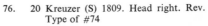

73. 1 Convention taler (S) 1809. Head right, L at truncation. Rev. Crowned arms within palm and laurel branches — 45.00

77. 10 Kreuzer (S) 1808. Type of #76 — 4.50

78. 6 Kreuzer (B) 1819, 20. Crowned arms,
    GR: HERZOGTH. Rev. Value — 2.00

79. 6 Kreuzer (B) 1821–33. As #78, but
    GROSHERZOGTHUM — 2.50

80. 5 Kreuzer (B) 1807. Crowned L. Rev.
    Value. Reeded edge — 3.00

81. 5 Kreuzer (B) 1807. As #80, with
    curled edges on L — 8.50

82. 5 Kreuzer (B) 1808. Head right, with L
    at truncation. Rev. Crowned arms
    dividing date, R. IUSTIRT F. below — 3.50

83. 3 Kreuzer (S) 1808–17. Crowned arms,
    G.H.—L.M. Rev. Value — 3.00

84. 3 Kreuzer (B) 1819, 22. Crowned arms.
    Rev. Value — 1.25

85. I Kreuzer (S) 1806. Crowned lion be-
    tween HD. Rev. Value and LANDMUNZ — 1.75

86. I Kreuzer (S) 1806. Crowned lion
    with sword between HD. Rev. Type of
    #85 — 1.25

87. I Kreuzer (S) 1806, 07. Crowned lion
    between H.D.—L.M. Rev. Value — 1.25

88. I Kreuzer (S) 1807. Crowned lion with
    sword between H.D.—L.M. Rev. Value — 1.25

89. I Kreuzer (S) 1807, 08, 09. Crowned
    lion with sword between G.H.—L.M.
    Rev. Value — 1.00

90. I Kreuzer (S) 1809–19. Type of #83 — 3.75

91. ½ Kreuzer (C) 1809, 17. Crowned arms.
    Rev. Value — .75

92. ½ Kreuzer (C) 1817. Crowned arms,
    G.H.—S.M. Rev. Value — .75

93.　¼ Kreuzer (C) 1809, 16. Type of #91　　1.00

94.　¼ Kreuzer (C) 1809, 16, 17. Type of #92　　1.00

95.　I Pfennig (C) 1811, 19. Type of #92　　1.50

GRAND DUKE LUDWIG II, 1830–48

Born December 26, 1777, son of Ludwig I and his consort, his cousin, Luise Karoline Henriette of Hessen-Darmstadt. Ludwig II died June 16, 1848.

96.　10 Gulden (G) 1840, 41, 42. Head left, with c.v. below. Rev. Crowned draped arms with the Cross of Ludwig's Order　　250.00

97.　5 Gulden (G) 1835. As #96. Rev. With Cross of Ludwig's Order, AUS HESS. RHEINGOLD—"Struck from Hessian Rhine Gold"　　625.00

98.　5 Gulden (G) 1835, 40, 41. Type of #96　　137.50

99.　2 Taler—3½ gulden (S) 1839–42. Head left, with ST at truncation. Rev. Value within oak wreath. Edge: CONVENTION VOM 30 JULY 1838　　50.00

100.　2 Taler—3½ gulden (S) 1844. As #99. Rev. Crowned, draped arms supported by two lions with chains of the Ludwig's Order and the Philip's Order. Edge: Type of #99　　55.00

101. 2 Gulden (S) 1845, 46, 47. Head left, c. VOIGT below. Rev. Crowned arms supported by two lions   35.00

105. 1 Gulden (S) 1839–47. Head left, VOIGT below. Rev. Type of #103   12.50

106. ½ Gulden (S) 1838–46. Type of #105   8.50

107. 6 Kreuzer (B) 1833–37. Crowned, pointed arms. Rev. Value and SCHEIDEMUNZE   2.00

108. 6 Kreuzer (B) 1838–42. As #107. Rev. Value within oak wreath   1.50

109. 6 Kreuzer (B) 1843–47. Crowned, squared arms, GROSHERZOGTHUM HESSEN. Rev. Type of #108   1.25

110. 3 Kreuzer (B) 1833. Crowned arms, GR:HERZOGTH. Rev. Type of #107   2.50

102. 1 Kronentaler (S) 1833–37. As #101, but Rev. crowned, draped arms with the Cross of Ludwig's Order. Edge: GOTT EHRE VATERLAND—"God, Honor, Fatherland"   55.00

111. 3 Kreuzer (B) 1833–36. Type of #107   1.75

103. 1 Gulden (S) 1837. Head left. Rev. Value within oak wreath   10.00

104. 1 Gulden (S) 1838. Type of #103   16.50

112. 3 Kreuzer (B) 1838–42. Type of #111. Rev. Type of #108   1.50

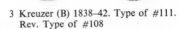

113.   3 Kreuzer (B) 1843–47. Type of #109   1.25

114.   1 Kreuzer (S) 1834–38. Type of #107   .75

115.   1 Kreuzer (S) 1837–42. Type of #107.
        Rev. Type of #108   .75

116.   1 Kreuzer (S) 1843–47. Type of #109   .75

117.   I Heller (C) 1824–47. As #107, but
        with G.H.—K.M. Rev. Value   1.50

118.   I Heller (C) 1847. As #109, but with
        G.H.—K.M. Rev. Value   .75

GRAND DUKE LUDWIG III, 1848–77

Born June 9, 1806, son of Ludwig II and his consort, Wilhelmine, Princess of Baden. Ludwig III died June 13, 1877.

119.   2 Taler—3½ gulden (S) 1854. Head
        left, KORN below. Rev. Crowned,
        draped arms supported by two lions
        with chains of the Ludwig's Order
        and the Philip's Order. Edge: CON-
        VENTION VOM 30 JULY 1838   112.50

120.   1 Vereinstaler (S) 1857–71. Head left.
        Rev. Crowned arms supported by
        two lions. Edge: MUNZVERTRAG VOM
        24 JANUAR 1857   20.00

126. 6 Kreuzer (B) 1864–67. Crowned arms,
GR.HESSISCHE-SCHEIDEMUNZE. Rev.
Type of #122   2.00

127. 3 Kreuzer (B) 1848–56. Type of #125   2.00

121. 2 Gulden (S) 1848–56. As #120, but
c. VOIGT below   27.50

122. 1 Gulden (S) 1848. As #120. Rev.
Value within oak wreath   7.50

128. 3 Kreuzer (B) 1864–67. Type of #126   2.00

129. 1 Kreuzer (S) 1848–56. Type of #125   .75

123. 1 Gulden (S) 1854, 55, 56. Type of
#120 but VOIGT. Rev. Type of #122   6.50

130. 1 Kreuzer (S) 1858–72. Type of #126   .75

131. I Heller (C) 1848–55. Crowned,
squared arms G.H.—K.M. Rev. Value   .75

132. 1 Pfennig (C) 1857–72. Type of #125.
Rev. Value, SCHEIDEMUNZE   .75

COMMEMORATIVE ISSUES

124. ½ Gulden (S) 1855. Type of #123   27.50

125. 6 Kreuzer (B) 1848–56. Crowned arms,
GROSHERZOGTHUM HESSEN. Rev. Type
of #122   2.00

133. 1 Konzertgulden (S) 1843. Head left,
VOIGT below. Rev. ZUR ERINNERUNG
within laurel and oak branches   55.00

     Marks the visit of the Crown Prince
of Russia, later Czar Alexander II.

140. 10 Mark (G) 1875, 76, 77. As #138.
      Edge: Vines and stars   45.00

141. 5 Mark (G) 1877. As #138, but smooth
      edge   162.50

134. 1 Prize Freedoms gulden (S) 1848.
      Head left. Rev. PRESSFREIHEIT   45.00

      Marks the public freedoms through
      the German parliament.

135. 6 Kreuzer (B) 1848. As #125. Rev.
      Crowned L and H monograms   —

      Marks the visit of Princes Ludwig
      and Heinrich to the mint at Darm-
      stadt.

136. 6 Kreuzer (B) 1859. As #125. Rev.
      Crowned A and W monograms   —

      Marks the visit of Prince Wilhelm
      and Princess Anna to the mint at
      Darmstadt.

AFTER INCORPORATION INTO THE EMPIRE

137. 20 Mark (G) 1872, 73. Head right, H
      below. Rev. Type 1 eagle. Edge:
      GOTT MIT UNS   62.50

142. 5 Mark (S) 1875, 76. Type of #138   45.00

138. 20 Mark (G) 1874. As #137, but Rev.
      Type 2 eagle. Edge: Type of #137   80.00

139. 10 Mark (G) 1872, 73. As #137. Edge:
      Vines and stars   45.00

143. 2 Mark (S) 1876, 77. As #138, but
      reeded edge   80.00

126 • **Hesse-Darmstadt**

GRAND DUKE LUDWIG IV, 1877–92

Born September 12, 1837, son of Karl of Hessen-Darmstadt (a brother of Ludwig III) and his consort, Elisabeth of Prussia. Ludwig IV died March 13, 1892.

144.   20 Mark (G) 1892. Bearded head right, H below. Rev. Type 3 eagle. Edge: GOTT MIT UNS   150.00

145.   10 Mark (G) 1878, 79, 80. As #144. Rev. Type 2 eagle. Edge: Vines and stars   70.00

146.   10 Mark (G) 1888. As #145, but A below   105.00

147.   10 Mark (G) 1890. As #144, but Edge: Vines and stars   100.00

148.   5 Mark (G) 1877. As #145, but smooth edge   175.00

149.   5 Mark (S) 1888. Head right, A below. Rev. Type 2 eagle. Edge: GOTT MIT UNS   562.50

150.   5 Mark (S) 1891. As #149, but Rev. type 3 eagle   250.00

151.   2 Mark (S) 1888. As 149, but reeded edge   200.00

152.   2 Mark (S) 1891. As #151, but Rev. type 3 eagle   150.00

GRAND DUKE ERNST LUDWIG, 1892–1918

Born November 25, 1866, son of Ludwig IV and his consort, Alice, Princess of Great Britain. He abdicated his throne in 1918. Ernst Ludwig died October 9, 1937.

153.   20 Mark (G) 1893. Head left, A below. Rev. Type 3 eagle. Edge: GOTT MIT UNS   130.00

154.   20 Mark (G) 1896–1903. As #153, but head turned slightly more to left   62.50

155.   20 Mark (G) 1905–11. Type of #154   52.50

160.   2 Mark (S) 1895–1900. As #158, but
        reeded edge   112.50

COMMEMORATIVE ISSUES

161.   5 Mark (S) 1904. Conjoined heads left,
        PHILIPP. LANDGRAF. Rev. Type 3
        eagle. Edge: GOTT MIT UNS   45.00

156.   10 Mark (G) 1893. As #153, but Edge:
        vines and stars   120.00

162.   2 Mark (S) 1904. As #161, but reeded
        edge   20.00

        The above two coins commemorate
        the 400th anniversary of the birth of
        Philip the Magnanimous.

157.   10 Mark (G) 1896, 98. As #154, but
        Edge: vines and stars   80.00

158.   5 Mark (S) 1895–1900. Head left, A
        below. Rev. Type 3 eagle. Edge:
        GOTT MIT UNS   80.00

163.   3 Mark (S) 1917. Head left, laurel
        branch and A at truncation and 1892,
        1917, left. Rev. Type 3 eagle. Edge:
        Type of #161   550.00

        Marks the 25th anniversary of the
        reign.

159.   3 Mark (S) 1910. Type of #158   25.00

HESSE-HOMBURG

Capital: Bad Homburg

Hesse-Homburg was created from part of Hesse-Darmstadt in 1622 but again made subordinate to Darmstadt in 1806. Restored to independence in 1815, it was enlarged by the addition of the lordships of Meisenheim and Kreuznach. The Homburg line became extinct with the death of Landgrave Ferdinand in 1866. The property passed to Darmstadt but was almost immediately annexed to Prussia.

Coins for Hesse-Homburg were struck in Darmstadt.

COUNT LUDWIG WILHELM FRIEDRICH, 1829–39

Born August 29, 1770, son of Count Friedrich V. Ludwig Wilhelm Christian and his consort, Caroline of Hessen-Darmstadt. Ludwig Wilhelm Friedrich died January 9, 1839.

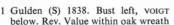

164.   1 Gulden (S) 1838. Bust left, VOIGT
       below. Rev. Value within oak wreath   37.50

165.   ½ Gulden (S) 1838. Type of #164   30.00

COUNT PHILIPP AUGUST FRIEDRICH, 1839–46

Born March 11, 1779, son of Count Friedrich V and his consort, Caroline of Hessen-Darmstadt. Philipp August Friedrich died December 15, 1846.

168.	½ Gulden (S) 1840–46. Type of #167	15.00
169.	6 Kreuzer (B) 1840. Crowned arms. Rev. Type of #167	12.50
170.	3 Kreuzer (B) 1840. Type of #169	16.50
171.	1 Kreuzer (S) 1840. Type of #169	4.50

166.	2 Gulden (S) 1846. Head left, C. VOIGT below. Rev. Crowned, draped arms	65.00

COUNT FERDINAND, 1848–66

Born April 26, 1783, son of Count Friedrich V Ludwig and his consort, Caroline of Hessen-Darmstadt. He was never married. Ferdinand died March 24, 1866.

167.	1 Gulden (S) 1841–46. As #166, but RS at truncation. Rev. value within oak wreath	20.00

172.	1 Vereinstaler (S) 1858–63. Head right, C.SCHNITZ-SPAHN at truncation. Rev. Crowned, draped arms. Edge: MUNZVERTRAG VOM 24 JANUAR 1857	17.50

HOHENZOLLERN

The Hohenzollern family took its name from its castle on Zollern hill in southern Germany. One branch of the family gained the Electorate of Brandenburg, eventually becoming kings of Prussia and emperors of Germany. The sons of Count Karl I of the Swabian branch divided their inheritance in 1576 into the lines of Hechingen and Sigmaringen.

HOHENZOLLERN-HECHINGEN

Capital: Hechingen

Founded in 1576, the Hechingen line endured into the 19th century when Prince Friedrich Wilhelm Constantin was forced to abdicate during the political upheavals of 1848. The principality passed to Prussia in 1849.

Coins for Hohenzollern-Hechingen were struck in:
Stuttgart
Munich (1839–47)

HERMANN FRIEDRICH OTTO, 1798–1810

Born November 6, 1748, son of Prince Friedrich Xaver and his consort, Anna of Hoensbroech. Hermann Friedrich Otto died November 2, 1810.

1. 1 Convention taler (S) 1804. Bust left. Rev. Crowned arms within laurel and palm branches   250.00

1.

FRIEDRICH WILHELM CONSTANTIN, 1838–49

Born February 16, 1801, son of Prince Friedrich and his consort, Pauline of Kurland. Friedrich Wilhelm Constantin died September 8, 1869.

4.   1 Gulden (S) 1839–47. As #2, but VOIGT below. Rev. Value within oak wreath   25.00

2.   2 Taler—3½ gulden (S) 1844, 45, 46. Head right, C.VOIGT below. Rev. Crowned, draped shield with Hohenzollern arms. Edge: CONVENTION VOM 30 JULY 1838   225.00

5.   ½ Gulden (S) 1839–47. Type of #4   22.50

6.   6 Kreuzer (S) 1841–47. Crowned arms. Rev. Type of #4   17.50

3.   2 Gulden (S) 1846, 47. Type of #2   125.00

7.   3 Kreuzer (S) 1845, 46, 47. Type of #6   12.50

HOHENZOLLERN-SIGMARINGEN

Capital: Sigmaringen

Dating from 1576, the line of Hohenzollern-Sigmaringen endured into the 19th century when Prince Carl Anton was forced to abdicate during the political upheavals of 1848. The principality passed to Prussia in 1849.

Coins for Hohenzollern-Sigmaringen were struck in:
Wiesbaden (1–6 kreuzers)
Karlsruhe ($\frac{1}{2}$ gulden up)
Berlin (1852)   Mintmark A

CARL, 1831–48

Born February 20, 1785, son of Prince Anton Alois and his consort, Amalie of Salm-Kyburg. Carl died March 11, 1853.

9.   3½ Gulden—2 taler (S) 1844, 46, 47. As #8. Rev. Crowned, draped arms supported by two dogs   212.50

8.   3½ Gulden—2 taler (S) 1841, 42, 43. Head left, DOELL F. below. Rev. Value within oak wreath. Edge: CONVENTION VOM 30 JULY 1838   237.50

10.   2 Gulden (S) 1845–48. As #8, but D below. Rev. Crowned arms supported by two dogs over palm branches   105.00

11.   1 Gulden (S) 1838. As #8, but D below   50.00

12.   1 Gulden (S) 1838–48. As #8 but
        DOELL   60.00

13.   ½ Gulden (S) 1838–48. Type of #11   32.50

14.   6 Kreuzer (S) 1839–47. Crowned arms.
        Rev. Value within oak wreath   7.50

15.   3 Kreuzer (S) 1839–47. Type of #14   10.00

16.   1 Kreuzer (C) 1842, 46. Type of #14.
        Rev. I KREUZER within oak wreath   8.75

17.   1 Kreuzer (S) 1842, 46. Type of #14.
        Rev. EIN KREUZER within oak wreath   3.75

CARL ANTON, 1848–49

Born September 7, 1811, son of Prince Carl and his
consort, Marie Antoinette, niece of King Joachim
Murat of Naples. Carl Anton died June 2, 1885.

18.   2 Gulden (S) 1849. Head left, BALBACH
        below. Rev. Crowned arms sup-
        ported by two dogs over palm
        branches   450.00

19.   1 Gulden (S) 1849. As #18. Rev. Value
        within oak wreath   25.00

FRIEDRICH WILHELM IV, KING OF PRUSSIA, 1849–61

(Because of the 1848 revolution in Europe, the King of Prussia accepted the areas of Hechlingen and Sigmaringen when both princes abdicated in his favor in 1849.)

22.   6 Kreuzer (S) 1852. Eagle with shield. Rev. Value within oak wreath   12.50

20.   1 Gulden (S) 1852. Head right, A below. Rev. Value within oak wreath   40.00

23.   3 Kreuzer (S) 1852. Type of #22   13.75

21.   ½ Gulden (S) 1852. Type of #20   22.50

24.   1 Kreuzer (C) 1852. Type of #22   3.75

ISENBURG

The territories of the Isenburg family were consolidated in 1806 under Carl Friedrich Ludwig Moritz of the Birstein line who was made a sovereign prince of the Rhine Confederation. The 1815 Congress of Vienna put the principality under Austrian domination. It was passed in turn to Hesse-Darmstadt and eventually went to Prussia.

Coins for Isenburg were struck in Frankfurt am Main.

CARL FRIEDRICH LUDWIG MORITZ, 1806–13

Born June 29, 1766, son of Prince Wolfgang Ernst II and his consort, Sophie Charlotte Ernestine of Anhalt-Bernburg. Carl Friedrich died March 21, 1820.

1.   1 Ducat (G) 1811. Head left, J. LAROQUE F. at truncation. Rev. Crowned, draped arms with chains of the orders of Malta, Legion of Honor and St. Anne of Russia   875.00

#2

2.   1 Reichstaler (S) 1811. As #1. Rev. Value within laurel wreath   300.00

3.   12 Kreuzer (S) 1811. Type of #2   80.00

4.   6 Kreuzer (S) 1811. Crowned C. Rev. Value within laurel wreath   72.50

KNYPHAUSEN

The house of Bentinck in the person of Count Wilhelm zu Rhoon and Pendrecht acquired the lordship of Knyphausen in 1732 through Wilhelm's wife Charlotte Sophie von Oldenburg. Their grandson was the only ruler to issue coins. The land came under the control of Oldenburg in 1818.

Coins for Knyphausen were struck in:
  St. Petersburg (gold)
  London (silver)

WILHELM GUSTAV FRIEDRICH, 1768–1835

Born July 21, 1762, son of Count Anton of Knyphausen and his consort, Marie van Tuyl of Serooskerken, Holland. Wilhelm Gustav Friedrich died October 22, 1835.

1. 10 Taler (G) 1806. Crowned arms within Order band and clasp, GUILIEL MUS. Rev. Value, SACR. ROM. —

2. 5 Taler (G) 1806. Type of #1 —

3. 2½ Taler (G) 1806. As #1 but GUILIEL. Rev. As #1 but S.ROM. —

4. 9 Grote—⅛ taler (S) 1807. Crowned, double headed eagle dividing 9 GR. Rev. Crowned lion rampant 20.00

5. 9 Grote—⅛ taler (S) 1807. Crowned arms. Rev. Value, crowned lion rampant 45.00

LAUENBURG

Hannover inherited the duchy of Lauenburg in 1705 but lost it after the Napoleonic Wars when the 1815 Congress of Vienna assigned the property to Prussia. Although the Prussians traded it to Denmark for Swedish Pomerania, Lauenburg remained within the German Confederation. A special coin was struck for the duchy in 1830 in the name of the Danish king. Prussia regained Lauenburg when it annexed Holstein in 1864.

The coin for Lauenburg was struck in Altona.

FREDERICK VI OF DENMARK, 1808–39

Born January 28, 1768, son of King Christian VII and his consort, Mathilde of Great Britain. At the close of the Congress of Vienna, Lauenburg was given to Denmark by Prussia and King Frederick VI of Denmark also became the Duke of Lauenburg. Frederick VI died December 3, 1839.

1.	⅔ Taler (S) 1830. Head left, F.A. at truncation. Rev. Value within oak wreath	30.00

LEININGEN-DAGSBURG-HARTENBURG

France annexed the Leiningen possessions on the west side of the Rhine in 1801 but compensated the principality by giving it Mosbach, Amorbach and Miltenberg, properties in the Rhineland and Wurttemberg. In 1806, however, the family lands were mediatized to Baden. A further division in 1810 gave parts to Bavaria and Hesse.

Coins for Leiningen were struck in Darmstadt.

KARL FRIEDRICH WILHELM, 1756–1807

Born August 14, 1724, son of Count Friedrich Magnus of Leiningen-Hartenburg and his consort, Anna Christine Eleonore, Countess of Wurmbrand. Karl Friedrich Wilhelm died January 9, 1807.

1.   6 Kreuzer (S) 1804. Crowned arms within laurel and palm branches. Rev. Value, palm branch below   17.50

2.   6 Kreuzer (S) 1805. Three eagles below crown within laurel and palm branches. Rev. Value, laurel branch below   15.00

3.   3 Kreuzer (S) 1804. Type of #1   12.50

4.   3 Kreuzer (S) 1805. Type of #2   12.50

5.   2 Pfennig (S) 1805. Crowned arms. Rev. Value, palm branch below   17.50

6.   1 Pfennig (S) 1805. As #2. Rev. Value   15.00

LIPPE

Capital: Detmold

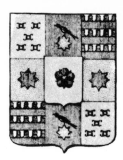

The Lippe family history goes back to the 12th century. The lords became counts in 1528, princes in 1720. The principality joined the German Empire in 1871 and endured until Leopold IV abdicated in 1918.

Coins for Lippe were struck in:
Detmold (1803–12)
Lemgo (1812–20)
Blomberg (1820–40)
Berlin (1843–1913)   Mintmark A

PAUL ALEXANDER LEOPOLD II, 1802–51

Born November 6, 1796, son of Prince Friedrich Wilhelm Leopold I and his consort, Pauline of Anhalt-Bernburg. Paul Alexander Leopold II died January 1, 1851.

UNDER THE GUARDIANSHIP OF HIS MOTHER FROM 1802 UNTIL 1820

2.   1 Pfennig (C) 1802. Type of #1   4.50

3.   1 Pfennig (C) 1818. As #1. Rev. т
     under date   2.50

1.   2 Pfennig (C) 1802. Blooming rose.
       Rev. Value, rosette under date   4.00

4.   1 Heller (C) 1802–16. Type of #3   2.00

140 • Lippe

AS INDEPENDENT PRINCE

5.   1 Double taler (S) 1843. Head right, A
below. Rev. Crowned, draped arms.
Edge: CONVENTION VOM 30 JULY 1838   150.00

6.   2½ Silbergroschen (B) 1847. Head right.
Rev. Value, A below   6.50

7.   1 Silbergroschen (B) 1847. Type of #6   4.50

8.   ½ Silbergroschen (B) 1847. Type of #6   3.00

9.   3 Pfennig (C) 1847. Crowned shield
with blooming rose. Rev. Value   1.50

10.   1½ Pfennig (C) 1821–25. Blooming rose.
Rev. PFEN-NING., T below   2.00

11.   1 Pfennig (C) 1820–25. As #10, but ST
below on reverse   1.75

12.   1 Pfennig (C) 1824. As #11. Rev.
PFENNING   2.50

13.   1 Pfennig (C) 1828–40. As #11, but
Rev. PFENNIG   2.50

14.   1 Pfennig (C) 1847. Crowned shield
with blooming rose. Rev. Value   1.50

15.   1 Heller (C) 1821–40. Blooming rose.
Rev. Value   1.50

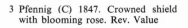

PAUL FRIEDRICH EMIL LEOPOLD III, 1851–75

Born September 1, 1821, son of Prince Paul Alexander Leopold II and his consort, Emilie of Schwarzburg-Sondershausen. Paul Friedrich Emil died December 8, 1875.

LEOPOLD IV, 1905–18

Born May 30, 1871, son of Count Ernst of Lippe-Biesterfeld and his consort, Caroline, Countess of Wartensleben. With the death of Prince Alexander of Lippe-Detmold on January 13, 1905, his line became extinct and reverted to Lippe-Biesterfeld. Leopold IV abdicated his throne in 1918, and died in 1949.

16.   1 Vereinstaler (S) 1860, 66. Head right, C.P. at truncation, A below. Rev. Crowned, draped arms. Edge: MUNZVERTRAG VOM 24 JANUAR 1857   45.00

17.   2½ Silbergroschen (B) 1860. Head right. Rev. Value   4.50

18.   1 Silbergroschen (B) 1860. Type of #17   4.00

19.   3 Pfennig (C) 1858. Crowned shield with blooming rose. Rev. Value   3.00

20.   1 Pfennig (C) 1851, 58. Type of #19   1.50

21.   3 Mark (S) 1913. Head left, A below. Rev. Type 3 eagle. Edge: GOTT MIT UNS   112.50

22.   2 Mark (S) 1906. Type of #21. Reeded edge   87.50

LUBECK
Free City

The present town of Lubeck dates from 1143, founded five years after the old town was destroyed. Made a free city of the Empire in 1188, it became one of the leading members of the Hanseatic League. Occupied by the French during the Napoleonic Wars, Lubeck was restored as a free city in 1813. The city became part of the German Empire in 1871 but retained its right to mint coins.

Coins for Lubeck were struck in Berlin: Mintmark A

1.   10 Mark (G) 1901, 04. Narrow double eagle with breast shield. Rev. Type 3 eagle   187.50

2.   10 Mark (G) 1905–10. Broad double eagle with breast shield. Rev. Type of #1   187.50

3.   5 Mark (S) 1904–13. Type of #2   100.00

4.   3 Mark (S) 1908–14. Type of #2   25.00

5.   2 Mark (S) 1901. Type of #1   65.00

6.   2 Mark (S) 1904–12. Type of #2   45.00

MECKLENBURG

The Mecklenburg dynasty which dates from the 12th century divided in 1658 into the Schwerin and Strelitz lines. The 1815 Congress of Vienna elevated the duchies to the status of grand duchies. Both became part of the German Empire in 1871 and endured until 1918. Grand Duke Friedrich Adolf VI of Strelitz died on February 24, 1918 without heirs and his title passed to Friedrich Franz IV of Schwerin who was forced to abdicate before the lands could be united.

MECKLENBURG-SCHWERIN

Coins for Mecklenburg-Schwerin were struck in:

Schwerin (to 1848)
Berlin (from 1855)   Mintmark A
Dresden (1872)

FRIEDRICH FRANZ I, 1785–1837

Born December 10, 1756, the son of Duke Ludwig and his consort, Charlotte of Sachsen-Coburg-Saalfeld. Friedrich Franz took the title of Grand Duke June 9, 1815. He died February 1, 1837.

2.   5 Taler (G) 1828–35. As #1, but arms have no supporters   250.00

To commemorate the Grand Duke's visit to the Schwerin mint, a special strike was made of the 1828 5 Taler gold coin bearing the date, 28 MAERZ 1828. Only five or six pieces were struck.

1.   10 Taler (G) 1828–33. Head left. Rev. Crowned, draped arms supported by a bull and griffin   400.00

3.   2½ Taler (G) 1831, 33, 35. Type of #2   150.00

4.　2 Taler (G) 1830. Head left. Rev.
　　Crowned arms within collar of the
　　Danish Order of the Elephant and
　　the Prussian Order of the Black
　　Eagle　　　　　　　　　　　500.00

5.　1 Ducat (G) 1830. As #4 but bull and
　　griffin supporting the shield　　500.00

8.　⅔ Taler—gulden (S) 1817. As #6 but
　　G.G. GROSHERZOG　　　　　137.50

6.　⅔ Taler—gulden (S) 1808, 10.
　　Crowned arms, G.G. HERZOG. Rev.
　　Value　　　　　　　　　　　20.00

9.　⅔ Taler—gulden (S) 1825. As #6 but
　　G.G. GR. HERZ.　　　　　　45.00

7.　⅔ Taler—gulden (S) 1813. As #6 but
　　DEM VATERLANDE below value　　30.00

10.　⅔ Taler—gulden (S) 1825, 26. Uni-
　　formed bust left. Rev. Value　　25.00

Mecklenburg-Schwerin　•　145

11. ⅔ Taler—gulden (S) 1828, 29. Head left. Rev. Crowned, draped arms   27.50

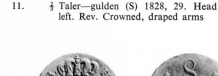

12. 8 Schillinge—1/6 taler (S) 1827. Crowned FF monogram. Rev. Value, LAND. MUNZ.   16.50

13. 4 Schillinge—1/12 taler (S) 1809. Crowned FF monogram on cartouche. Rev. Value, MUNZE   45.00

14. 4 Schillinge—1/12 taler (S) 1826. Type of #8   8.50

15. 4 Schillinge—1/12 taler (S) 1828–33. Head left. Rev. Value   8.50

16. 1 Schilling—1/48 taler (B) 1806–17. Crowned FF monogram. Rev. Value   2.50

17. 1 Schilling—1/48 taler (B) 1826, 27. Crowned FF monogram, GR. HZ. U.M.S. Rev. Value   6.50

18. 1 Schilling—1/48 taler (B) 1829–37. Crowned FF monogram, GR. HERZOG v. Rev. Value   3.00

19. 1 Sechsling—6 pfennige (B) 1809–17. Type of #16   3.00

20. 1 Sechsling—6 pfennige (B) 1820–24. Type of #16   2.50

146 • Mecklenburg-Schwerin

21. 1 Sechsling—6 pfennige (B) 1828, 29.
Type of #18   5.50

28. 1 Pfennig (C) 1831. Type of #22   2.00

22. 1 Sechsling—6 pfennige (B) 1831.
Crowned FF monogram. Rev. Value   5.00

PAUL FRIEDRICH, 1837–42

Born September 15, 1800, the son of Grand Duke
Friedrich Ludwig and his consort, Helene, Grand
Duchess of Russia. Paul Friedrich died March 7, 1842.

23. 1 Dreiling—3 pfennige (B) 1810–19.
Type of #22   2.50

24. 1 Dreiling—3 pfennige (B) 1819–24.
Type of #22   2.50

29. 10 Taler (G) 1839. Head right. Rev.
Crowned, draped arms supported by
a bull and a griffin   300.00

25. 1 Dreiling—3 pfennige (B) 1828, 29, 30.
Crowned FF monogram, G.R. HERZOG
v. Rev. Value   1.35

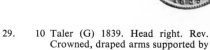

30. 5 Taler (G) 1840. As #29. Rev. Arms
without supporters   500.00

26. 1 Dreiling—3 pfennige (B) 1831–36.
Type of #22   1.50

27. 2 Pfennige (C) 1831. Type of #22   2.00

31. 2½ Taler (G) 1840. Type of #30   212.50

36. Commemorative medals (2½ and 5 taler sizes) 1842. Head right. Rev. Within mourning wreath, VOLLENDET D. 7 MAERZ 1842   25.00

Marks the death of the Grand Duke, March 7, 1842.

32. ⅔ Taler—gulden (S) 1839, 40, 41. Head right. Rev. Crowned arms within two crossed laurel branches   22.50

FRIEDRICH FRANZ II, 1842–83

Born February 28, 1823, son of Grand Duke Paul Friedrich and his consort, Alexandrine of Prussia. Friedrich Franz died April 15, 1883.

33. 4 Schillinge—1/12 taler (S) 1838, 39. Crowned arms within two crossed laurel branches. Rev. Value   6.50

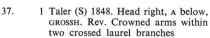

37. 1 Taler (S) 1848. Head right, A below, GROSSH. Rev. Crowned arms within two crossed laurel branches   32.50

34. 1 Schilling—1/48 taler (B) 1838–42. Crowned PF monogram, inscription. Rev. Value   4.00

38. 1 Taler (S) 1864. Head right with sideburns. Rev. Type of #37. Edge: PER ASPERA AD ASTRA—"Through Difficulties to the Stars"   25.00

35. 1 Dreiling—3 pfennige (B) 1838–42. Crowned PF monogram, no inscription. Rev. Value   2.50

43. 1 Schilling—1/48 taler (B) 1848. As #42, but GR. HERZOG — 2.50

44. 1 Schilling—1/48 taler (B) 1852–66. As #42, but GROSSH. — 1.50

39. ⅔ Taler—gulden (S) 1845. As #37, but no A below head and GROSSHERZOG. Rev. Crowned arms within two laurel branches — 120.00

45. 5 Pfennige (C) 1872. As #42, but V.G.G. GROSSHERZOG — 3.00

40. 1/6 Taler (S) 1848. Type of #37 — 6.50

46. 3 Pfennige (B) 1842–46. Crowned FF monogram. Rev. Value, III PFENNINGE — 3.00

41. 1/12 Taler (S) 1848. Head right. Rev. Value — 2.50

47. 3 Pfennige (C) 1843–48. As #6 but 3 PFENNINGE — 2.50

42. 1 Schilling—1/48 taler (B) 1842–46. Crowned FF monogram, GROSSHERZOG. Rev. Value — 3.00

48. 3 Pfennige (C) 1852–64. Type of #47 — 1.50

49.   2 Pfennige (C) 1872. Crowned FF
        monogram, V.G.G. GROSSH. Rev.
        Value   1.50

50.   1 Pfennig (C) 1872. Type of #49   1.50

AFTER INCORPORATION INTO THE EMPIRE

51.   20 Mark (G) 1872. Head right. Rev.
        Type 1 eagle. Edge: GOTT MIT UNS   155.00

52.   10 Mark (G) 1872. As #51, but vines
        and stars on edge   200.00

53.   10 Mark (G) 1878. As #51, but Rev.
        Type 2 eagle   187.50

54.   2 Mark (S) 1876. Head right. Rev.
        Type 2 eagle   90.00

COMMEMORATIVE ISSUE

55.   1 Taler (S) 1867. Head right. Rev.
        Crowned arms within two crossed
        laurel branches, ZUR FEIER. Edge:
        EIN THALER 30 EIN PFUND FEIN   50.00

        Commemorates the 25th anniversary
        of the reign.

FRIEDRICH FRANZ III, 1883–97

Born March 19, 1851, son of Grand Duke Friedrich
Franz II and his consort, Auguste of Reuss-Kostritz.
Friedrich Franz III died April 10, 1897.

56.   10 Mark (G) 1890. Head right. Rev.
        Type 2 eagle   105.00

FRIEDRICH FRANZ IV, 1897–1918

Born April 9, 1882, son of Grand Duke Friedrich Franz III and his consort, Anastasia, Grand Duchess of Russia. Friedrich Franz was under the Regency of his uncle, Johann Albrecht from 1897–1901. Upon the death of Grand Duke Adolf Friedrich VI of Mecklenburg-Strelitz, he also assumed the rule of that dynasty. Friedrich Franz IV renounced his throne November 14, 1918.

58.   10 Mark (G) 1901. Type of #57   212.50

57.   20 Mark (G) 1901. Head right. Rev. Type 3 eagle   312.50

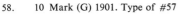

59.   2 Mark (S) 1901. Type of #57   125.00

COMMEMORATIVE ISSUES

#60

60.   5 Mark (S) 1904. Conjoined heads of the Duke and Duchess. Rev. Type 3 eagle   65.00

61.   2 Mark (S) 1904. Type of #60   27.50

The above two coins commemorate the marriage of the Grand Duke to Alexandra, Princess of Great Britain and Duchess of Braunschweig-Luneburg.

62.   5 Mark (S) 1915. Conjoined heads of Friedrich Franz I and IV, left. Rev. Type 3 eagle   150.00

63.   3 Mark (S) 1915. Type of #62   70.00

The above two coins commemorate the centennial of the Grand Duchy.

MECKLENBURG-STRELITZ

Coins for Mecklenburg-Strelitz were struck in:
Schwerin (to 1848)
Berlin (from 1855)   Mintmark A
Dresden (1872)

GEORG, 1816–60

Born August 12, 1779, the son of Grand Duke Karl II and his consort, Frederike Caroline Louise of Hessen-Darmstadt. Georg died September 6, 1860.

67.   3 Pfennige (C) 1832–47. Crowned G, V.G.G.G.R., rosette below. Rev. Value 3.00

64.   4 Schillinge—1/12 taler (B) 1846, 47, 49. Head right. Rev. Value   4.50

68.   3 Pfennige (C) 1855, 59. As #66   2.00

65.   1/48 Taler (B) 1838–47. Crowned G, V.G.G.GR. Rev. Value   3.00

69.   1½ Pfennige (C) 1838. Crowned G. Rev. Value   10.00

66.   1/48 Taler (B) 1855, 59. As #65, with A below date   2.50

70.   1 Pfennig (C) 1838. Type of #69   7.50

FRIEDRICH WILHELM, 1860–1904

Born October 17, 1819, son of Grand Duke Georg and his consort, Marie of Hessen-Kassel. Friedrich Wilhelm died May 30, 1904.

71.   1 Taler (S) 1870. Head left. Rev. Crowned arms within buckled Order of the Garter inscribed HONI SOIT QUI MAL Y PENSE—"Evil to Him Who Thinks Evil." Edge: GOTT SCHIRME MECKLENBURG—"God Protect Mecklenburg"   27.50

72.   1/48 Taler (B) 1862,64. Crowned F W monogram, G. GR. Rev. Value   2.00

73.   5 Pfennige (C) 1872. Crowned F W monogram, G. GROSSHERZOG. Rev. Value   3.00

74.   3 Pfennige (C) 1862, 64. Type of #72   2.00

75.   2 Pfennige (C) 1872. Crowned F W monogram, G. GROSSH. Rev. Value   2.50

76.   1 Pfennig (C) 1872. Type of #75   2.00

AFTER INCORPORATION INTO THE GERMAN EMPIRE

77.   20 Mark (G) 1873. Head left. Rev. Type 1 eagle. Edge: GOTT MIT UNS   565.00

78.   20 Mark (G) 1874. As #77, but Rev. type 2 eagle   575.00

79.   10 Mark (G) 1873. As #77. Edge: Vines and stars   700.00

80.   10 Mark (G) 1874, 80. As #79, but Rev. type 2 eagle   600.00

81.   2 Mark (S) 1877. As #77. Rev. Type 2 eagle. Reeded edge   125.00

ADOLF FRIEDRICH V, 1904–14

Born July 22, 1848, son of Grand Duke Friedrich Wilhelm and his consort, Auguste Karoline, Princess of Great Britain, Hannover and Ireland. Adolf died June 11, 1914.

85.   2 Mark (S) 1905. Type of #82   125.00

CITY OF ROSTOCK

Located within the Grand Duchy of Mecklenburg-Schwerin.

82.   20 Mark (G) 1905. Head left. Rev. Type 3 eagle. Edge: GOTT MIT UNS   750.00

86.   3 Pfennige (C) 1815, 24. Griffin striding left, inscription. Rev. Value, mint mark A.S.   4.00

83.   10 Mark (G) 1905. As #82. Edge: Vines and stars   800.00

87.   3 Pfennige (C) 1843. As #86, but mint mark B.S.   1.75

88.   3 Pfennige (C) 1855. Two arms of Rostock, separated. Rev. Type of #87   3.75

84.   3 Mark (S) 1913. Head left. Rev. Type 3 eagle. Edge: GOTT MIT UNS   162.50

89.   3 Pfennige (C) 1859. Type of #87   3.00

90.   3 Pfennige (C) 1862, 64. As #86, but mint mark H.K.   2.50

91.   1 Pfennig (C) 1815, 24. Type of #86   5.00

92.   1 Pfennig (C) 1848. Griffin striding left, no inscription. Rev. Value, mint mark B.S.   8.00

CITY OF WISMAR

Located within the confines of the Grand Duchy of Mecklenburg-Schwerin, the city was acquired in 1803 from Swedish King Gustaf IV Adolf.

93.   3 Pfennige (C) 1824–45. City arms. Rev. Value within arabesques   4.50

94.   3 Pfennige (C) 1854. Crowned arms. Rev. Value, mint mark s   3.00

NASSAU

Capital: Wiesbaden

The duchy of Nassau originated in the 12th century and the lands were frequently divided and combined. In 1806, the remaining lines, Nassau-Usingen and Nassau-Weilburg, united under a common administration. The Usingen line became extinct in 1816 leaving a fully united duchy under the Weilburg rulers. Nassau sided with Austria in the Austro-Prussian War of 1866. Prussia invaded without resistance and annexed the duchy.

Coins for Nassau were struck in:
Darmstadt (1808–09)
Ehrenbreitstein near Coblenz (from 1809)
Frankfurt (1822)
Limburg/Lahn (1815–28)
Wiesbaden (1830–66)

Since 1808, a common or mutual minting agreement existed between Duke Friedrich August and Prince Friedrich Wilhelm.

1.   1 Ducat (G) 1809. Crowned arms with garland. Rev. Value within square tablet — 225.00

2.   24 Kreuzer (S) 1809. Crowned arms, CONVENTIONS. Rev. Value within two bound oak branches — 7.50

3.   24 Kreuzer (S) 1809. As #2 but CONVENT and Rev. L below branches — 11.00

4.   24 Kreuzer (S) 1809. As #2. Rev. No bow on wreath and prancing horse below — 12.50

5.   24 Kreuzer (S) 1809. Crowned arms, HERZ:NASS:CONV:MUNZ. Rev. Value within two bound oak branches — 6.50

6.   12 Kreuzer (S) 1809. Crowned arms, HERZ. NASSAUISCHE. Rev. Value within two bound oak branches, L below   5.00

16.   1 Kreuzer (C) 1808. Crowned arms. Rev. Value within oak wreath, L below (Wide planchet—22-24 mm)   2.00

7.   12 Kreuzer (S) 1809. As #6, but HERZ. NASSAU. and Rev. no L   4.50

8.   6 Kreuzer (S) 1808, 09. As #7, but Rev. L below   4.50

9.   6 Kreuzer (S) 1808. As #8 but HERZOGL   4.00

10.   3 Kreuzer—groschen (S) 1809. Crowned arms, HERZ. NASS. Rev. Value   2.00

17.   1 Kreuzer (C) 1808, 09. As #16, but period after -ZER. on reverse (Thick, narrow planchet—19 mm)   6.50

11.   3 Kreuzer—groschen (S) 1810. As #10 but HERZ. NASSAU. SCHEIDE M. Rev. As #10, but period after date   2.50

18.   1 Kreuzer (C) 1809, 10, 13. Crowned arms, HERZ: Rev. Type of #17 (Wide planchet—22-24 mm)   2.00

12.   3 Kreuzer—groschen (S) 1811. As #11, but Rev. no period after date   2.50

13.   3 Kreuzer—groschen (S) 1812. Type of #12   1.50

19.   ½ Kreuzer (C) 1813. Crowned arms, HERZ. Rev. Value within oak wreath   1.50

14.   3 Kreuzer—groschen (S) 1813. As #11 but SCHEIDE.M. and Rev. with or without period after date   1.50

20.   ¼ Kreuzer (C) 1808. Crowned arms, HERZOGL:NASS. Rev. Value within oak wreath   1.75

15.   3 Kreuzer—groschen (S) 1814, 15, 16. As #14   1.50

21.   ¼ Kreuzer (C) 1808-14. Crowned arms, HERZ. Rev. As #20 but no L   1.50

DUKE FRIEDRICH AUGUST, 1803–16

Born April 23, 1738, son of Prince Karl and his consort, Christiane Wilhelmine of Sachsen-Eisenach. Friedrich August died March 24, 1816.

22.   1 Convention taler (S) 1809. Head right, L at truncation. Rev. Crowned arms within bound laurel and oak branches, MARK. Edge: UT SIT SUO PONDERE TUTUS—"That He May Be Safe by His Own Weight"   50.00

25.   1 Convention taler (S) 1810–15. As #22, but date dividing C.T. on reverse   100.00

26.   ½ Convention taler (S) 1809. As #23, but L below truncation and period after MARK   20.00

27.   24 Kreuzer (S) 1809. Head right, L at truncation. Rev. Crowned arms dividing date   7.50

23.   1 Convention taler (S) 1809. As #22, but Rev. laurel and palm branches and no period after MARK   62.50

24.   1 Convention taler (S) 1809–12. Type of #22   50.00

28.   12 Kreuzer (S) 1809. Type of #27   12.50

PRINCE FRIEDRICH WILHELM, 1788–1816

Born October 25, 1768, son of Prince Karl Christian and his consort, Karoline of Nassau-Dietz-Oranien. Friedrich Wilhelm died January 9, 1816.

33.	1 Convention taler (S) 1812. Type of #30. Rev. Type of #32	55.00

29.	1 Convention taler (S) 1809. Head right, L on truncation. Rev. Crowned arms within bound laurel and oak branches. Edge: UT SIT SUO PONDERE TUTUS	62.50
30.	1 Convention taler (S) 1809. As #29, but L at truncation. Rev. As #29 but laurel and palm branches	62.50
31.	1 Convention taler (S) 1809, 10. As #30. Rev. As #29	55.00

34.	1 Convention taler (S) 1813, 15. As #29 but older portrait. Rev. Type of #32	55.00
35.	½ Convention taler (S) 1809. Type of #29. Rev. Type of #30	22.50

36.	24 Kreuzer (S) 1809, 10. Type of #29. Rev. Crowned arms dividing date	7.50
37.	12 Kreuzer (S) 1809. Type of #30. Rev. Type of #36	15.00

32.	1 Convention taler (S) 1810, 11, 12. As #29 but date dividing C.T. on reverse	60.00

DUKE WILHELM, 1816–39

Born June 14, 1792, son of Prince Friedrich Wilhelm
and his consort, Luise. Wilhelm died August 20, 1839.

38. 1 Ducat (G) 1818. Head right. Rev.
Crowned, draped arms, date below
dividing C.T. 325.00

39. 1 Kronentaler (S) 1816. Type of #38,
but L below head —

42. 1 Kronentaler (S) 1831–37. Head right,
deep ZOLLMANN.F at truncation.
Rev. Crowned arms supported by
two lions. Edge: ZUR SICHERUNG DES
GEWICHTS — "To Guarantee the
Weight" 95.00

40. 1 Kronentaler (S) 1817. Crowned,
draped arms. Rev. Value within two
bound laurel branches 70.00

43. 1 Gulden (S) 1838, 39. Head right,
older portrait, Z at truncation. Rev.
Value within two bound oak branches 25.00

41. 1 Kronentaler (S) 1818, 25. Head right,
hair neatly in rows, P.Z. at truncation. Rev. Crowned, draped arms 95.00

44. ½ Gulden (S) 1838, 39. Type of #43 5.00

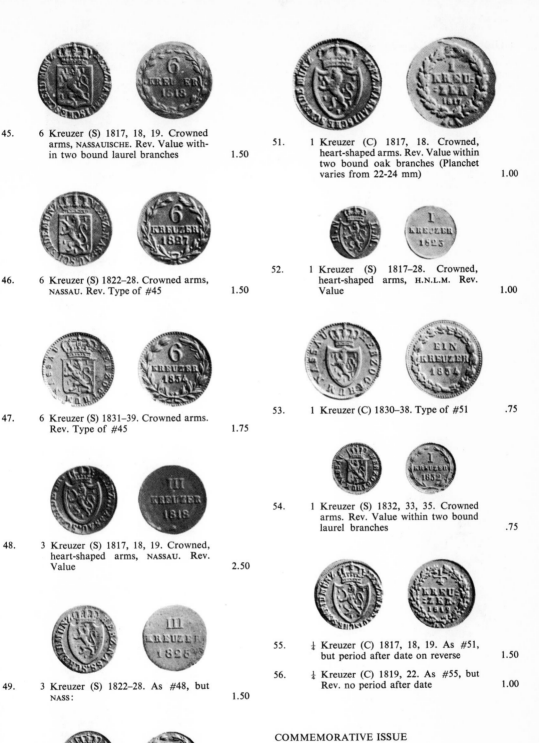

45.　6 Kreuzer (S) 1817, 18, 19. Crowned
arms, NASSAUISCHE. Rev. Value within two bound laurel branches　　1.50

46.　6 Kreuzer (S) 1822–28. Crowned arms,
NASSAU. Rev. Type of #45　　1.50

47.　6 Kreuzer (S) 1831–39. Crowned arms.
Rev. Type of #45　　1.75

48.　3 Kreuzer (S) 1817, 18, 19. Crowned,
heart-shaped arms, NASSAU. Rev.
Value　　2.50

49.　3 Kreuzer (S) 1822–28. As #48, but
NASS:　　1.50

50.　3 Kreuzer (S) 1831–36. Crowned,
heart-shaped arms. Rev. Value within
two laurel branches　　1.75

51.　1 Kreuzer (C) 1817, 18. Crowned,
heart-shaped arms. Rev. Value within
two bound oak branches (Planchet
varies from 22-24 mm)　　1.00

52.　1 Kreuzer (S) 1817–28. Crowned,
heart-shaped arms, H.N.L.M. Rev.
Value　　1.00

53.　1 Kreuzer (C) 1830–38. Type of #51　　.75

54.　1 Kreuzer (S) 1832, 33, 35. Crowned
arms. Rev. Value within two bound
laurel branches　　.75

55.　¼ Kreuzer (C) 1817, 18, 19. As #51,
but period after date on reverse　　1.50

56.　¼ Kreuzer (C) 1819, 22. As #55, but
Rev. no period after date　　1.00

COMMEMORATIVE ISSUE

57.　1 Kronentaler (S) 1831. As #42. Rev.
BESUCHT ZUM. Edge: Type of #42　　125.00

Marks the visit of the Duke to the
mint.

DUKE ADOLPH, 1839–66

Born July 24, 1817, son of Duke Wilhelm and his consort, Louise, Duchess of Sachsen-Altenburg. He was dispossessed by Prussia in 1866. Adolph died November 17, 1905, as Grand Duke of Luxembourg.

58.   1 Double taler—3½ gulden (S) 1840. Head right, ZOLLMANN at truncation. Rev. Value within two oak branches. Edge: CONVENTION VOM 30 JULY 1838   88.50

60.   1 Double taler—3½ gulden (S) 1844, 54. As #58 but without ZOLLMANN. Rev. Type of #59   100.00

59.   1 Double taler—3½ gulden (S) 1844, 47. As #58. Rev. Crowned, draped arms. Edge: Type of #58   95.00

61.   1 Double taler (S) 1860. Head left, C. ZOLLMANN at truncation. Rev. Type of #59. Edge: MUNZVERTRAG VOM 24 JANUAR 1857   75.00

62. 2 Gulden (S) 1846, 47. Head right, C. ZOLLMANN at truncation. Rev. Crowned arms supported by two lions   22.50

65. 1 Gulden (S) 1840–55. As #63. Rev. Value within oak wreath   15.00

63. 1 Vereinstaler (S) 1859, 60. Head left, z at truncation. Rev. As #62. Edge: As #61   22.50

66. 1 Gulden (S) 1855, 56. Type of #65   22.50

67. ½ Gulden (S) 1840–45. As #65 but no z   15.00

64. 1 Vereinstaler (S) 1863. As #63 but F.KORN at truncation   30.00

68. ½ Gulden (S) 1856, 60. Type of #65   15.00

69.   6 Kreuzer (S) 1840–55. Crowned arms. Rev. Type of #65   2.50

74.   1 Heller (C) 1842. Crowned arms. Rev. Value   1.50

70.   3 Kreuzer (S) 1839–55. Type of #69   2.50

75.   1 Pfennig (C) 1859, 60, 62. Crowned arms supported by two lions. Rev. Type of #71   2.00

COMMEMORATIVE ISSUES

71.   1 Kreuzer (C) 1842–56. Crowned, heart-shaped arms. Rev. Value within two bound oak branches   1.50

76.   1 Taler (S) 1861. Head left, F.KORN at truncation. Rev. DEM EDLEN   —

Marks the visit of the Grand Duke to the mint.

72.   1 Kreuzer (C) 1859–63. Crowned arms supported by two lions. Rev. Type of #71   2.00

73.   1 Kreuzer (S) 1861. Crowned arms. Rev. Type of #71   1.50

77.   1 Taler (S) 1864. Head left in laurel wreath, F.KORN at truncation. Rev. DEN 21 AUGUST within two bound oak branches. Edge: EIN GEDENK-THALER XXX EIN PFUND FEIN   55.00

Marks the 25th anniversary of the reign.

OLDENBURG

The county of Oldenburg dates back to 1180. Christian VIII of the ruling line became king of Denmark in 1448. Oldenburg passed to the Holstein-Gottorp line in 1773 and it was raised to the status of a duchy in 1777. In 1803, the Bishopric of Lubeck was joined to it. The territory was annexed to France in 1810 but restored by the 1815 Congress of Vienna which also elevated the duke to the rank of grand duke. The grand duchy entered the German Empire in 1871 and endured until Friedrich August was forced to abdicate in 1918.

Coins for Oldenburg were struck in:
Berlin (1815–18, 91, 1900, 01)　　Mintmark A
Bremen (1845, 46)
Hannover (1835–66, 74)　　Mintmark B
Oldenburg
Wiesbaden (1840, 41)

PETER FRIEDRICH WILHELM, 1785–1823

Born January 3, 1754, son of Count Friedrich August of Oldenburg and his consort, Friederike of Hesse-Kassel. Peter Friedrich Wilhelm died July 2, 1823.

The government was under his cousin, Peter Friedrich Ludwig (Bishop of Lubeck, 1786–1803), Grand Duke of Oldenburg, 1823–29. He was born January 17, 1755, son of Duke Georg Ludwig of Holstein-Gottorp and his consort, Sophie of Holstein-Beck. Peter Friedrich Ludwig died May 21, 1829.

1.　1 Dritteltaler (S) 1816, 18. Crowned, draped arms. Rev. Value　　12.50

2.　1/6 Taler—12 grote (S) 1816, 18. As #1 but shield with garlands　　7.50

PAUL FRIEDRICH AUGUST, 1829–53

Born July 13, 1783, son of Grand Duke Peter Friedrich Ludwig and his consort, Friederike of Wurttemberg. He took the title of Grand Duke in 1829. Paul Friedrich August died February 27, 1853.

3. 1/12 Taler—6 grote (B) 1816, 18. Type of #2   4.00

4. 1/18 Taler—4 grote (B) 1816, 18. Crowned arms with garlands, N.D.C.F. Rev. Value   2.50

5. 1/36 Taler—2 grote (B) 1815. Type of #4   2.00

8. 1 Double taler—3½ gulden (S) 1840. Head left, ZOLLMAN under truncation. Rev. Value within two bound oak branches. Edge: CONVENTION VOM 30 IULY 1838   300.00

6. 1 Grote (B) 1817. Type of #4   2.00

7. 1/2 Grote (C) 1802, 16. Type of #4   2.50

9. 1 Taler (S) 1846. Head left, B below. Rev. Crowned arms within crossed laurel and oak branches. Edge: EIN GOTT EIN RECHT EINE WAHRHEIT— "One God, One Justice, One Truth"   30.00

10. 1/6 Taler—12 grote (S) 1846. As #9. Rev. Value. Edge: Type of #9   6.50

15. ½ Grote (C) 1831, 35, 40. Crowned arms of Oldenburg-Delmenhorst with garlands. Rev. Value   2.50

11. 1/18 Taler—4 grote (B) 1840. Crowned arms of Oldenburg-Delmenhorst, SCHEIDE-M. Rev. Value   2.50

16. ½ Grote (C) 1846. As #15, HERZOG-THUM OLDENBURG   2.00

12. 1/24 Taler—3 grote (B) 1840. Type of #11   2.00

17. 1 Pfennig—¼ grote (C) 1846. Crowned PFA monogram. Rev. Value   2.00

13. 1 Grote (B) 1836. As #11 but SCHEIDE M.   1.50

18. 1 Schwaren (C) 1846. Type of #17   1.75

14. 1 Grote (B) 1849, 50. Type of #11   1.50

19. 1 Schwaren (C) 1852. Type of #17   1.75

NICOLAUS FRIEDRICH PETER, 1853–1900

Born July 8, 1827, son of Grand Duke Paul Friedrich August and his consort, Ida, Princess of Anhalt-Bernberg-Schaumburg-Hoym. Nicolaus Friedrich Peter died June 13, 1900.

20. 2½ Silbergroschen—1/12 taler—6 grote (B) 1848. Crowned arms. Rev. Value   9.50

21. 1 Silbergroschen (B) 1848. Type of #20   6.50

25. 1 Taler (S) 1858, 60, 66. Head left, BREHMER.F. at truncation, B below. Rev. Crowned arms within crossed laurel and oak branches. Edge: EIN GOTT EIN RECHT EINE WAHRHEIT   38.50

22. 3 Pfennig (C) 1848. Crowned PFA monogram. Rev. Value   4.00

26. ½ Taler—2½ silbergroschen (B) 1858. Crowned arms. Rev. Value   2.50

23. 2 Pfennig (C) 1848. Crowned PFA monogram. Rev. Value   2.50

24. 1 Pfennig (C) 1848. Type of #23   2.50

27. 1/24 Taler—3 grote (B) 1856. Crowned arms. Rev. Value   2.00

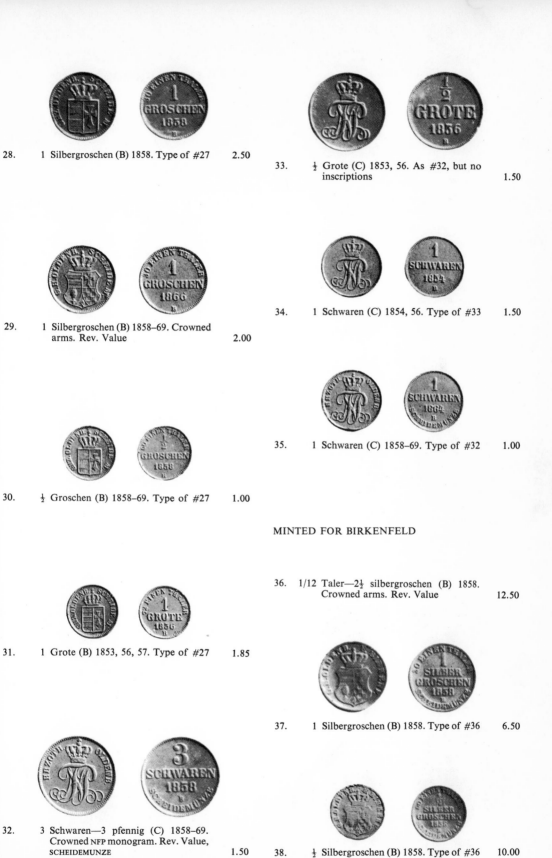

28.   1 Silbergroschen (B) 1858. Type of #27   2.50

33.   ½ Grote (C) 1853, 56. As #32, but no inscriptions   1.50

29.   1 Silbergroschen (B) 1858–69. Crowned arms. Rev. Value   2.00

34.   1 Schwaren (C) 1854, 56. Type of #33   1.50

35.   1 Schwaren (C) 1858–69. Type of #32   1.00

30.   ½ Groschen (B) 1858–69. Type of #27   1.00

MINTED FOR BIRKENFELD

36.   1/12 Taler—2½ silbergroschen (B) 1858. Crowned arms. Rev. Value   12.50

31.   1 Grote (B) 1853, 56, 57. Type of #27   1.85

37.   1 Silbergroschen (B) 1858. Type of #36   6.50

32.   3 Schwaren—3 pfennig (C) 1858–69. Crowned NFP monogram. Rev. Value, SCHEIDEMUNZE   1.50

38.   ½ Silbergroschen (B) 1858. Type of #36   10.00

Oldenburg • 169

39.   3 Pfennige (C) 1858. Crowned NFP
       monogram. Rev. Value   4.50

40.   2 Pfennige (C) 1858. Type of #39   3.00

41.   1 Pfennig (C) 1859. Type of #39   5.00

AFTER INCORPORATION INTO THE EMPIRE

42.   10 Mark (G) 1874. Head left, B below.
       Rev. Type 3 eagle   450.00

43.   2 Mark (S) 1891. As #42, but A below
       head   87.50

FRIEDRICH AUGUST, 1900–18

Born November 16, 1852, son of Grand Duke Nicolaus Friedrich Peter and his consort, Ida. He abdicated his throne in 1918. Friedrich August died February 24, 1931.

44.   5 Mark (S) 1900, 01. Head left, A
       below. Rev. Type 3 eagle. Edge:
       GOTT MIT UNS   175.00

45.   2 Mark (S) 1900, 01. Type of #44.
       Reeded edge   75.00

PRUSSIA

Capital: Berlin

The Kingdom of Prussia came into being in 1701. Elector Friedrich I of Brandenburg was allowed to take the title of King in Prussia in return for his support of the emperor in the War of the Spanish Succession. During the Napoleonic Wars, Prussia at first remained neutral, then allied itself with Saxony. Defeated at Jena in 1806, Prussia was forced to pay reparations and to cede a large portion of its territory. The French were expelled in 1813, however, and the post-war Congress of Vienna restored the ceded lands and granted Prussia additional important territories as well. Wars with Denmark and Austria in 1864 and 1866 led to the acquisition of more territory. Following Prussia's victory in the 1870–71 war with France, King Wilhelm I of Prussia was proclaimed emperor of all Germany. The 25 states and cities of the union continued their own coinage of higher denomination coins but the values from 1 pfennig to 1 mark were the same throughout the empire. World War I brought an end to the Empire and the Kingdom of Prussia in 1918.

Coins for Prussia were struck in:

Berlin	Mintmark A	Dusseldorf (1817–48)	Mintmark D
Breslau (1799–1825)	B	Glatz (1807–09)	G
Hannover (1866–78)	B	Hamburg (1805–12)	J
Frankfurt am Main (1866–79)	C		

FRIEDRICH WILHELM III, 1797–1840

Born August 3, 1770, son of King Friedrich Wilhelm II and his consort, Frederike of Hessen-Darmstadt. Friedrich Wilhelm died June 7, 1840.

2. 2 Frederick d'or (G) 1825–40. Head right. Rev. Crowned eagle on cannon with flags and trophies in background   212.50

1. 2 Frederick d'or (G) 1806–14. Uniformed bust left, L at truncation. Rev. Crowned eagle on weapons with scepter and orb   225.00

3. 1 Frederick d'or (G) 1806–16. Type of #1   125.00

4.　1 Frederick d'or (G) 1817–22. Uniformed bust, left. Rev. Crowned eagle on cannon with flags and drums　115.00

5.　1 Frederick d'or (G) 1825–40. Type of #2　110.00

9.　1 Double taler—3½ gulden (S) 1839, 40, 41. Head right. Rev. Crowned, draped arms with Chain of the Order of the Black Eagle　87.50

6.　½ Frederick d'or (G) 1806, 14, 16. Type of #1　80.00

10.　1 Taler (S) 1806–09. Uniformed bust left. Rev. Crowned arms flanked by two wild men, king's monogram on eagle's breast　25.00

7.　½ Frederick d'or (G) 1817. Type of #4　125.00

8.　½ Frederick d'or (G) 1825–40. Type of #2　80.00

11.　1 Taler (S) 1809–16. Head right. Rev. Value within oak wreath　45.00

12. 1 Taler (S) 1816, 17. Uniformed bust left, FR. WILH. Rev. Crowned eagle on cannon with flags and drums. Edge: GOTT MIT UNS 175.00

16. 1 Mining taler (S) 1826, 27, 28. As #14. Rev. Value, inscription. Edge: GOTT MIT UNS 32.50

13. 1 Taler (S) 1816–22. As #12, but FRIEDR. 25.00

17. 1 Taler (S) 1828–40. As #14, but older portrait 32.50

14. 1 Taler (S) 1823–26. Head right. Rev. Crowned arms on laurel wreath with Chain of the Order of the Black Eagle. Edge: Type of #12 .... 30.00

18. 1 Mining taler (S) 1829–40. As #16, but older portrait 38.50

15. 1 Taler (S) 1827, 28. As #14, except arms of different design 30.00

19. 2/3 Taler—gulden (S) 1810. Crowned, oval arms with crowned eagle holding scepter and orb within two laurel branches. Rev. Value 50.00

20. 1/3 Taler (S) 1807, 09. Uniformed bust left, L at truncation. Rev. Crowned arms above laurel branches   15.00

26. 1/6 Taler—4 groschen (S) 1822–40. Head right. Rev. Crowned arms with crowned eagle holding scepter and orb with Chain of the Order of the Black Eagle. Edge: GOTT MIT UNS   5.50

21. 1/3 Taler (S) 1809. Head right. Rev. Value within oak wreath   45.00

22. 1/5 Taler—6 silbergroschen (S) 1819. Uniformed bust left, FRIEDR. Rev. Value (Essay)   —

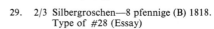

27. 1 Silbergroschen (B) 1821–40. As #26, but Rev. value   3.00

28. 5/6 Silbergroschen—10 pfennige (B) 1818. Crowned arms with crowned eagle holding scepter and orb. Rev. Value (Essay)   —

29. 2/3 Silbergroschen—8 pfennige (B) 1818. Type of #28 (Essay)   —

23. 1/6 Taler—4 groschen (S) 1806–09. Uniformed bust left, FRIDERICUS. Rev. As #20, but no laurel branches   10.00

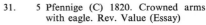

30. ½ Silbergroschen (B) 1821–40. Type of #27   3.75

31. 5 Pfennige (C) 1820. Crowned arms with eagle. Rev. Value (Essay)   —

24. 1/6 Taler—4 groschen (S) 1809–18. Type of #21   9.50

32. 4 Pfennige (C) 1821–40. Crowned arms with eagle. Rev. Value   2.50

25. 1/6 Taler—4 groschen (S) 1816, 17, 18. Uniformed bust left, FRIEDR. Rev. Value   20.00

33. 3 Pfennige (C) 1821–40. Type of #32   2.50

34. 2 Pfennige (C) 1821–40. Type of #32   2.00

MINTED FOR WESTPHALIA

41. 1 Pfennig (C) 1806. Crowned FW monogram. Rev. Value   4.50

35. 1 Pfennig (C) 1821–40. Type of #32   2.00

MINTED FOR EAST AND WEST PRUSSIA

MINTED FOR BRANDENBURG

36. 1 Silbergroschen (B) 1806, 07, 08. Uniformed bust left. Rev. Crowned flying eagle with scepter and orb   7.00

42. 1 Groschen (C) 1810, 11. Crowned arms with eagle within two crossed oak branches. Rev. Value   4.50

37. 3 Pfennige (B) 1806. Crowned F W R monogram. Rev. Value   4.50

43. ½ Groschen (C) 1811. Type of #42   5.50

38. 2 Pfennige (C) 1810, 14, 16. Crowned arms with scepter within two crossed oak branches. Rev. Value   3.75

44. 1 Schilling (C) 1806. Crowned FW monogram. Rev. Value, PR: SCHEIDE MUNZE   5.00

39. 1 Pfennig (B) 1806. Type of #37   3.75

45. 1 Schilling (C) 1810. As #44. Rev. Value, PREUSS   6.50

40. 1 Pfennig (C) 1810–16. Type of #38   2.50

46. 18 Kreuzer (S) 1808. Uniformed bust left. Rev. Crowned eagle with scepter and orb   37.50

52. 3 Groschen (C) 1816, 17. Crowned arms with eagle, within two crossed oak branches. Rev. Value   6.00

47. 9 Kreuzer (B) 1808. Type of #46   20.00

53. 1 Groschen (C) 1816, 17. Type of #52   8.75

48. 1 Kreuzer (B) 1806, 08. As #46. Rev. Crowned arms with eagle   7.50

COMPENSATION COINAGE

49. 1 Kreuzer (C) 1810. Type of #42   7.00

54. 10 Pfennige (C) 1812. Borussia seated on rock with monogram FWR, eagle in background, fruit on floor, within oak wreath. Rev. Value. Edge: IEDEM DAS SEINIGE—"To Each His Own"   3.75

50. 1 Groschel (B) 1806, 08, 09. Crowned FWR monogram. Rev. Value   5.00

51. ½ Kreuzer (C) 1806. Crowned FW monogram. Rev. Value   6.00

55. 5 Pfennige (C) 1812. Type of #54   2.50

56.   5 Pfennige (C) 1812. Crowned FW
       monogram, date below. Rev. Value.
       Edge: Type of #54   2.50

57.   2 Pfennige (C) 1812. Type of #54   2.50

58.   1 Pfennig (C) 1812. Type of #54   3.00

59.   1 Pfennig (C) 1812. Crowned FW
       monogram. Rev. Value   3.00

COMMEMORATIVE ISSUE

60.   1 Taler (S) 1812. Head right. Rev.
       GOTT SCHUTZE IHN within oak wreath   612.50

       Marks the visit of Crown Prince
       Friedrich Wilhelm IV to the Berlin
       mint.

FRIEDRICH WILHELM IV, 1840–61

Born October 15, 1795, son of King Friedrich
Wilhelm III and his consort, Luise of Mecklenburg-
Strelitz. Friedrich Wilhelm died January 2, 1861.

61.   1 Double Frederick d'or (G) 1841–52.
       Head right, WILH. Rev. Crowned
       eagle on cannon with standards and
       flags in background   200.00

62.   1 Double Frederick d'or (G) 1853, 54,
       55. As #61, but older head and
       WILHELM   250.00

63.   1 Frederick d'or (G) 1841–52. Type of
       #61   105.00

64.   1 Frederick d'or (G) 1853, 54, 55. Type
       of #62   130.00

65.   ½ Frederick d'or (G) 1841–49. Type of #61   85.00

66.   ½ Frederick d'or (G) 1853. As #61, but older head   162.50

67.   1 Krone (G) 1858, 59, 60. Head right. Rev. Value within oak wreath. Edge: GOTT MIT UNS   275.00

68.   ½ Krone (G) 1858. Type of #67   425.00

#69

69.   1 Double taler—3½ gulden (S) 1841–51. Head right. Rev. Crowned, draped arms with Chain of the Order of the Black Eagle. Edge: GOTT MIT UNS   55.00

70.   1 Double taler—3½ gulden (S) 1853–56. As #69, but older head   70.00

71.   1 Double taler (S) 1858, 59. As #70. Rev. Crowned eagle with scepter and orb, arms and Chain of the Order of the Black Eagle. Edge: Type of #69   100.00

72. 1 Taler (S) 1841. Head right. Rev. Crowned arms on laurel wreath with Chain of the Order of the Black Eagle   22.50

76. 1 Taler (S) 1853–56. As #74, but older head   20.00

73. 1 Mining taler (S) 1841. As #72. Rev. Value, SEGEN DES. Edge: Type of #69   22.50

77. 1 Mining taler (S) 1853–56. As #73, but older head   25.00

74. 1 Taler (S) 1842–52. As #72, but different crown   30.00

78. 1 Taler (S) 1857–61. Head right. Rev. Crowned eagle with scepter and orb, Chain of the Order of the Black Eagle. Monogram FR on eagle breast. Edge: GOTT MIT UNS   20.00

75. 1 Mining taler (S) 1842–52. Type of #73   27.50

79. 1 Mining taler (S) 1857–60. As #78, but Rev. SEGEN DES   25.00

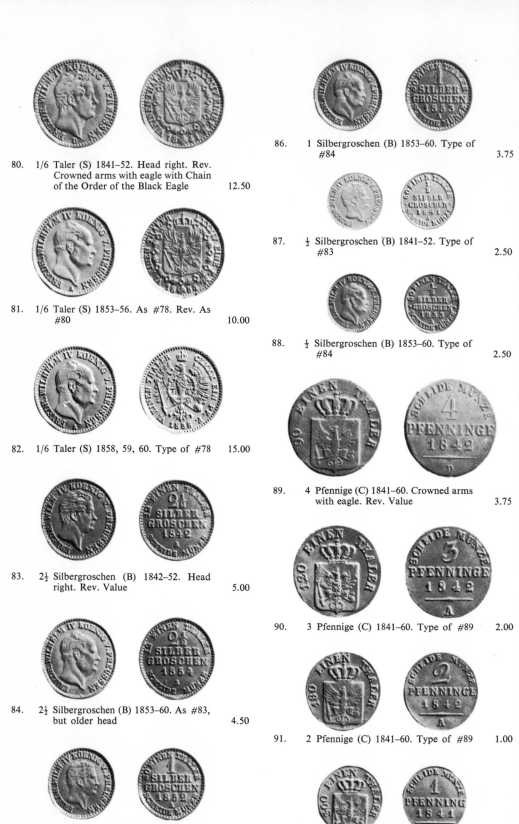

80. 1/6 Taler (S) 1841–52. Head right. Rev. Crowned arms with eagle with Chain of the Order of the Black Eagle — 12.50

81. 1/6 Taler (S) 1853–56. As #78. Rev. As #80 — 10.00

82. 1/6 Taler (S) 1858, 59, 60. Type of #78 — 15.00

83. 2½ Silbergroschen (B) 1842–52. Head right. Rev. Value — 5.00

84. 2½ Silbergroschen (B) 1853–60. As #83, but older head — 4.50

85. 1 Silbergroschen (B) 1841–52. Type of #83 — 3.75

86. 1 Silbergroschen (B) 1853–60. Type of #84 — 3.75

87. ½ Silbergroschen (B) 1841–52. Type of #83 — 2.50

88. ½ Silbergroschen (B) 1853–60. Type of #84 — 2.50

89. 4 Pfennige (C) 1841–60. Crowned arms with eagle. Rev. Value — 3.75

90. 3 Pfennige (C) 1841–60. Type of #89 — 2.00

91. 2 Pfennige (C) 1841–60. Type of #89 — 1.00

92. 1 Pfennig (C) 1841–60. Type of #89 — 1.00

WILHELM I, 1861–88

Younger brother of Friedrich Wilhelm IV. Born March 22, 1797, son of King Friedrich Wilhelm III and his consort, Luise of Mecklenburg-Strelitz. Proclaimed German Emperor on January 18, 1871. Wilhelm I died March 9, 1888.

93.   1 Krone (G) 1861–70. Head right. Rev. Value within oak wreath. Edge: GOTT MIT UNS   250.00

94.   ½ Krone (G) 1862–69. Type of #93   200.00

96.   1 Double taler (S) 1865–71. As #95, but larger head and eagle has monogram FR on breast   112.50

97.   1 Taler (S) 1861, 62, 63. As #95, but with monogram FR on eagle breast   13.75

95.   1 Double taler (S) 1861, 62, 63. Head right. Rev. Crowned eagle with scepter and orb, Chain of the Order of the Black Eagle. Edge: GOTT MIT UNS   140.00

98.   1 Mining taler (S) 1861, 62. As #95, but Rev. SEGEN DES   17.50

103.   1 Silbergroschen (B) 1861–73. Type of
         #102   2.00

104.   ½ Silbergroschen (B) 1861–72. Type of
         #102   1.75

99.   1 Taler (S) 1864–71. Type of #96   13.75

105.   4 Pfennige (C) 1861–71. Crowned arms
         with eagle. Rev. Value   1.00

100.   1/6 Taler (S) 1861–64. Type of #97   1.75

106.   3 Pfennige (C) 1861–73. Type of #105   1.75

101.   1/6 Taler (S) 1865, 67, 68. Type of #95
         but larger head. Rev. Type of #96.
         Edge: Type of #95   1.50

107.   2 Pfennige (C) 1861–73. Type of #105   1.00

102.   2½ Silbergroschen (B) 1861–73. Head
         right. Rev. Value   2.65

108.   1 Pfennig (C) 1861–73. Type of #105   .50

109.   20 Mark (G) 1871, 72, 73. Head right.
Rev. Type 1 eagle. Edge: GOTT MIT
UNS   30.00

110.   20 Mark (G) 1874–88. As #109. Rev.
Type 2 eagle. Edge: Type of #109   25.00

114.   5 Mark (S) 1874, 75, 76. Head right.
Rev. Type 2 eagle. Edge: GOTT MIT
UNS   20.00

111.   10 Mark (G) 1872, 73. Type of #109.
Edge: Vines and stars   25.00

115.   2 Mark (S) 1876–84. Type of #110.
Reeded edge   10.00

COMMEMORATIVE ISSUES

112.   10 Mark (G) 1874–88. Type of #110.
Edge: Type of #111   22.50

113.   5 Mark (G) 1877, 78. Type of #110.
Edge: Type of #111   105.00

116.   1 Taler (S) 1861. Conjoined heads
right. Rev. Crowned eagle with
scepter and orb. Edge: GOTT MIT UNS   15.00

Commemorates the coronation of
Wilhelm and Augusta at Konigsberg
on October 18, 1861.

117. 1 Taler (S) 1866. Laureated head right. Rev. Crowned eagle with scepter and orb, chain and jewel from collar of the Order of the Black Eagle, monogram FW on eagle breast. Edge: Type of #116   17.50

Marks the victory over Austria in 1866.

121. 5 Mark (S) 1888. Type of #119 (Issued after death of the Kaiser)   35.00

118. 1 Taler (S) 1871. Head right. Rev. Enthroned Borussia with crown, sword and eagle shield. Edge: Type of #116   10.00

Marks the victory over France in 1871.

122. 2 Mark (S) 1888. Type of #119 (Issued after death of the Kaiser)   17.50

FRIEDRICH III, March 9, 1888, to June 15, 1888

Born October 18, 1831, son of Kaiser Wilhelm I and his consort, Augusta of Sachen-Weimar-Eisenach. Friedrich III died June 15, 1888.

WILHELM II, 1888–1918

Born January 27, 1859, son of Kaiser Friedrich III and his consort, Victoria of Great Britain and Ireland. He abdicated his throne November 28, 1918.

119. 20 Mark (G) 1888. Head right. Rev. Type 2 eagle. Edge: GOTT MIT UNS   32.50

120. 10 Mark (G) 1888. Type of #119. Edge: Vines and stars   37.50

123. 20 Mark (G) 1888, 89. Head right. Rev. Type 2 eagle. Edge: GOTT MIT UNS   40.00

124.   20 Mark (G) 1890–1912. As #123, but
       Rev. type 3 eagle   25.00

125.   20 Mark (G) 1913, 14, 15. Uniformed
       bust right. Rev. Type of #124. Edge:
       GOTT MIT UNS (1915 mintage was not
       issued due to World War I)   35.00

126.   10 Mark (G) 1889. Type of #123. Edge:
       Vines and stars   412.50

127.   10 Mark (G) 1890–1912. Type of #124.
       Edge: Vines and stars   32.50

128.   5 Mark (S) 1888. Head right. Rev.
       Type 2 eagle. Edge: GOTT MIT UNS 120.00

129.   5 Mark (S) 1891–1908. As #128, but
       type 3 eagle   7.50

130.   5 Mark (S) 1913, 14. Bust in curassier
       uniform with collar of Order of the
       Black Eagle. Rev. Type 3 eagle.
       Edge: Type of #128   12.50

131.   3 Mark (S) 1908–12. Type of #129 (The 1911 date is known counter-stamped M for Mozambique)   4.50

135.   5 Mark (S) 1901. Conjoined busts left. Rev. Type 3 eagle. Edge: GOTT MIT UNS   22.50

132.   3 Mark (S) 1914. Type of #130   7.50

136.   2 Mark (S) 1901. As #135, but reeded edge   6.50

    The above two coins commemorate the 200th anniversary of the Kingdom of Prussia.

133.   2 Mark (S) 1914. Type of #128, but reeded edge   75.00

137.   3 Mark (S) 1910. Conjoined heads left, UNIVERSITAT BERLIN. Rev. and edge: Type of #135   32.50

    Commemorates the 100th anniversary of the founding of the Berlin University.

134.   2 Mark (S) 1891–1912. Type of #129, but reeded edge   6.50

138. 3 Mark (S) 1911. Conjoined heads left, UNIVERSITAT BRESLAU. Rev. and edge: Type of #135   22.50

Commemorates the 100th anniversary of the University of Breslau.

141. 3 Mark (S) 1913. As #130, but with 1888–1913 and laurel branches below bust. Edge: Type of #135   7.50

142. 2 Mark (S) 1913. As #141, but reeded edge   6.50

The above two coins commemorate the 25th anniversary of the reign.

139. 3 Mark (S) 1913. Friedrich Wilhelm III on horseback surrounded by jubilant people, beneath design: MIT GOTT. Rev. Eagle left with serpent in claws. Edge: Type of #135   7.50

140. 2 Mark (S) 1913. As #139, but reeded edge   6.50

The above two coins commemorate the 100th anniversary of the War of Liberation.

143. 3 Mark (S) 1915. St. George killing dragon, arms of Mansfeld on saddle cover, inscription between crossed mining hammers. Rev. Type 3 eagle. Edge: GOTT MIT UNS   125.00

Commemorates the 100th anniversary of the absorption of Mansfeld by Prussia.

PRUSSIAN ANSBACH-BAYREUTH

The territories of Ansbach-Bayreuth passed to King Friedrich Wilhelm III of Prussia in 1791. The French occupied both areas in 1806 and, together with Cleves and other territories, created the grand duchy of Berg for Napoleon's field marshal, Joachim Murat. Berg became part of Westphalia in 1808, and part of Prussia in 1814.

FRIEDRICH WILHELM III OF PRUSSIA, 1797–1840

144.   6 Kreuzer (B) 1797–1802. Arms within two laurel branches. Rev. Value   7.50

145.   3 Kreuzer (B) 1798–1802. Crowned eagle, FWR monogram on breast, over weapons and flags. Rev. Value above laurel and palm branches   6.50

146.   1 Kreuzer (B) 1798, 99, 1800. Crowned eagle, FWR monogram on breast, with scepter and orb. Rev. Value in decorated frame   3.75

147.   1 Kreuzer (B) 1802, 03, 04. As #146. Rev. Value within garlands   3.75

148.   1 Pfennig (B) 1799, 1801, 03. Crowned FWR monogram. Rev. Value   4.50

COMMEMORATIVE ISSUE

149.   1 Ducat (G) 1803. Arms within laurel branches. Rev. AUS DER FURSTEN-ZECHE—"From the Mint of the Principality," palm and oak branches below   Rare

REGENSBURG

Also known as Ratisbon, the town of Regensburg became a free city of the Empire in 1180. It was the meeting place of the Imperial Diet from 1663 until the end of the Holy Roman Empire in 1806. Regensburg lost its independence in 1803 and was given to the archchancellor of the empire, Carl Theodor von Dalberg, who was also the Bishop of Regensburg. Made a principality in 1806, the city was annexed to Bavaria in 1810 and Dalberg was given the newly created duchy of Frankfurt in exchange.

Coins for the principality were struck in Regensburg.

CARL THEODOR VON DALBERG, 1804–10 (Bishop of Regensburg, 1804–17)

1.   1 Ducat (G) 1809. Bust right. Rev. Crowned arms with crozier and sword   550.00

3.   1 Convention taler (S) 1809. As #2. Rev. As #1, REGENSBURG below   87.50

2.   1 Convention taler (S) 1809. Bust right. Rev. Value within palm and laurel branches   75.00

4.   1 Gulden (S) 1809. Type of #2   87.50

REUSS (Elder Line)

The Reuss family traces its history back to the 11th century. Originally known as the lords of Weida, the name Reuss came from Heinrich III who was known as "der Russe" (the Russian). The family followed the confusing custom of calling all of its male children Heinrich. The main branches of the family—Greiz (Elder Line) and Schleiz (Younger Line)—date from the 16th century. Lobenstein-Selbitz and Lobenstein-Ebersdorf were sub-branches of the younger line.

Coins for Reuss were struck in:

Saalfeld (before 1840)	Mintmark S
Berlin (from 1840)	A
Hannover (1875, 1877)	B

The elder line of Reuss was divided into Upper and Lower Greiz until 1768 when the territories were again united. In 1778, Heinrich XI was made a prince of the Holy Roman Empire. The principality endured until 1918. All Reuss males were named Heinrich and, in the elder line, were given numbers from 1 to 100 at which point the sequence was started over again.

HEINRICH XIII, 1800–17

Born February 16, 1747, son of Prince Heinrich XI and his first consort, Konradin, Countess of Reuss zu Kostritz. He was a general of the Imperial Army. Heinrich died January 29, 1817.

1.   1 Taler (S) 1806, 07. Uniformed bust right, D. G. HENR., DOELL F. at arm. Rev. Crowned, draped, heart-shaped arms within chain and jewel of the Hungarian Order of St. Stephen   125.00

2.   1 Taler (S) 1807, 12. As #1, but V.G.G. HEINRICH and D.F. at arm   162.50

8.   1 Pfennig (C) 1806–16. Type of #6   2.50

9.   1 Heller (C) 1812, 15. Crowned lion on oval shield. Rev. Value   3.00

3.   1 Taler (S) 1812. As #2, but no D.F. Rev. Value within two tied oak branches   150.00

HEINRICH XIX, 1817–36

Born March 1, 1790, son of Prince Heinrich XIII and his consort, Wilhelmine of Nassau-Weilburg. Heinrich died October 31, 1836.

4.   1/3 Taler (S) 1809. Crowned, draped, heart-shaped arms within chain and jewel of the Hungarian Order of St. Stephen. Rev. Type of #3   115.00

10.   3 Pfennige (C) 1817–33. Long, tapered, crowned shield with crowned lion. Rev. Value   2.00

5.   1/6 Taler (S) 1808. As #4. Rev. Value within two crossed oak branches   85.00

6.   1 Groschen (B) 1812. Crowned lion on pointed shield. Rev. Value   5.00

11.   1 Pfennig (C) 1817–32. Oval crowned shield with crowned lion. Rev. Value   1.75

7.   3 Pfennige (C) 1808–16. Type of #6   2.50

12.   1 Heller (C) 1819. Type of #11   3.00

HEINRICH XX, 1836–59

Younger brother of Heinrich XIX. Born June 29, 1794, son of Prince Heinrich XIII and his consort, Wilhelmine of Nassau-Weilburg. Heinrich XX died November 8, 1859.

13.　1 Double taler—3½ gulden (S) 1841–51. Head left, LIN SOUVERAIN. Rev. Crowned, draped arms. Edge: OMNIA CUM DEO—"Everything with God"　　215.00

14.　1 Taler (S) 1858. As #13, but L. SOUV.　37.50

HEINRICH XXII, 1859–1902

Born March 28, 1846, son of Heinrich XX and his consort, Caroline of Hessen-Hamburg. From 1859–67, he was under the guardianship of his mother. Heinrich XXII died April 19, 1902.

15.　1 Taler (S) 1868. Head right. Rev. Crowned, draped arms. Edge: Type of #13　　45.00

16.　1 Silbergroschen (B) 1868. Crowned shield with crowned lion. Rev. Value　6.50

17.　3 Pfennige (C) 1864, 68. Type of #16　3.50

18.　1 Pfennig (C) 1864, 68. Type of #16　3.50

AFTER INCORPORATION INTO THE EMPIRE

19.　20 Mark (G) 1875. Head right. Rev. Type 2 eagle. Edge: GOTT MIT UNS　1,625.00

20.　2 Mark (S) 1877. As #19, but reeded edge　　125.00

HEINRICH XXIV, 1902–18

Born March 20, 1878, son of Prince Heinrich XXII and his consort, Ida of Schaumburg-Lippe. Due to the inability of the government to function properly, a regency was established under Prince Heinrich XXVII of Reuss, Younger Line, until November, 1918.

21.	2 Mark (S) 1892. As #20, but Rev. type 3 eagle	175.00

22.	2 Mark (S) 1899, 1901. Head right. Rev. Type of #21	137.50
23.	3 Mark (S) 1909. Head right. Rev. Type 3 eagle. Edge: GOTT MIT UNS	112.50

REUSS (Younger Line)

The younger line of Reuss was divided into the Gera, Schleiz and Lobenstein branches during the 17th century. The first died out in 1802, and was then administered jointly by the two remaining branches. The division of the lands came to an end in 1848 when Heinrich LXXII of Lobenstein-Ebersdorf renounced his throne in favor of Heinrich LXII of Schleiz. The principality endured until 1918. All Reuss males were named Heinrich and, in the younger line, were given numbers beginning with 1 for the first male born in each century.

HEINRICH XLII, 1784–1818

Born February 27, 1752, son of Count Heinrich XII and his consort, Christine of Erbach-Schonberg. Elevated to Prince April 9, 1806. Heinrich XLII died April 17, 1818.

24.	1 Groschen (B) 1815, 16. Oval crowned arms. Rev. Value	5.00
25.	3 Pfennige (C) 1815, 16. Oval crowned shield with crowned lion. Rev. Value	3.75

HEINRICH LXII, 1818–54

Born May 31, 1785, son of Prince Heinrich XLII and his consort, Caroline Henriette of Hohenlohe-Kirchberg. Heinrich LXII died June 19, 1854. All males of the Younger Line of Reuss were named Heinrich with the numbering system starting anew in each century.

29.   1 Silbergroschen (B) 1850. Type of #27   6.50

30.   3 Pfennige (C) 1841, 44. Type of #28   5.00

31.   3 Pfennige (C) 1850. Type of #27   4.00

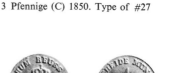

26.   1 Double taler—3½ gulden (S) 1840–54. Head right. Rev. Crowned, draped arms supported by two crowned lions. Edge: ICH BAU AUF GOTT—"I Build On God"   125.00

32.   1 Pfennig (C) 1841, 47. Type of #28   2.50

27.   2 Silbergroschen (B) 1850. Crowned shield with crowned lion, IUNGERER LINIE. Rev. Value   20.00

33.   1 Pfennig (C) 1850. Type of #27   2.50

28.   1 Silbergroschen (B) 1841, 44, 46. As #27, but SCHLEIZ   6.50

34.   ½ Pfennig—heller (C) 1841. Crowned arms. Rev. Value   4.00

37. 2 Silbergroschen (B) 1855. Crowned shield with crowned lion. Rev. Value 7.50

38. 1 Silbergroschen (B) 1855. Type of #37 5.00

39. 3 Pfennige (C) 1855–64. Type of #37 2.50

40. 1 Pfennig (C) 1855–64. Type of #37 2.50

35. 1 Double taler (S) 1843. As #26, but Rev. D. 17 APRIL 1843. Edge: ZWEI THALER VII E.F.M. DREI EIN. HALB GULDEN 500.00

Commemorates the 25th anniversary of the reign.

HEINRICH LXVII, 1854–67

Younger brother of Heinrich LXII. Born October 20, 1789, son of Prince Heinrich XLII and his consort, Caroline Henriette of Hohenlohe-Kirchberg. Heinrich LXVII died July 11, 1867.

HEINRICH XIV, 1867–1913

Born May 28, 1832, son of Prince Heinrich LXVII and his consort, Adelheid, Princess of Reuss zu Ebersdorf. Heinrich XIV died March 29, 1913.

36. 1 Taler (S) 1858, 62. Head right. Rev. Crowned arms supported by two lions within band inscribed ICH BAU AUF GOTT—"I Build On God." Edge: MUNZVERTRAG VOM 24 JANUAR 1857 —"Currency Treaty of 24 January 1857" 50.00

41. 1 Taler (S) 1868. Head right. Rev. Crowned arms supported by two lions, within band inscribed ICH BAU AUF GOTT. Edge: MUNZ VERTRAG VOM 24 JANUAR 1857 87.50

42.   3 Pfennige (C) 1868. Crowned shield with crowned lion. Rev. Value   3.75

43.   1 Pfennig (C) 1868. Type of #42   2.50

AFTER INCORPORATION INTO THE EMPIRE

44.   20 Mark (G) 1881. Head left. Rev. Type 2 eagle. Edge: GOTT MIT UNS   450.00

45.   10 Mark (G) 1882. As #44, but vines and stars on edge   750.00

46.   2 Mark (S) 1884. As #44, but reeded edge   100.00

REUSS-LOBENSTEIN-SELBITZ

HEINRICH LIV, 1805–24

Born October 8, 1767, son of Count Heinrich XXV and his consort, Marie Elisabeth, Countess of Reuss zu Ebersdorf. Elevated to rank of Prince on April 9, 1806. Heinrich LIV died May 7, 1824.

47.   3 Pfennige (B) 1807. Crowned lion. Rev. Value   10.00

REUSS-LOBENSTEIN-EBERSDORF

HEINRICH LI, 1779–1822

Born May 16, 1761, son of Count Heinrich XXIV and his consort, Caroline Ernestine of Erbach-Schonberg. From May 13, 1779, to May 16, 1782, he was under the guardianship of his mother. Heinrich LI died July 10, 1822.

51.   6 Pfennige (B) 1812. Type of #50   7.50

52.   4 Pfennige (C) 1812. Type of #50   6.25

48.   1 Taler (S) 1812. Crowned, draped, heart-shaped arms. Rev. Value   150.00

53.   3 Pfennige (C) 1812. Type of #50   7.00

49.   1 Groschen (B) 1812, 14. Crowned, heart-shaped arms. Rev. Value   7.50

54.   2 Pfennige (C) 1812. Type of #50   3.75

50.   8 Pfennige (B) 1812. Crowned shield with hound's head. Rev. Value   7.00

55.   1 Pfennig (C) 1812. Type of #50   3.00

HEINRICH LXXII, 1822–48

Born March 27, 1797, son of Prince Heinrich LI and his consort, Luise, Countess of Hoym. He abdicated the throne October 1, 1848 in favor of Prince Heinrich LXII of Schleiz. Heinrich LXXII died February 17, 1853.

| 59. | 3 Pfennige (C) 1841, 44. Type of #57 | 3.75 |

| 60. | 1 Pfennig (C) 1841, 44. Type of #57 | 3.75 |

COMMEMORATIVE ISSUE

| 56. | 1 | Double taler—3½ gulden (S) 1840, 47. Head left. Rev. Crowned, draped arms supported by two crowned lions. Edge: ICH BAU AUF GOTT | 162.50 |

| 57. | 1 | Silbergroschen (B) 1841, 44. Crowned shield with crowned lion. Rev. Value | 8.50 |

| 58. | ½ | Silbergroschen (B) 1841. Type of #57 | 7.50 |

| 61. | 1 | Double taler (S) 1847. Head left. Rev. Crowned, draped arms supported by two crowned lions. Edge: ZWEI THALER VII E. F. M. DREI EIN HALB GULDEN | 250.00 |

Commemorates the 25th anniversary of the reign.

RHEINBUND

Napoleon, in 1806, created the Confederation of the Rhine, made up of most of the south and west German states. The Holy Roman Empire was dissolved and in place of the emperor, Napoleon named a prince primate—Baron Carl Theodor von Dalberg. Dalberg had formerly been arch chancellor of the empire and was also the prince and bishop of Regensburg. With Napoleon's decline, the Confederation broke up in 1813.

Coins for the confederation were struck in Frankfurt am Main.

CARL THEODORE VON DALBERG, 1806–10
(See: Regensburg)

1. 1 Ducat (G) 1809. Bust left, B.H. below. Rev. Crowned arms   190.00

2. 1 Convention taler (S) 1808. Bust right, B below. Rev. Crowned arms with crozier and sword   150.00

3. I Kreuzer (S) 1808, 09, 10. Crowned arms. Rev. Value   5.00

4. I Heller (C) 1808, 10, 12. Type of #3   3.75

#2

SAXONY

Capital: Dresden

The name Saxony comes from a pagan tribe that occupied this area in southeast Germany during the time of Charlemagne. In 1423, Friedrich the Warlike was made an elector of the Holy Roman Empire. His grandsons, Ernst and Albert, divided the family lands in 1485 into the Ernestine and Albertine lines. The younger Albertine line acquired the electoral dignity in 1547, and in 1806 the electorate was made a kingdom. The Ernestine lands were frequently divided, exchanged and united over the centuries with the kingdom and the duchies of Saxe-Weimar-Eisenacht, Saxe-Altenburg, Saxe-Coburg-Gotha and Saxe-Meiningen all entering the German Empire in 1871 as separate states.

Coins for Saxony were struck in:
Dresden (until 1886)   Mintmark E
Muldenhutten bei Freiberg (from 1887)   E

FRIEDRICH AUGUST I, 1806–27 (As Friedrich August III, Elector from 1763–1806; from 1763–68 under guardianship of his uncle Xaver)

Born December 23, 1750, the son of Elector Friedrich Christian and his consort, Maria Antonia, a daughter of Emperor Karl VII. Friedrich August I died May 5, 1827.

2.   10 Taler—double August d'or (G) 1818. Uniformed bust left, FRIEDRICH. Rev. As #1   500.00

1.   10 Taler—double August d'or (G) 1806–17. Head right. Rev. Crowned, oval arms with laurel branches within two crossed palm branches   375.00

3.   10 Taler—double August d'or (G) 1825, 26, 27. As #2 but FRIEDR. Rev. Crowned arms   375.00

4. 5 Taler—August d'or (G) 1806–17.
Type of #1   250.00

10. 1 Ducat (G) 1824. As #9. Rev.
Crowned arms dividing date   150.00

5. 5 Taler—August d'or (G) 1818. Type of
#2   400.00

11. 1 Ducat (G) 1825, 26, 27. Type of #10   125.00

6. 5 Taler—August d'or (G) 1825, 26, 27.
Type of #3   250.00

7. 1 Ducat (G) 1806. Head right. Rev.
Crowned, oval arms with laurel
branches within two crossed palm
branches (Essay)   250.00

12. 1 Specie taler (S) 1806–16. Head right.
Rev. Crowned, oval arms with laurel
branches within two crossed palm
branches   37.50

8. 1 Ducat (G) 1806–22. Type of #7   125.00

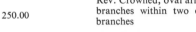

9. 1 Ducat (G) 1823. Uniformed bust
left. Rev. Type of #7   250.00

13. 1 Mining taler (S) 1807–16. As #12, but
Rev. DER SEEGEN DES around arms   65.00

14.   1 Specie taler (S) 1808. Head right with closed mouth. Rev. As #12, but no inscription (Essay)   —

17.   1 Specie taler (S) 1813. As #12. Rev. As #16, but no inscription (Essay)   —

15.   1 Specie taler (S) 1808. As #14, except mouth open and different throat design (Essay)   —

18.   1 Specie taler (S) 1814. As #12. Rev. Rectangular crowned arms within two crossed palm branches (Essay)   —

16.   1 Mining taler (S) 1807. Uniformed bust right. Rev. Crowned, oval arms on four-cornered shield with upper edges rolled in cartouche, DER SEEGEN (Essay)   —

19.   1 Specie taler (S) 1814. As #12. Rev. As #18 except two crossed oak branches (Essay)   —

20. 1 Specie taler (S) 1816. Head right. Rev. Crowned, oval arms with laurel branches within two crossed palm branches (Essay) —

21. 1 Specie taler (S) 1816. Uniformed bust right, without epaulettes. Rev. Type of #20. Edge: GOTT SEGNE SACHSEN— "God Bless Saxony" 212.50

22. 1 Specie taler (S) 1816–21. Uniformed bust left with epaulettes. Rev. Type of #20. Edge: Type of #21 25.00

23. 1 Mining taler (S) 1817–21. As #22, but Rev. DER SEGEN. Edge: Type of #21 50.00

24. 1 Specie taler (S) 1822, 23. Uniformed bust left. Rev. Type of #20. Edge: Type of #21 25.00

25. 1 Mining taler (S) 1822, 23. Type of #24. Rev. Type of #23. Edge: Type of #21 45.00

26.　1 Specie taler (S) 1824. Uniformed bust
　　　left. Rev. Crowned arms in circle.
　　　Edge: As #21 (Essay)　　　—

29.　1 Specie taler (S)　As #28, but arms
　　　within oak branches (Essay)　　　—

27.　1 Mining taler (S) 1824. As #26, but
　　　Rev. DER SEGEN　　　120.00

30.　1 Specie taler (S) 1824–27. Military
　　　bust left. Rev. Crowned arched arms,
　　　date below. Edge: GOTT SEGNE SACH-
　　　SEN　　　27.50

28.　1 Specie taler (S) Head right. Rev.
　　　Crowned, rectangular arms within
　　　two laurel branches, s 182 below,
　　　proof with partial date. Edge: GOTT
　　　SEGNE SACHSEN (Essay)　　　—

31.　1 Mining taler (S) 1824–27. As #30.
　　　Rev. Crowned arched arms dividing
　　　date, DER SEGEN　　　65.00

32. 2/3 Taler—gulden (S) 1806–17. Head right. Rev. Crowned, oval arms with laurel branches within two crossed palm branches. Edge: Type of #30   15.00

33. 2/3 Taler—gulden (S) 1821, 22. Uniformed bust left. Rev. and edge: Type of #32   45.00

34. 1/3 Taler (S) 1806. Crowned, oval arms with laurel branches within crossed palm branches. Rev. Crowned Austrian double-eagle with shield on breast (Essay)   —

35. 1/3 Taler (S) 1806–17. Type of #32   7.50

36. 1/3 Taler (S) 1818, 21. Uniformed bust left. Rev. Type of #32   27.50

37. 1/6 Taler (S) 1806–17. Head right. Rev. Type of # 32   6.50

38. 1/6 Taler (S) 1825. As #30, but arms divide date on reverse   11.50

39. 1/12 Taler—double groschen (B) 1806–18. Crowned, oval arms with laurel branches, within crossed palm branches, FRID. Rev. Value   5.50

40. 1/12 Taler—double groschen (B) 1819–23. As #39, but FRIED.   8.75

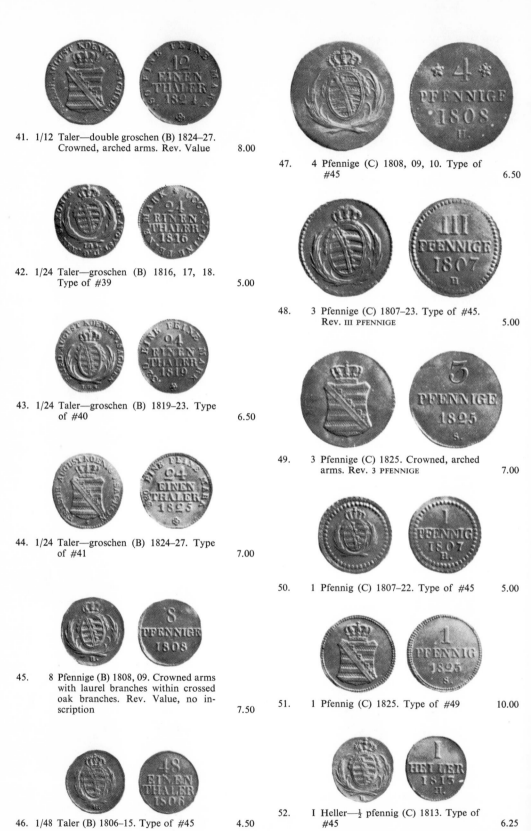

41. 1/12 Taler—double groschen (B) 1824–27. Crowned, arched arms. Rev. Value   8.00

42. 1/24 Taler—groschen (B) 1816, 17, 18. Type of #39   5.00

43. 1/24 Taler—groschen (B) 1819–23. Type of #40   6.50

44. 1/24 Taler—groschen (B) 1824–27. Type of #41   7.00

45.   8 Pfennige (B) 1808, 09. Crowned arms with laurel branches within crossed oak branches. Rev. Value, no inscription   7.50

46. 1/48 Taler (B) 1806–15. Type of #45   4.50

47.   4 Pfennige (C) 1808, 09, 10. Type of #45   6.50

48.   3 Pfennige (C) 1807–23. Type of #45. Rev. III PFENNIGE   5.00

49.   3 Pfennige (C) 1825. Crowned, arched arms. Rev. 3 PFENNIGE   7.00

50.   1 Pfennig (C) 1807–22. Type of #45   5.00

51.   1 Pfennig (C) 1825. Type of #49   10.00

52.   I Heller—½ pfennig (C) 1813. Type of #45   6.25

206 • Saxony

53. 1 Ducat (G) 1809. Bust of Elector Friedrich I (The Valiant) in coronet with fur cape, right. Rev. SALVA SIT   375.00

Marks the Jubilee of Leipzig University.

56. 1 Mining Specie taler (S) 1827. Type of #55. Edge: SEGEN DES BERGBAUS   80.00

57. 1/6 Taler (S) 1827. Type of #55. Edge: Smooth   10.00

The above three coins commemorate the death of King Friedrich August on May 5, 1827.

54. 1 Prize Specie taler (S) 1815. Head right. Rev. K. S. BERGAKADEMIE, in oak wreath DEM FLEISSE with crossed mine hammers   400.00

Commemorates the Berg Academy.

ANTON, 1827–36

Younger brother of King Friedrich August I. Born December 27, 1755, the son of Elector Friedrich Christian and his consort, Maria Antonia, a daughter of Emperor Karl VII. Anton died June 6, 1836.

55. 1 Specie taler (S) 1827. Head right. Rev. PSALM 91 V. 14–16 within crossed cypress branches, VOLLENDET DEN 5. MAI 1827. Edge: GOTT SEGNE SACHSEN   40.00

58. 10 Taler—double Anton d'or (G) 1827, 28. Head right. Rev. Crowned, arched arms within two crossed branches   500.00

59. 10 Taler—double Anton d'or (G) 1829–36. Type of #58   400.00

60. 5 Taler—Anton d'or (G) 1827, 28. Type of #58   450.00

64. 1 Specie taler (S) 1827, 28. Head right. Rev. Crowned, arched arms within two crossed branches. Edge: GOTT SEGNE SACHSEN   32.50

61. 5 Taler—Anton d'or (G) 1829–36. Type of #58   300.00

65. 1 Mining Specie taler (S) 1828. As #64, but Rev. SEGEN DES BERGBAUS. Edge: Type of #64   68.50

62. 1 Ducat (G) 1827, 28. Type of #58   215.00

63. 1 Ducat (G) 1829–36. Type of #58   115.00

66. 1 Specie taler (S) 1829–36. Type of #64   22.50

208 • **Saxony**

70. 2/3 Taler—gulden (S) 1829. Type of #64   30.00

67. 1 Mining Specie taler (S) 1829–36.
Type of #65   50.00

71. 1/3 Taler (S) 1827, 28. As #64, but
smooth edge   16.25

72. 1/3 Taler (S) 1829, 30. Type of #71   20.00

68. 1 Specie taler (S) As #64, but rectangular arms and partial date below
(Essay)   —

73. 1/6 Taler (S) 1827, 28. Type of #71   11.25

69. 2/3 Taler—gulden (S) 1827, 28. Type of
#64   22.50

74. 1/6 Taler (S) 1829. Type of #71   12.50

75. 1/12 Taler—double groschen (B) 1827, 28. Crowned, arched arms within two crossed branches. Rev. Value ... 7.50

76. 1/12 Taler—double groschen (B) 1829–32. As #75, but no crossed branches ... 4.50

81. 1 Prize Specie taler (S) 1829. Head right. Rev. BERGAKADEMIE, DEM FLEISSE and crossed hammers within oak wreath. Edge: GOTT SEGNE DEN BERGBAU—"God Bless the Mines" ... 750.00

Commemorates the Berg Academy of Frieberg.

77. 1/24 Taler—groschen (B) 1827, 28. Type of #75 ... 7.50

78. 3 Pfennige (C) 1831–33. Crowned, arched arms, no inscription. Rev. Value ... 4.50

82. 1 Prize Specie taler (S) 1830. As #81. Rev. FORSTINSTITUT, DEM FLEISSE UND GESITTETEN BETRAGEN in oak wreath ... —

Commemorates the Forstin Institute.

79. 3 Pfennige (C) 1834. Crowned, arched arms, inscription. Rev. Value ... 4.50

83. 1 Prize Specie taler (S) 1830. As #81, but Rev. LANDWIRTSCHAFTL ... —

Marks the Agriculture Educational establishment at Tharant.

80. 1 Pfennig (C) 1831, 32, 33. Type of #78 ... 4.00

84. 1 Specie taler (S) 1831. Conjoined heads right, ANTON KOENIG UND FRIEDRICH. Rev. Constitution with inscription: AM 4. SEPTBR. 1831 within crossed oak and laurel branches. Edge: ZEHN EINE FEINE MARK   75.00

Commemorates the new constitution of German States.

85. 1 Specie taler (S) 1836. Head right, DEN 6 JUNI 1836. Rev. Crowned, arched arms and crossed torches within cypress branches. Edge: GOTT SEGNE SACHSEN   43.50

86. 1 Mining Specie taler (S) 1836. Type of #85. Edge: SEGEN DES BERGBAUS   112.50

87. 1/6 Taler (S) 1836. Type of #85. Smooth edge   11.25

The above three coins commemorate the death of King Anton.

FRIEDRICH AUGUST II, 1836–54

Nephew of Friedrich August I and Anton. Born May 18, 1797, the son of Prince Maximilian and his consort, Karoline of Parma. Friedrich August II died August 9, 1854.

88. 10 Taler—double August d'or (G) 1836–39. Head right. Rev. Crowned, rectangular arms within two crossed branches. Edge: GOTT SEGNE SACHSEN   300.00

89. 10 Taler—double August d'or (G) 1845–54. Head right. Rev. Crowned, draped arms with insignia of the Order of the Jeweled Crown. Edge: Type of #88   325.00

90. 5 Taler—August d'or (G) 1837, 38, 39. Type of #88   375.00

91. 5 Taler—August d'or (G) 1842–54. Type of #89   250.00

92. 1 Ducat (G) 1836, 37, 38. Type of #88. Reeded edge   400.00

93.   2½ Taler—½ August d'or (G) 1842–54.
        Type of #89. Reeded edge   250.00

94.   1 Double taler—3½ gulden (S) 1839–54.
        Head right, mint mark below. Rev.
        Crowned, draped arms with insignia
        of the Order of the Jeweled Crown.
        Edge: GOTT SEGNE SACHSEN   55.00

96.   1 Mining Specie taler (S) 1836. As #95,
        but Rev. SEGEN DES   137.50

97.   1 Specie taler (S) 1837, 38. Type of #95   45.00

95.   1 Specie taler (S) 1836, 37. As #94, but
        no mint mark. Rev. Crowned arms
        within two crossed branches, mint
        mark below. Edge: Type of #94   62.50

98.   1 Mining Specie taler (S) 1837, 38.
        Type of #96   75.00

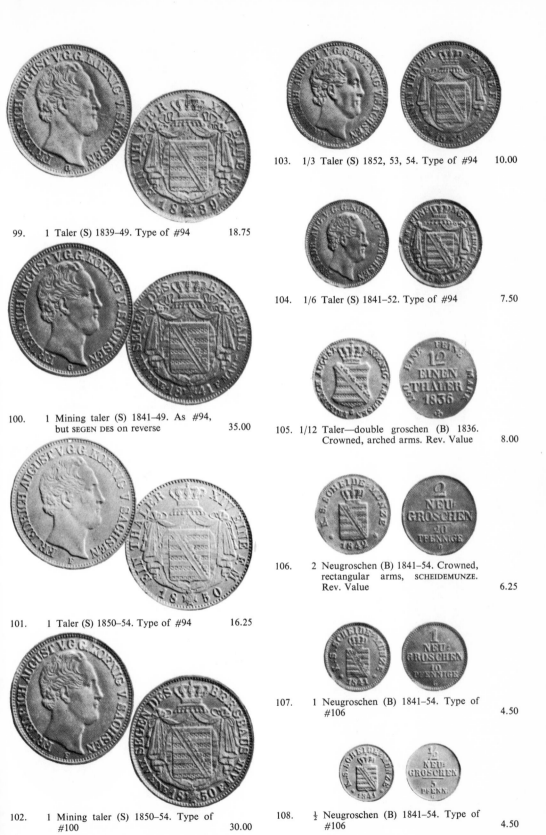

99.   1 Taler (S) 1839–49. Type of #94   18.75

100.   1 Mining taler (S) 1841–49. As #94,
but SEGEN DES on reverse   35.00

101.   1 Taler (S) 1850–54. Type of #94   16.25

102.   1 Mining taler (S) 1850–54. Type of
#100   30.00

103.   1/3 Taler (S) 1852, 53, 54. Type of #94   10.00

104.   1/6 Taler (S) 1841–52. Type of #94   7.50

105.   1/12 Taler—double groschen (B) 1836.
Crowned, arched arms. Rev. Value   8.00

106.   2 Neugroschen (B) 1841–54. Crowned,
rectangular arms, SCHEIDEMUNZE.
Rev. Value   6.25

107.   1 Neugroschen (B) 1841–54. Type of
#106   4.50

108.   ½ Neugroschen (B) 1841–54. Type of
#106   4.50

109. 3 Pfennige (C) 1836, 37. Type of #106   5.00

110. 2 Pfennige (C) 1841–54. As #106, but
K.S.S.M.   3.75

111. 1 Pfennig (C) 1836, 37, 38. As #106,
but no inscription   3.15

112. 1 Pfennig (C) 1841–51. Type of #110   4.00

COMMEMORATIVE ISSUES

113. 1 Mint Visit taler (S) 1839. Head right,
mint mark below. Rev. DEM PRINZEN
ALBERT. Edge: GOTT SEGNE SACHSEN   750.00

Marks the visit to the Dresden mint
by the Princes Albert, Ernst, and
Georg, and Princess Elizabeth.

114. 1 Prize double taler (S) 1841. As
#113. Rev. K. S. BERGAKADEMIE, DEM
FLEISSE and crossed mining hammers
within crossed oak branches. Edge:
GOTT SEGNE DEN BERGBAU, crossed
hammers   625.00

Commemorates the Mining Academy
at Freiberg.

115. 1 Prize double taler (S) 1847. Type of
#113. Rev. K. S. ACADEMIE, DEM
FLEISSE UND GESITTETEN BETRAGEN
within crossed oak branches. Edge:
Smooth   1,000.00

Commemorates the Forest and Agriculture Educational establishment at
Tharant.

116. 1 Double taler (S) 1854. Head right,
below D. 9. AUG. 1854. Rev. Two
female figures, personifying Justice
and Love, seated, between them two
crossed torches and the Saxon arms.
Edge: VII EINE FEINE MARK   87.50

117.   1 Taler (S) 1854. Type of #116. Edge:
        XIV EINE FEINE MARK   30.00

118.   1 Mining taler (S) 1854. Type of #116.
        Edge: SEGEN DES BERGBAUS, crossed
        hammers, XIV E.F.M.   70.00

119.   1/3 Taler (S) 1854. As #116. Rev. ER
        SAEETE. Edge: XLII EINE FEINE MARK   15.00

120.   1/6 Taler (S) 1854. Type of #119. Edge:
        LXXXIV EINE F. MARK   7.50

        The above five coins commemorate
        the death of King Friedrich August II
        in 1854.

JOHANN, 1854–73

Younger brother of Friedrich August II. Born
December 12, 1801, son of Prince Maximilian and his
consort, Karoline of Parma. Johann died October 29,
1873.

121.   20 Mark—double krone (G) 1872, 73.
        Head left, E below. Rev. Type 1
        eagle. Edge: GOTT MIT UNS   43.75

122.   1 Krone (G) 1857–71. As #121. Rev.
        Value within oak wreath. Edge: GOTT
        SEGNE SACHSEN   450.00

123.   10 Mark—1 krone (G) 1872, 73. Type of
        #121. Edge: Smooth   43.75

124.   ½ Krone (G) 1857–70. Type of #122   375.00

#125

125.   1 Double taler—3½ gulden (S) 1855, 56.
        Head left, mint mark below. Rev.
        Crowned, draped, rectangular arms
        with insignia of the Order of the
        Jeweled Crown. Edge: GOTT SEGNE
        SACHSEN   50.00

128.   1 Taler (S) 1854. Type of #125   40.00

126.   1 Double taler (S) 1857, 58, 59. As
        #125, but arched arms on reverse   47.50

129.   1 Mining taler (S) 1854. As #125, but
        SEGEN DES BERGBAUS on reverse   55.00

130.   1 Taler (S) 1855, 56. Type of #125   18.75

127.   1 Double taler (S) 1861. As #125. Rev.
        In circle: crowned arms supported by
        two lions, with insignia of the Order
        of the Jeweled Crown. Edge: Type of
        #125   95.00

131.   1 Mining taler (S) 1855, 56. Type of
        #129   27.50

132.   1 Taler (S) 1857, 58, 59. Type of #126   27.50

133.   1 Mining taler (S) 1857, 58. As #126, but SEGEN DES BERGBAUS on reverse   45.00

134.   1 Mining taler (S) 1858–61. Head left, mint mark below. Rev. Crowned arms supported by two men, SEGEN DES BERGBAUS. Edge: GOTT SEGNE SACHSEN   27.50

135.   1 Mining taler (S) 1861–71. Type of #134   21.50

136.   1 Taler (S) 1860, 61. As #127, but no circle   22.50

137.   1 Taler (S) 1861–71. Type of #127   18.75

138.   1/3 Taler (S) 1856. Head left, mint mark below. Rev. Crowned, draped, rectangular arms with insignia of the Order of the Jeweled Crown   12.50

139.   1/3 Taler (S) 1858, 59. As #138, but arched arms on reverse   7.50

140.   1/3 Taler (S) 1860. As #138. Rev. Crowned arms on cartouche   11.25

Saxony • 217

141. 1/6 Taler (S) 1855, 56. Type of #138   6.25

142. 1/6 Taler (S) 1860–71. Type of #140   7.00

143. 2 Neugroschen (B) 1855, 56. Rectangular, crowned arms. Rev. Value.
Edge: Deep squares   5.50

144. 2 Neugroschen (B) 1863–66. Crowned
arms on cartouche in circle. Rev.
Value in circle. Edge: Type of #143   7.00

145. 2 Neugroschen (B) 1868–73. Head left,
mint mark below. Rev. Value. Edge:
Type of #143   5.00

146. 1 Neugroschen (B) 1855, 56, 61. Type
of #143   3.75

147. 1 Neugroschen (B) 1863, 65, 67. Type
of #144   5.50

148. 1 Neugroschen (B) 1867–73. Type of
#145   5.00

149. ½ Neugroschen (B) 1855, 56. Type of
#143. Smooth edge   4.50

150. 5 Pfennige (C) 1857. Crowned rectangular arms within pearl circle.
Rev. Value, PROBE-STUCK (Essay)   —

151. 5 Pfennige (C) 1862–69. Crowned arms
on cartouche within circle. Rev.
Value within circle. Smooth edge   4.50

152.　2 Pfennige (C) 1855–61. Crowned rect-
　　　angular arms, K.S.S.M. Rev. Value.
　　　Smooth edge　　　　　　　　　　2.50

153.　2 Pfennige (C) 1862–73. Type of #151　4.50

154.　1 Pfennig (C) 1855–61. Type of #152　3.75

155.　1 Pfennig (C) 1862–73. Type of #151　3.00

COMMEMORATIVE ISSUES

156.　1 Mint Visit taler (S) 1855. Head left,
　　　mint mark below. Rev. GEPRAEGT IN
　　　GEGENWART in circle. Edge: GOTT
　　　SEGNE SACHSEN　　　　　　　　70.00

　　　Marks the visit to the mint by King
　　　Johann, April 24, 1855.

157.　1 Prize double taler (S) 1857. Head
　　　left, mint mark below. Rev. K.S.
　　　BERGAKADEMIE, DEM FLEISSE and
　　　crossed hammers, within oak wreath.
　　　Edge: GOTT SEGNE DEN BERGBAU,
　　　crossed hammers　　　　　　　700.00

　　　Commemorates the Mining Academy
　　　at Freiberg.

158.　1 Medal in weight of a double taler (S)
　　　1866. Conjoined busts in circle, left.
　　　Rev. Three allegorical figures, in
　　　back a smoking chimney, in circle.
　　　Smooth edge　　　　　　　　400.00

　　　Commemorates the 100th anniver-
　　　sary of the Mining Academy at
　　　Freiberg.

159. 1 Victory taler (S) 1871. As #157. Rev. Winged spirit with German flag, left, background 11 flags, date below with palm branches and laurel wreath. Edge: GOTT SEGNE SACHSEN 32.50

Commemorates the victory over France in 1871.

160. 1 Double taler (S) 1872. Conjoined heads right, in circle, arabesque below. Rev. 1822 10. NOVEMBER 1872 within crossed oak and myrtle branches. Edge: XV EIN PFUND FEIN ... 50.00

Marks the golden wedding anniversary of the royal couple.

161. 1 Taler (S) 1873. As #157. Rev. Cartouche, two crossed torches within branches, inscribed VOLLENDET 29. OCTOBER 1873, book, crown and scepter below —

Commemorates the death of King Johann on October 29, 1873.

ALBERT, 1873–1902

Born April 23, 1828, the son of King Johann and his consort, Amalie of Bavaria. Albert died June 19,1902.

162. 20 Mark (G) 1874–78. Head right, E below. Rev. Type 2 eagle. Edge: GOTT MIT UNS 50.00

163. 20 Mark (G) 1894, 95. As #162, but type 3 eagle on reverse 45.00

164. 10 Mark (G) 1874–88. Type of #162. Edge: Vines and stars 41.25

165. 10 Mark (G) 1891–1902. Type of #163. Edge: Type of #164 .... 36.50

166. 5 Mark (G) 1877. Type of #162. Smooth edge 112.50

170.   2 Mark (S) 1891–1902. Type of #169   15.00

COMMEMORATIVE ISSUES

167.   5 Mark (S) 1875, 76, 89. Type of #162   35.00

171a.   5 Mark size (S) 1889. Head right. Rev. Saxonia enthroned, with sword and shield. Wreath below: 1089/1889. Smooth edge   500.00

171b.   5 Mark size (C) 1889. Type of #171a   150.00

    The above two coins commemorate the 800th anniversary of the House of Wettin.

168.   5 Mark (S) 1891–1902. Type of #163   20.00

172.   2 Mark size (S) 1892. As #171a. Rev. GEPTRAGT IN GEGENWART   200.00

    Marks the visit of the king to the mint in 1892.

169.   2 Mark (S) 1876–88. Type of #163. Reeded edge   30.00

176. 10 Mark (G) 1903, 04. Type of #175.
      Edge: Vines and stars   42.25

173. 5 Mark (S) 1902. Head right, 23. IV.
      1828 19. VI. 1902. below. Rev. Type 3
      eagle. Edge: GOTT MIT UNS   37.50

174. 2 Mark (S) 1902. Type of #173.
      Reeded edge   16.25

      The above two coins commemorate
      the death of King Albert in 1902.

177. 5 Mark (S) 1903, 04. Type of #175   21.50

GEORG, 1902–04

Younger brother of King Albert. Born August 8,
1832, son of King Johann and his consort, Amalie of
Bavaria. Georg died October 15, 1904.

175. 20 Mark (G) 1903. Head right. Rev.
      Type 3 eagle. Edge: GOTT MIT UNS   50.00

178. 2 Mark (S) 1903, 04. Type of #175.
      Reeded edge   18.75

179.   2 Mark size (S) 1903. As #175. Rev.
        GEPRAGT IN GEGENWART   250.00

       Marks the visit of the King to the
       mint in 1903.

180.   5 Mark (S) 1904. Head right, 8. VIII.
       1832, 15. X. 1904 to right and left of
       head. Rev. Type 3 eagle. Edge: GOTT
       MIT UNS   47.50

181.   2 Mark (S) 1904. Type of #180.
       Reeded edge   21.25

       The above two coins commemorate
       the death of King Georg in 1904.

FRIEDRICH AUGUST III, 1904–18

Born May 25, 1865, the son of King Georg and his consort, Maria Anna of Portugal. He abdicated his throne November 13, 1918.

182.   20 Mark (G) 1905, 13, 14. Head right.
       Rev. Type 3 eagle. Edge: GOTT MIT
       UNS   40.00

183.   10 Mark (G) 1905–12. Type of #182.
       Edge: Vines and stars   46.50

184.   5 Mark (S) 1907, 08, 14. Type of #182   18.75

185.   3 Mark (S) 1908–13. Type of #182   7.50

Saxony • 223

186. 2 Mark (S) 1905–14. Type of #182.
Reeded edge 15.00

190. 3 Mark (S) 1913. National Battle Monument at Leipzig, 18 OCTOBER 1813–1913. Rev. and edge: Type of #188 10.00

Commemorates the 100th anniversary of the Battle of Leipzig in 1913.

COMMEMORATIVE ISSUES

187. 2 Mark size (S) 1905. Type of #182.
Rev. ZUR ERINNERUNG 225.00

Marks the visit of the King to the mint in 1905.

191. 3 Mark (S) 1917. Capped, robed bust right, FRIEDRICH DER WEISE, in circle: EINE FESTE BURG. Rev. and edge: Type of #188 10,000.00

Commemorates the 400th anniversary of the Reformation.

188. 5 Mark (S) 1909. Conjoined busts left, FRIEDRICH DER STREITBARE. Rev. Type 3 eagle. Edge: GOTT MIT UNS 50.00

192. 1 Sophien ducat (G) coin, 1827–38; medallion 1846–73. Monogram CS under elector's cap, WOL DEM DER FREVD AN SEIN KIND ERLEBT— "Praised Be He Who Derives Joy From His Children." Rev. HILF DV HEILIGE DREYFALTIGKEIT 1616—"Help From the Holy Trinity" and symbols of the Holy Trinity. Edge: Reeded 87.50

Meant to be given as a gift from a godparent to his godchild.

189. 2 Mark (S) 1909. Type of #188.
Reeded edge 18.75

The above two coins commemorate the 500th anniversary of the University of Leipzig.

224 • **Saxony**

SAXON DUCHIES

Saxe-Weimar-Eisenacht

CARL AUGUST, 1775–1828

Born September 3, 1757, son of Duke Ernst August Constantin and his consort, Anna Amalie of Braunschweig-Wolfenbuttel. He was under the guardianship of his mother from May 28, 1758, to August 3, 1775. He was elevated to Grand Duke in 1815. Carl August died June 14, 1828.

1.　1 Taler (S) 1813. Crowned, tapered arms within palm and laurel branches. Rev. Value　137.50

2.　1 Taler (S) 1815. Crowned, tapered arms. Rev. DEM VATERLANDE within two crossed oak branches　125.00

3.　1 Gulden—2/3 taler (S) 1813. Type of #1　35.00

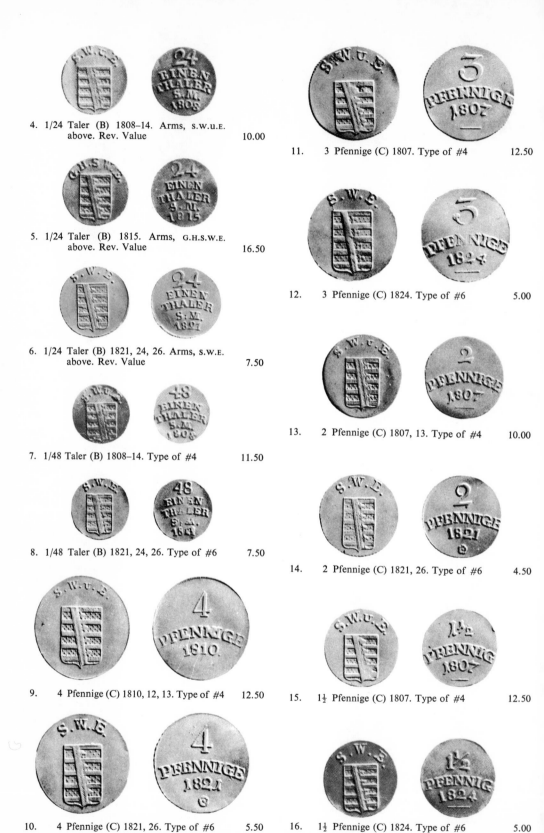

4. 1/24 Taler (B) 1808–14. Arms, s.w.u.e. above. Rev. Value ... 10.00

5. 1/24 Taler (B) 1815. Arms, g.h.s.w.e. above. Rev. Value ... 16.50

6. 1/24 Taler (B) 1821, 24, 26. Arms, s.w.e. above. Rev. Value ... 7.50

7. 1/48 Taler (B) 1808–14. Type of #4 ... 11.50

8. 1/48 Taler (B) 1821, 24, 26. Type of #6 ... 7.50

9. 4 Pfennige (C) 1810, 12, 13. Type of #4 ... 12.50

10. 4 Pfennige (C) 1821, 26. Type of #6 ... 5.50

11. 3 Pfennige (C) 1807. Type of #4 ... 12.50

12. 3 Pfennige (C) 1824. Type of #6 ... 5.00

13. 2 Pfennige (C) 1807, 13. Type of #4 ... 10.00

14. 2 Pfennige (C) 1821, 26. Type of #6 ... 4.50

15. 1½ Pfennige (C) 1807. Type of #4 ... 12.50

16. 1½ Pfennige (C) 1824. Type of #6 ... 5.00

17.   1 Pfennig (C) 1807, 10, 13. Type of #4   6.50

18.   1 Pfennig (C) 1821, 24, 26. Type of #6   3.75

19.   1 Heller (C) 1813. Type of #4   7.50

CARL FRIEDRICH, 1828–53

Born February 2, 1783, son of Grand Duke Carl August and his consort, Luise of Hessen-Darmstadt. Carl Friedrich died July 8, 1853.

20.   1 Double taler—3½ gulden (S) 1840–48. Head left, A below, FRIEDR. Rev. Crowned, draped arms with the Order of the White Falcon. Edge: GOTT UND RECHT—"God and Right"   125.00

21.   1 Taler (S) 1841. As #20, but inscription has FRIEDRICH   45.00

22.   1/24 Taler (B) 1830. Arms, S.W.E. above. Rev. Value. Reeded edge.   7.00

23.   1/48 Taler (B) 1831. As #22, but smooth edge   6.50

24.   1 Silbergroschen (B) 1840. Crowned arms. Rev. Value   5.50

25.   ½ Silbergroschen (B) 1840. Type of #24   5.00

26.   3 Pfennige (C) 1830. Type of #22   4.50

27.   3 Pfennige (C) 1840. Type of #24   5.50

28.   2 Pfennige (C) 1830. Arms, S.W.E.
       above. Rev. Value   3.75

29.   1½ Pfennige (C) 1830. Type of #28   4.50

30.   1 Pfennig (C) 1830. Type of #28   3.00

31.   1 Pfennig (C) 1840–51. Crowned arms.
       Rev. Value   2.50

CARL ALEXANDER, 1853–1901

Born June 24, 1818, son of Grand Duke Carl Friedrich
and his consort, Maria Paulowna, Grand Duchess of
Russia. Carl Alexander died January 5, 1901.

32.   1 Double taler—3½ gulden (S) 1855.
       Head left, A below. Rev. Crowned,
       draped arms with Order of the White
       Falcon. Edge: GOTT UND RECHT—
       "God and Right"   200.00

33.   1 Taler (S) 1858, 66, 70. Type of #32   37.50

34. 1 Silbergroschen (B) 1858. Crowned
     arms. Rev. Value   3.75

35. ½ Silbergroschen (B) 1858. Type of #34   3.75

36. 2 Pfennige (C) 1858, 65. Type of #34   2.50

37. 1 Pfennig (C) 1858, 65. Type of #34   2.00

AFTER INCORPORATION INTO THE EMPIRE

38. 20 Mark (G) 1892, 96. Head left, A
     below. Rev. Type 3 eagle. Edge:
     GOTT MIT UNS   250.00

39. 2 Mark (S) 1892, 98. Type of #38.
     Reeded edge   62.50

WILHELM ERNST, 1901–18

Born June 10, 1876, son of Grand Duke Carl August
and his consort, Pauline, Duchess of Sachsen.
Wilhelm Ernst abdicated his throne November 9,
1918.

40. 20 Mark (G) 1901. Head left, A below.
     Rev. Type 3 eagle. Edge: GOTT MIT
     UNS   425.00

41. 2 Mark (S) 1901. Type of #40. Reeded
     edge   100.00

COMMEMORATIVE ISSUES

42. 5 Mark (S) 1903. Conjoined heads left,
     30 IV WILHELM ERNST-CAROLINE. Rev.
     Type 3 eagle. Edge: GOTT MIT UNS   70.00

43. 2 Mark (S) 1903. As #42, but reeded
     edge   27.50

     The above two coins commemorate
     the first marriage of the Grand Duke
     in 1903.

46. 3 Mark (S) 1910. Conjoined heads left,
     IV. I. WILHELM ERNST-FEODORA. Rev.
     and edge: Type of #42   22.50

     Commemorates the second marriage
     of the Grand Duke in 1910.

44. 5 Mark (S) 1908. Bust of Johann Fried-
     richs with cape and cap, holding
     sword, right, JOH. FRIED. . . . D. UNIV.
     JENA. 1558/1908. Rev. and edge:
     Type of #42   62.50

45. 2 Mark (S) 1908. As #44, but reeded
     edge   25.00

     The above two coins commemorate
     the 350th anniversary of the Univer-
     sity of Jena, 1908.

47. 3 Mark (S) 1915. Conjoined uniformed
     busts, WILHELM ERNST MCMXV CARL
     AUGUST MDCCCXV. Rev. and edge:
     Type of #42   50.00

     Marks the 100th anniversary of the
     Grand Duchy in 1915.

SAXON DUCHIES (continued)

Saxe-Altenburg

JOSEPH, 1826–48

Born August 27, 1789, son of Duke Friedrich of
Sachsen-Hildburghausen (from November 12, 1826,
Duke of Sachsen-Altenburg) and his consort, Char-
lotte of Mecklenburg-Strelitz. He abdicated his throne
in favor of his brother Georg on November 30, 1848.
Joseph died November 25, 1868.

49. 1 Taler (S) 1841. Type of #48   42.50

48. 1 Double taler (S) 1841–47. Head left,
     mint mark below. Rev. Crowned,
     draped arms. Edge: GOTT SEGNE
     SACHSEN   212.50

50. 1/6 Taler (S) 1841, 42. Type of #48   18.75

Saxe-Altenburg • **231**

51. 2 Neugroschen—20 pfennige (B) 1841.
     Crowned arms. Rev. Value   10.00

52. 1 Neugroschen—10 pfennige (B) 1841,
     42. Type of #51   8.75

53. ½ Neugroschen—5 pfennige (B) 1841,
     42. Type of #51   8.00

54. 2 Pfennige (C) 1841. Type of #51   6.25

55. 2 Pfennige (C) 1843. Crowned, heart-
     shaped arms. Rev. Value   10.00

56. 1 Pfennig (C) 1841. Type of #51   5.00

57. 1 Pfennig (C) 1843. Type of #55   3.75

GEORG, 1848–53

Younger brother of Joseph. Born July 24, 1796, son
of Duke Friedrich of Sachsen-Hildburghausen (from
November 12, 1826, Duke of Sachsen-Altenburg) and
his consort, Charlotte of Mecklenburg-Strelitz. He
assumed the throne upon the abdication of his
brother Joseph on November 30, 1848. Georg died
August 3, 1853.

58. 1 Double taler—3½ gulden (S) 1852.
     Head right, F below. Rev. Crowned,
     draped arms. Edge: GOTT SEGNE
     SACHSEN   300.00

59. 2 Pfennige (C) 1852. Crowned, heart-
     shaped arms. Rev. Value   5.00

60. 1 Pfennig (C) 1852. Type of #59   2.50

ERNST I, 1853–1908

Born September 16, 1826, son of Duke Georg and his consort, Marie of Mecklenburg-Schwerin. Ernst I died February 7, 1908.

61. 1 Taler (S) 1858, 64, 69. Head right, mint mark below. Rev. Crowned, draped arms. Edge: GOTT SEGNE SACHSEN 40.00

62. 2 Pfennige (C) 1856. Crowned, heart-shaped arms. Rev. Value 7.50

63. 1 Pfennig (C) 1856–65. Type of #62 2.50

AFTER INCORPORATION INTO THE EMPIRE

64. 20 Mark (G) 1887. Head right, A below. Rev. Type 2 eagle. Edge: GOTT MIT UNS 300.00

65. 5 Mark (S) 1901. As #64, but Rev. type 3 eagle 200.00

66. 2 Mark (S) 1901. Type of #65 100.00

COMMEMORATIVE ISSUE

67. 5 Mark (S) 1903. Head right with laurel branch, 1853 1903. Rev. Type of #65 100.00

Marks the 50th anniversary of the reign.

SAXON DUCHIES (continued)

Saxe-Coburg-Gotha

ERNST I, 1806–44

Born January 2, 1784, son of Duke Franz of Sachsen-Coburg-Saalfeld and his consort, Auguste. On December 9, 1806, he became Duke of Sachsen-Coburg-Saalfeld. On November 12, 1826, he became Duke of Sachsen-Coburg and Gotha. Ernst I died January 29, 1844.

68.　1 Ducat (G) 1831. Head left, z.s. Rev. Crowned arms within two bound laurel branches　550.00

69.　1 Ducat (G) 1836, 42. Head left, ZU SACHSEN. Rev. Crowned arms on shield with Ernst House Order. Reeded edge　250.00

70.　1 Double taler—3½ gulden (S) 1841, 42, 43. Head left, mint mark below. Rev. Crowned, draped arms within wreath. Edge: NACH DER CONVENTION VOM 30 JULY 1838　200.00

71.   1 Taler (S) 1827. Bust left in armor with ermine cape. Rev. Crown, scepter and sword within two bound laurel branches   400.00

74.   ½ Taler—gulden (S) 1830–35. As #72, but reeded edge   45.00

75.   1/6 Taler (S) 1841, 42, 43. Head left, mint mark below. Rev. Crowned arms within wreath. Edge: Type of #70   22.50

76.   20 Kreuzer (S) 1827, 28, 30. Crowned arms. Rev. Value within two crossed palm branches   25.00

72.   1 Taler (S) 1829. As #70, but no mint mark. Rev. Crowned arms within two bound laurel branches. Smooth edge   250.00

77.   20 Kreuzer (S) 1831, 34. Head left. Rev. Crowned arms within two crossed laurel branches. Edge: Deep squares   16.50

73.   1 Taler (S) 1841, 42. Type of #70   45.00

78.   20 Kreuzer (S) 1835, 36. Type of #77   15.00

Saxe-Coburg-Gotha • **235**

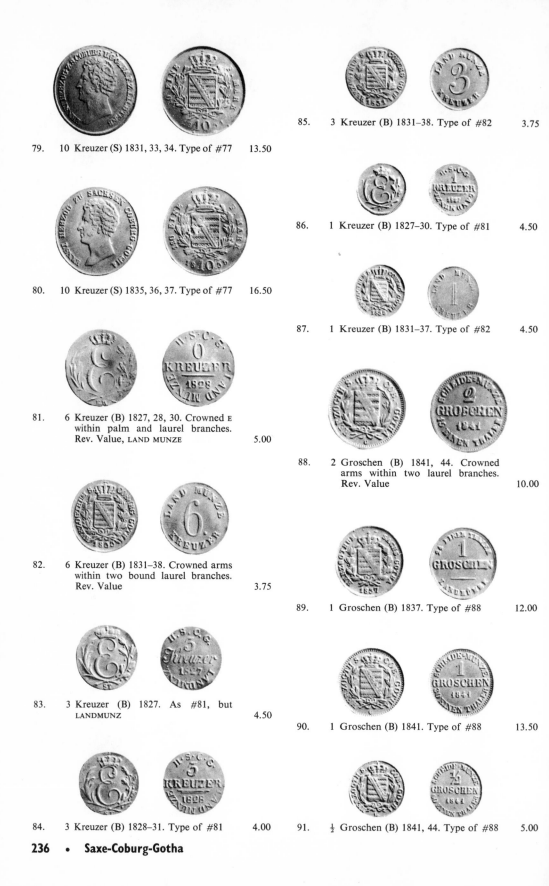

79.   10 Kreuzer (S) 1831, 33, 34. Type of #77   13.50

80.   10 Kreuzer (S) 1835, 36, 37. Type of #77   16.50

81.   6 Kreuzer (B) 1827, 28, 30. Crowned E within palm and laurel branches. Rev. Value, LAND MUNZE   5.00

82.   6 Kreuzer (B) 1831–38. Crowned arms within two bound laurel branches. Rev. Value   3.75

83.   3 Kreuzer (B) 1827. As #81, but LANDMUNZ   4.50

84.   3 Kreuzer (B) 1828–31. Type of #81   4.00

85.   3 Kreuzer (B) 1831–38. Type of #82   3.75

86.   1 Kreuzer (B) 1827–30. Type of #81   4.50

87.   1 Kreuzer (B) 1831–37. Type of #82   4.50

88.   2 Groschen (B) 1841, 44. Crowned arms within two laurel branches. Rev. Value   10.00

89.   1 Groschen (B) 1837. Type of #88   12.00

90.   1 Groschen (B) 1841. Type of #88   13.50

91.   ½ Groschen (B) 1841, 44. Type of #88   5.00

92. 3 Pfennige (C) 1834. Crowned arms.
Rev. Value   2.50

93. 2 Pfennige (C) 1834, 35. Type of #92   2.00

94. 2 Pfennige (C) 1841. Type of #88   4.50

95. 1½ Pfennige (C) 1834, 35. Type of #92   5.00

96. 1 Pfennig (C) 1833–37. Type of #92   2.00

97. 1 Pfennig (C) 1841. Type of #88   3.00

ERNST II, 1844–93

Born June 21, 1818, son of Duke Ernst I of Sachsen-Coburg-Saalfeld (Duke of Sachsen-Coburg and Gotha from November 12, 1826) and his consort, Luise of Sachsen-Gotha-Altenburg. Ernst II died August 22, 1893.

98. 1 Double taler—3½ gulden (S) 1847.
Head left. Rev. Crowned, draped
arms with the Ernst House Order.
Edge: NACH DER CONVENTION VOM
30 IULY 1838   275.00

99. 1 Double taler—3½ gulden (S) 1854.
Head left. Rev. As #98, but crown of
different design. Edge: Type of #98   200.00

100. 1 Taler (S) 1846. As #98. Rev.
Crowned, draped arms. Edge: Type
of #98   46.50

104. 1/6 Taler (S) 1845. Head left. Rev.
Crowned arms within wreath   10.00

101. 1 Taler (S) 1848. As #99. Rev. As #100,
but crown of different design. Edge:
Type of #98   100.00

105. 1/6 Taler (S) 1848. Head left. Rev.
Arched arms within band, crown
above, on the band is the motto of
the Ernst House Order: FIDELITER ET
CONSTANTER. Edge: Type of #100   12.50

102. 1 Taler (S) 1852. Type of #99. Rev.
and edge: Type of #101   75.00

106. 1/6 Taler (S) 1852, 55. Type of #99. Rev.
and edge: Type of #105   18.75

103. 1 Taler (S) 1862, 64, 70. Head left,
with long moustache. Rev. Crowned,
draped arms on cartouche shield.
Edge: FIDELITER ET CONSTANTER—
"Faithfully and Constantly"   37.50

107. 1/6 Taler (S) 1864. Type of #103   16.50

108. 2 Groschen (B) 1847–58. Crowned
arms. Rev. Value   4.50

109. 2 Groschen (B) 1865, 68, 70. Head left.
Rev. Value   4.00

110. 1 Groschen (B) 1847–58. Type of #108   3.75

111. 1 Groschen (B) 1865, 68, 70. Type of
#109   3.00

112. ½ Groschen (B) 1851–70. Type of #108   4.00

113. 2 Pfennige (C) 1847–70. Crowned arms
within two laurel branches. Rev.
Value   2.50

114. 1 Pfennig (C) 1847–70. Type of #113   2.00

115. 20 Mark (G) 1872. Head left. Rev. Type
1 eagle. Edge: GOTT MIT UNS   1,375.00

116. 20 Mark (G) 1886. As #115, but Rev.
Type 2 eagle   300.00

COMMEMORATIVE ISSUES

117. 1 Taler (S) 1869. Head left. Rev. DEN
29 IANUAR 1869. Edge: FIDELITER ET
CONSTANTER   75.00

118. 1/6 Taler (S) 1869. Type of #117   50.00
The above two coins commemorate
the 25th anniversary of the reign.

Saxe-Coburg-Gotha • **239**

ALFRED, 1893–1900

Born August 6, 1844, son of Queen Victoria of Great Britain and Ireland and her consort, Prince Albert of Sachsen-Coburg-Gotha. Alfred died July 30, 1900.

CARL EDUARD, 1900–18

Born July 19, 1884, son of Prince Leopold, Duke of Albany, and his consort, Helene of Waldeck. He was under the regency of Prince Ernst of Hohenlohe-Langenburg. Carl Eduard abdicated his throne on November 14, 1918.

119. 20 Mark (G) 1895. Head right. Rev.
      Type 3 eagle. Edge: GOTT MIT UNS   230.00

122. 20 Mark (G) 1905. Head right. Rev.
      Type 3 eagle. Edge: GOTT MIT UNS   230.00

123. 10 Mark (G) 1905. Type of #122. Edge:
      Vines and stars   230.00

120. 5 Mark (S) 1895. Type of #119   312.50

124. 5 Mark (S) 1907. Type of #122   350.00

121. 2 Mark (S) 1895. As #119, but reeded
      edge   95.00

125. 2 Mark (S) 1905, 11. Type of #123   75.00

SAXON DUCHIES (continued)

Saxe-Coburg-Saalfeld

ERNST, 1806–26

Born January 2, 1784, son of Duke Franz and his consort, Auguste. On November 12, 1826, he became Duke of Sachsen-Coburg-Gotha. Ernst died January 29, 1844.

MINTED FOR SAALFELD

127. 1 Taler (S) 1825. Bust in armor left, ermine cape. Rev. Crown, scepter, sword and date within two bound laurel branches. Edge: Either with EIN KRONTHALER or without inscription   400.00

128. 1/24 Taler—groschen (B) 1808, 10, 18. Crowned E within two crossed oak branches. Rev. Value   7.50

126. 1 Taler (S) 1817. Uniformed bust left, ermine cape. Rev. Crowned arms. Edge: Either with leaves or with deep letters: EIN SPECIES THALER   212.50

129. 6 Pfennige (B) 1808, 10, 20. Type of #128   8.00

130.   4 Pfennige (C) 1809–20. Crowned E
       within two crossed laurel branches.
       Rev. Value   6.50

131.   3 Pfennige (C) 1807, 08. Arms on
       crowned cartouche with festoons.
       Rev. III PFENNIG   5.00

132.   3 Pfennige (C) 1821–26. As #131, but
       Rev. 3 PFENNIG   3.00

133.   2 Pfennige (C) 1810, 17, 18. Type of
       #130   2.25

134.   1 Pfennig (B) 1808. Crowned, heart-
       shaped arms within crossed palm and
       laurel branches. Rev. 1 PFENNIG   2.50

135.   1 Pfennig (C) 1808–26. As #131, but
       Rev. I PFENNIG   2.00

136.   1 Pfennig (C) 1809. Type of #130   3.00

137.   1 Heller (C) 1809. Type of #130   3.75

138.   1 Heller (C) 1809–24. As #131. Rev.
       Value   2.00

MINTED FOR COBURG

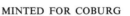

139.   20 Kreuzer (S) 1807. Crowned, pointed
       arms. Rev. Value within oak wreath,
       date below   27.50

140.   20 Kreuzer (S) 1807. As #139, but Rev.
       value and date within oak wreath   20.00

242 • **Saxe-Coburg-Saalfeld**

141.　20 Kreuzer (S) 1812–20. Crowned arms, SACHS. SOUV. Rev. Value within two bound palm branches　12.50

142.　20 Kreuzer (S) 1823–26. Crowned arms, SACHS: COBURG. Rev. Type of #141　11.50

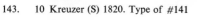

143.　10 Kreuzer (S) 1820. Type of #141　25.00

144.　10 Kreuzer (S) 1824. As #142, but SACHS. COBURG　31.50

145.　6 Kreuzer (B) 1808–20. Crowned E within crossed palm and laurel branches. Rev. Value, H.S.C.　6.50

146.　6 Kreuzer (B) 1821–26. As #145, but H.S.C.S. on reverse　6.50

147.　3 Kreuzer (B) 1808–19. Type of #145　4.50

148.　3 Kreuzer (B) 1820–26. Type of #146　6.50

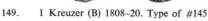

149.　1 Kreuzer (B) 1808–20. Type of #145　6.50

150.　1 Kreuzer (B) 1824, 25, 26. Type of #146　5.00

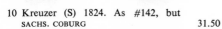

Saxe-Coburg-Saalfeld　•　243

SAXON DUCHIES (continued)

Saxe-Hildburghausen

FRIEDRICH, 1786–1826

Born April 29, 1763, son of Duke Ernst Friedrich Carl and his consort, Ernestine of Sachsen-Weimar-Eisenach. He was under the guardianship of General Field Marshal Prince Joseph Friedrich of Sachsen-Hildburghausen from September 22, 1780, to January 4, 1787. He was made Duke of Sachsen-Altenburg on January 12, 1826. Friedrich died September 29, 1834.

151.   6 Kreuzer (B) 1808–18. Crowned F within laurel wreath. Rev. Value and laurel branches   13.75

152.   6 Kreuzer (B) 1820–25. Crowned F within crossed palm and laurel branches. Rev. Value   10.00

153.   3 Kreuzer (B) 1808–20. Type of #151   11.50

154.   1 Kreuzer (B) 1806, 11. Crowned, oval arms within two palm branches. Rev. Value   8.75

155.   ½ Kreuzer (C) 1808, 09. Crowned arms. Rev. Value   4.50

156.   ½ Kreuzer (C) 1823. Crowned, heart-shaped arms, HERZ. Z.S. Rev. Type of #155   10.00

157.   ½ Kreuzer (C) 1823. Type of #156   6.50

158.   ½ Kreuzer (C) 1823. As #156. Rev.
       Value, KREUZER LANDMUNZE   6.50

159.   ¼ Kreuzer (C) 1825. Crowned F within
       crossed palm and laurel branches.
       Rev. Type of #158   2.50

160.   ¼ Kreuzer (C) 1825. As #156, but
       H.S.H.H. Rev. Type of #158   3.00

161.   1 Pfennig (C) 1823, 25, 26. As #156,
       but H.S. HHAEUSI. S.M. Rev. Value   5.00

162.   1 Pfennig (C) 1826. Crowned arms.
       Rev. Value   31.50

163.   ⅛ Kreuzer (C) 1825. Type of #159   3.75

164.   1 Heller (C) 1806. Crowned, oval arms
       within crossed palm and laurel
       branches. Rev. Value   3.75

165.   1 Heller (C) 1808–18. Crowned arms.
       Rev. Value   2.00

166.   1 Heller (C) 1820–25. Type of #159   2.50

Saxe-Hildburghausen • 245

SAXON DUCHIES (continued)

Saxe-Meiningen

BERNHARD II ERICH FREUND, 1803–66

Born December 17, 1800, son of Duke Georg I and his consort, Luise Eleonore of Hohenlohe-Langenburg. He was under the guardianship of his mother from 1803 to 1821. He retired in favor of his son, Georg II, on September 20, 1866. Bernhard II Erich Freund died December 3, 1882.

UNDER THE REGENCY OF LUISE ELEONORE, DUCHESS OF SAXE-MEININGEN

167.   20 Kreuzer (S) 1812. Bust right. Rev. Value within square frame entwined with flowers —

168.   6 Kreuzer (B) 1808, 12, 13. Crowned, draped arms, s.cob. Rev. Value within oak wreath   15.00

169.   6 Kreuzer (B) 1812, 13. As #168, but drape extends beneath crown   12.50

170.   3 Kreuzer (B) 1808. Type of #169   12.50

171.   3 Kreuzer (B) 1812, 13. As #170, but Rev. LAND MUNZE   10.00

172. 1 Kreuzer (B) 1808. As #168, but
      H.S.C.M. Rev. Value   5.00

173. 1 Kreuzer (B) 1812. As #169, but
      H.S.C.M. Rev. As #172   7.50

174. 1 Kreuzer (C) 1814, 18. Crowned,
      heart-shaped arms, HERZ. Rev. Value   5.50

175. ½ Kreuzer (C) 1812, 14, 18. As #174.
      Rev. Value   3.75

176. ¼ Kreuzer (C) 1812, 14, 18. As #174.
      Rev. Value   7.50

177. 1 Pfennig (C) 1818. Type of #174   11.00

178. 1 Heller (C) 1814. As #174, but H.
      Rev. Value   5.00

179. 1 Heller (C) 1814. Type of #174. Rev.
      Type of #178   6.25

180. 1 Double taler—3½ gulden (S) 1841.
      Head left, VOIGT below. Rev. Value
      within oak wreath. Edge: CONVEN-
      TION VOM 30 IULY 1838   225.00

181. 1 Double taler—3½ gulden (S) 1843, 46.
      As #180. Rev. Crowned, draped
      arms with Ernst House Order. Edge:
      Type of #180   205.00

182. 1 Double taler—3½ gulden (S) 1853–54.
      Head left with goatee, HELFRICHT be-
      low. Rev. and edge: Type of #181   162.50

Saxe-Meiningen • 247

187.   1 Gulden (S) 1838–41. Head left, rosette below. Rev. Value within oak
wreath   18.75

183.   1 Double gulden (S) 1854. As #182,
but different inscription on reverse   55.00

184.   1 Taler (S) 1859–66. Head left with
goatee, HELFRICHT F. on truncation.
Rev. Crowned, draped arms. Edge:
FIDELITER ET CONSTANTER   50.00

188.   1 Gulden (S) 1843, 46. Head left,
HELFRICHT below. Rev. Type of #187   17.50

185.   1 Gulden (S) 1829. Head left. Rev.
SEGEN DES SAALFELDER BERGBAUES   125.00
Note: The actual silver for these
coins did not come from the Saalfeld
mines, but the minting was paid for
out of the mines' profits.

189.   1 Gulden (S) 1854. As #188, but
bearded head   18.75

186.   1 Gulden (S) 1830–37. Head left.
Rev. Crown above two bound oak
branches   33.00

190.   ½ Gulden (S) 1838–41. Type of #187   12.50

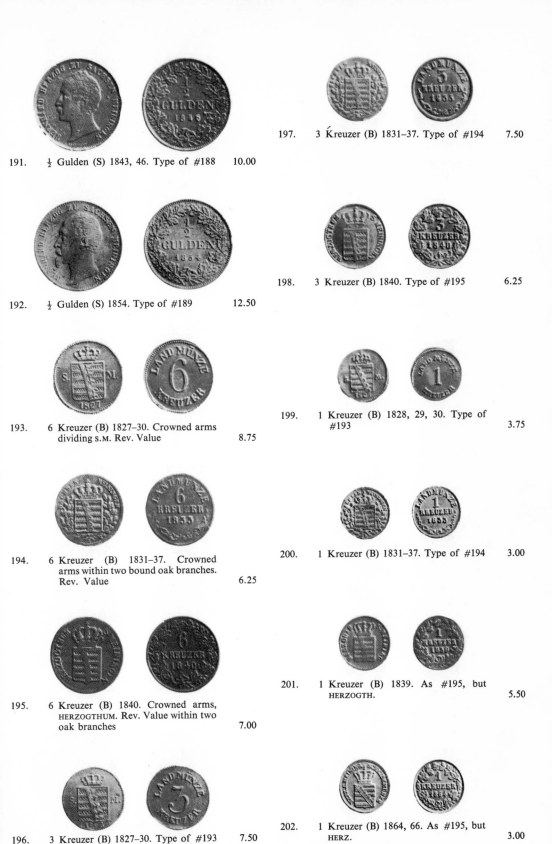

191.　½ Gulden (S) 1843, 46. Type of #188　10.00

192.　½ Gulden (S) 1854. Type of #189　12.50

193.　6 Kreuzer (B) 1827–30. Crowned arms
　　　dividing s.m. Rev. Value　8.75

194.　6 Kreuzer (B) 1831–37. Crowned
　　　arms within two bound oak branches.
　　　Rev. Value　6.25

195.　6 Kreuzer (B) 1840. Crowned arms,
　　　HERZOGTHUM. Rev. Value within two
　　　oak branches　7.00

196.　3 Kreuzer (B) 1827–30. Type of #193　7.50

197.　3 Kreuzer (B) 1831–37. Type of #194　7.50

198.　3 Kreuzer (B) 1840. Type of #195　6.25

199.　1 Kreuzer (B) 1828, 29, 30. Type of
　　　#193　3.75

200.　1 Kreuzer (B) 1831–37. Type of #194　3.00

201.　1 Kreuzer (B) 1839. As #195, but
　　　HERZOGTH.　5.50

202.　1 Kreuzer (B) 1864, 66. As #195, but
　　　HERZ.　3.00

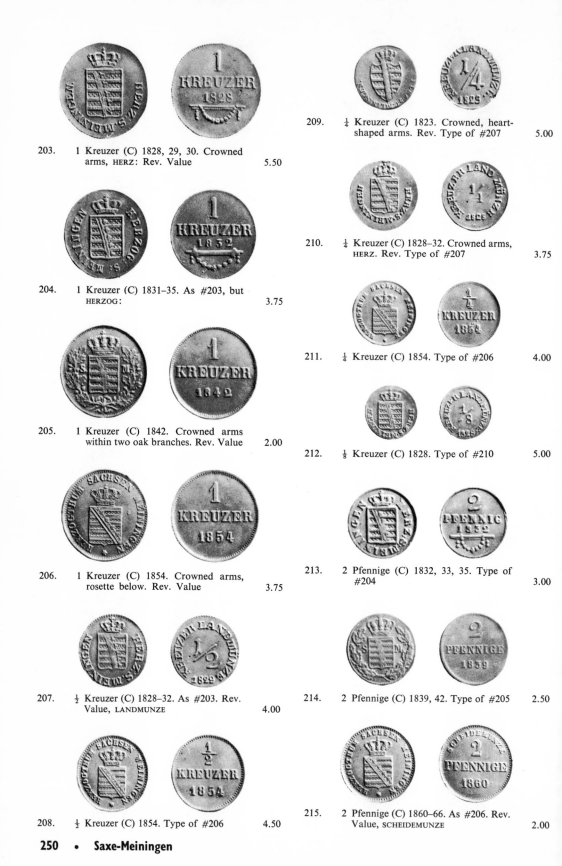

203.   1 Kreuzer (C) 1828, 29, 30. Crowned
arms, HERZ: Rev. Value   5.50

204.   1 Kreuzer (C) 1831–35. As #203, but
HERZOG: 3.75

205.   1 Kreuzer (C) 1842. Crowned arms
within two oak branches. Rev. Value   2.00

206.   1 Kreuzer (C) 1854. Crowned arms,
rosette below. Rev. Value   3.75

207.   ½ Kreuzer (C) 1828–32. As #203. Rev.
Value, LANDMUNZE   4.00

208.   ½ Kreuzer (C) 1854. Type of #206   4.50

209.   ¼ Kreuzer (C) 1823. Crowned, heart-
shaped arms. Rev. Type of #207   5.00

210.   ¼ Kreuzer (C) 1828–32. Crowned arms,
HERZ. Rev. Type of #207   3.75

211.   ¼ Kreuzer (C) 1854. Type of #206   4.00

212.   ⅛ Kreuzer (C) 1828. Type of #210   5.00

213.   2 Pfennige (C) 1832, 33, 35. Type of
#204   3.00

214.   2 Pfennige (C) 1839, 42. Type of #205   2.50

215.   2 Pfennige (C) 1860–66. As #206. Rev.
Value, SCHEIDEMUNZE   2.00

250 • **Saxe-Meiningen**

216. 1 Pfennig (C) 1832, 33, 35. Type of #213   3.75

217. 1 Pfennig (C) 1839, 42. Type of #214   4.50

218. 1 Pfennig (C) 1860–66. Type of #215   2.00

GEORG II, 1866–1914

Born April 2, 1826, son of Duke Bernhard Erich Freund and his consort, Marie of Hessen-Kassel. Georg II died June 25, 1914.

219. 1 Taler (S) 1867. Head right, HEL-FRICHT at truncation. Rev. Crowned, draped arms with Ernst House Order. Edge: FIDELITER ET CONSTANTER   65.00

220. 2 Pfennige (C) 1867–70. Crowned arms. Rev. Value   2.00

221. 1 Pfennig (C) 1867, 68. Type of #220   1.50

222. 20 Mark (G) 1872. Head right. Rev. Type 1 eagle. Edge: GOTT MIT UNS   900.00

223. 20 Mark (G) 1882. As #222, but Rev. type 2 eagle   712.50

224. 20 Mark (G) 1889. Head left, GEORG HERZOG. Rev. and edge: Type of #223   575.00

225. 20 Mark (G) 1900, 05. As #224, but Rev. type 3 eagle   900.00

226. 20 Mark (G) 1910, 14. Head left, GEORG II. Rev. and edge: Type of #225   1,000.00

227. 10 Mark (G) 1890, 98. Type of #225. Edge: Vines and stars   525.00

228. 10 Mark (G) 1902, 09, 14. Type of #226. Edge: Type of #227   650.00

229.   5 Mark (S) 1902, 08. Head left, D below. Rev. Type 3 eagle. Edge: GOTT MIT UNS   70.00

232.   5 Mark (S) 1901. Head right with small flowering spray and D at truncation. Rev. Type 3 eagle   100.00

230.   3 Mark (S) 1908, 13. Type of #229   87.50

233.   2 Mark (S) 1901. As #232, but reeded edge   87.50

The above two coins commemorate the 75th birthday of the Duke.

231.   2 Mark (S) 1902, 13. As #229, but reeded edge   100.00

234.   3 Mark (S) 1915. Head left, HERZOG V., 1826 + 1914 below. Rev. Type 3 eagle   62.50

COMMEMORATIVE ISSUES

#232

235.   2 Mark (S) 1914. Type of #234, but HERZOG VON   57.50

The above two coins commemorate the death of the Duke.

SCHAUMBURG-LIPPE

Capital: Buckeburg

This county, whose family took its name from an old castle, was raised to a principality in 1807 when it entered the Napoleonic Confederation of the Rhine. The principality endured until 1918.

Coins for Schaumburg-Lippe were struck in:

Hannover	Mintmark B	Arolsen (1824, 26, 28)
Brunswick	H	Altona (1829)
		Berlin Mintmark A

GEORG WILHELM, 1807–60

Born December 20, 1784, son of Count Philipp Ernst and his consort, Julie of Hessen-Philippsthal. From 1787 to 1807, he was under the guardianship of his mother. Georg Wilhelm died November 21, 1860.

UNDER GUARDIANSHIP OF HIS MOTHER

1.   1 Taler (S) 1802. Crowned arms. Rev. x and date on garlanded tablet   125.00

2.   1 Mariengroschen (B) 1802. Crowned arms, garlands and roses. Rev. Value, date, inscription begins GR: SCH: 9.50

3.   4 Pfennige (B) 1802. Type of #2   5.00

AS INDEPENDENT PRINCE

4.   10 Taler (G) 1829. Draped bust left, ALSING at truncation. Rev. Crowned, draped arms   750.00

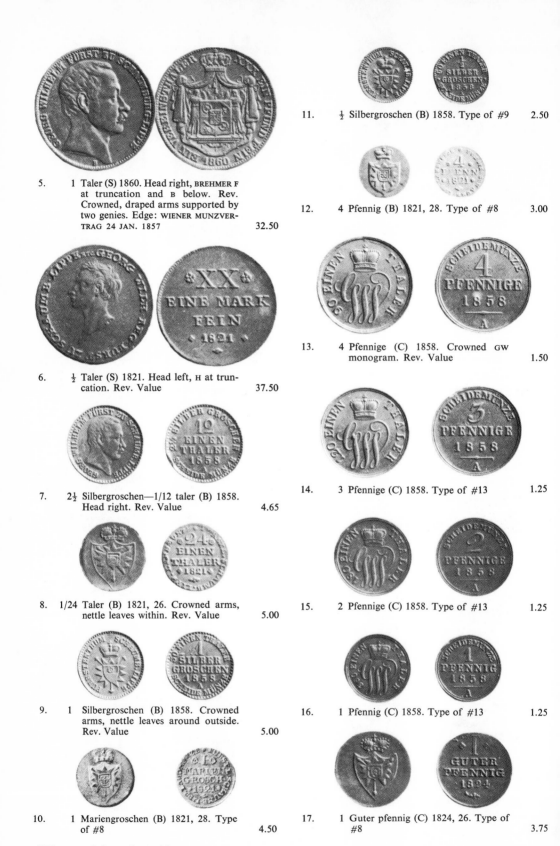

5.   1 Taler (S) 1860. Head right, BREHMER F at truncation and B below. Rev. Crowned, draped arms supported by two genies. Edge: WIENER MUNZVERTRAG 24 JAN. 1857   32.50

6.   ½ Taler (S) 1821. Head left, H at truncation. Rev. Value   37.50

7.   2½ Silbergroschen—1/12 taler (B) 1858. Head right. Rev. Value   4.65

8.   1/24 Taler (B) 1821, 26. Crowned arms, nettle leaves within. Rev. Value   5.00

9.   1 Silbergroschen (B) 1858. Crowned arms, nettle leaves around outside. Rev. Value   5.00

10.   1 Mariengroschen (B) 1821, 28. Type of #8   4.50

11.   ½ Silbergroschen (B) 1858. Type of #9   2.50

12.   4 Pfennig (B) 1821, 28. Type of #8   3.00

13.   4 Pfennige (C) 1858. Crowned GW monogram. Rev. Value   1.50

14.   3 Pfennige (C) 1858. Type of #13   1.25

15.   2 Pfennige (C) 1858. Type of #13   1.25

16.   1 Pfennig (C) 1858. Type of #13   1.25

17.   1 Guter pfennig (C) 1824, 26. Type of #8   3.75

COMMEMORATIVE ISSUE

18.   1 Double taler (S) 1857. As #5. Rev.
NACH FUNFZIG within two bow-tied
oak branches. Edge: MIT GOTTES
HULFE—"With God's Help"   150.00

    Commemorates the 50th anniversary
of the reign as Prince.

ADOLF GEORG, 1860–93

Born August 1, 1817, son of Prince Georg Wilhelm
and his consort, Ida of Waldeck and Pyrmont. Adolf
Georg died May 8, 1893.

19.   1 Taler (S) 1865. Head left, BREHMER.
F. at truncation and B below. Rev.
Arms supported by two genies. Edge:
WIENER MUNZVERTRAG 24 JAN. 1857   25.00

AFTER INCORPORATION INTO THE EMPIRE

20.   20 Mark (G) 1874. Head left, B below.
Rev. Type 2 eagle. Edge: GOTT MIT
UNS   1,150.00

GEORG, 1893–1911

Born October 10, 1846, son of Prince Adolf Georg
and his consort, Hermine of Waldeck and Pyrmont.
Georg died April 29, 1911.

21.   20 Mark (G) 1898, 1904. Head left, A
below. Rev. Type 3 eagle. Edge:
GOTT MIT UNS   450.00

22.   5 Mark (S) 1898, 1904. Type of #21   212.50

23.   2 Mark (S) 1898, 1904. As #21, but
reeded edge   87.50

COMMEMORATIVE ISSUE

24.   3 Mark (S) 1911. Head left, A below,
10 X 1846 + 29 IV 1911 under head.
Rev. Type 3 eagle. Edge: GOTT MIT
UNS   37.50

    Commemorates the death of the
Prince.

SCHLESWIG-HOLSTEIN

The duchy of Schleswig was historically Danish while Holstein was traditionally German. The 1773 Treaty of Zarskoje Selo, however, transferred the duchy of Holstein to the Danish crown in exchange for Oldenburg. On the premise that the two duchies were indissolubly united, the Danes maintained they had a right to hold both while the Germans pressed their claim as well. The so-called Schleswig-Holstein Question caused a great deal of trouble during the first half of the 19th century, settled only when Prussia annexed the territory in 1866 following its victory in the Austro-Prussian War.

Coins for Schleswig-Holstein were struck in Altona.

CHRISTIAN VII OF DENMARK, 1784–1808

Born January 29, 1749, son of King Frederick V of Denmark and his consort, Luise of Great Britain. Christian VII died March 13, 1808.

1. 1 Specie taler (S) 1800. Small head right, P.G. below. Rev. Crowned, oval arms dividing I.SP.   50.00

2. 1 Specie taler (S) 1800, 05. Larger head with bow-tied long hair and B at truncation. Rev. As #1, but larger, crowned, oval arms (Essay)   —

9.   16 Reichsbank schilling (S) 1816–39.
Crowned, interlaced FR monogram,
VI within. Rev. Value   10.50

3.   1 Specie taler (S) 1800–08. Head right,
bow-tied hair, B below. Rev. Type of
#1   45.00

10.   8 Reichsbank schilling (B) 1816, 18, 19.
Type of #9   3.00

11.   2½ Schilling Courant (B) 1809, 12. Type
of #9   6.50

PROVISIONAL GOVERNMENT

4.   2/3 Specie taler (S) 1808. Type of #3   20.00

5.   1/3 Specie taler (S) 1808. Type of #4   5.00

6.   1/12 Specie taler (S) 1800, 01. Crowned,
interlaced CR monogram, VII within.
Rev. Value   4.50

12.   1 Schilling (B) 1851. Crowned arms
within two crossed oak branches.
Rev. Value   —

7.   2½ Schilling Courant (B) 1800, 01. Type
of #6   3.00

13.   1 Sechsling (C) 1850, 51. Type of #12   2.00

8.   2 Sechsling (B) 1800. Type of #6   2.50

14.   1 Dreiling (C) 1850. Type of #12   2.50

SCHWARZBURG-RUDOLSTADT

The ruling family of the principality took its name from an old castle. It divided into two major branches in 1583. The Rudolstadt lands were made up of two separate pieces—the area around the town of Sonderhausen and that around Gehren. The principality became a member of the German Empire in 1871 and endured until 1909 when, on the death of Prince Karl Gunther, it passed to the Rudolstadt line.

Coins for Schwarzburg-Sonderhausen were struck in Berlin.

FRIEDRICH GUNTHER, 1807–67

Born November 6, 1793, son of Prince Ludwig Friedrich II and his consort, Caroline of Hessen-Homburg. He was under the guardianship of his mother from 1807 to 1814. Friedrich Gunther died June 28, 1867.

2.　1 Groschen (B) 1808. SCHWARZB.RUD. L.M. Rev. Value　3.75

3.　1 Groschen (B) 1812. As #2, but with rosette above and ledge below. Rev. As #2, with rosettes　3.75

4.　6 Pfennige (B) 1808. Type of #2. Rev. 6 PF.　3.00

1.　1 Taler (S) 1812, 13. Head right. Rev. Value within oak wreath　110.00

5.   6 Pfennige (B) 1808, 12, 13. Type of #3. Rev. Type of #4   3.00

6.   4 Pfennige (C) 1812, 13. Monogram FG within two crossed palm branches. Rev. Value   3.50

7.   3 Pfennige (C) 1813. Type of #6   3.75

11.   1 Double taler—3½ gulden (S) 1841, 45. Head right, VOIGT at truncation, A below. Rev. Helmeted arms with double eagle, flanked by wild male and female figures. Edge: GOTT MIT UNS   100.00

8.   3 Pfennige (C) 1825. Crowned FG monogram within two crossed laurel branches. Rev. Value   2.25

12.   1 Taler (S) 1858–63. Head right. Rev. Crowned double eagle with prince's crown on breast shield, holding scepter and orb. Edge: GOTT MIT UNS   21.25

9.   2 Pfennige (C) 1812. Type of #6   2.50

10.   1 Pfennig (C) 1825. Type of #8   2.00

13.   1 Taler (S) 1866. Type of #12   18.75

Schwarzburg-Rudolstadt • 259

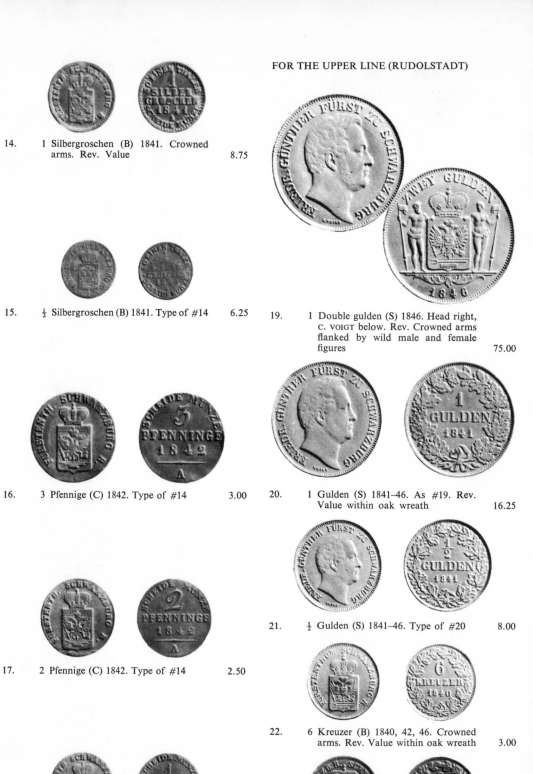

14.   1 Silbergroschen (B) 1841. Crowned arms. Rev. Value   8.75

15.   ½ Silbergroschen (B) 1841. Type of #14   6.25

16.   3 Pfennige (C) 1842. Type of #14   3.00

17.   2 Pfennige (C) 1842. Type of #14   2.50

18.   1 Pfennig (C) 1842. Type of #14. Rev. Type of #16   2.25

19.   1 Double gulden (S) 1846. Head right, C. VOIGT below. Rev. Crowned arms flanked by wild male and female figures   75.00

20.   1 Gulden (S) 1841–46. As #19. Rev. Value within oak wreath   16.25

21.   ½ Gulden (S) 1841–46. Type of #20   8.00

22.   6 Kreuzer (B) 1840, 42, 46. Crowned arms. Rev. Value within oak wreath   3.00

23.   6 Kreuzer (B) 1866. Type of #22   6.25

24. 3 Kreuzer (B) 1839–46. Type of #22   3.50

25. 3 Kreuzer (B) 1866. Type of #22   7.50

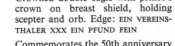

31. 1 Taler (S) 1864. Head right. Rev. Crowned double eagle with prince's crown on breast shield, holding scepter and orb. Edge: EIN VEREINS-THALER XXX EIN PFUND FEIN   35.00

Commemorates the 50th anniversary of the reign.

26. 1 Kreuzer (C) 1840. Crowned arms within two oak branches. Rev. Value   2.50

ALBERT, 1867–69

Younger brother of Friedrich Gunther. Born April 30, 1798, son of Prince Ludwig Friedrich II and his consort, Caroline of Hessen-Homburg. Albert died November 26, 1869.

27. 1 Kreuzer (C) 1864, 65, 66. As #26. Rev. Value, SCHEIDEMUNZE   3.75

32. 1 Taler (S) 1867. Head right. Rev. Crowned double eagle with prince's crown on breast shield, holding scepter and orb. Edge: GOTT MIT UNS   21.25

28. ¼ Kreuzer (C) 1840–56. Type of #26   2.50

29. ¼ Kreuzer (C) 1857–66. Type of #27   3.00

33. 1 Kreuzer (C) 1868. Crowned arms within two oak branches. Rev. Value   2.00

30. ⅛ Kreuzer (C) 1840, 55. Type of #26   2.00

34. ¼ Kreuzer (C) 1868. Type of #33   1.25

GUNTHER VIKTOR, 1890–1918

Born August 21, 1852, son of Prince Franz Friedrich Adolf and his consort, Mathilde of Schonburg-Waldenburg. He abdicated his throne in 1918.

35.	10 Mark (G) 1898. Head left. Rev. Type 3 eagle. Edge: Vines and stars	500.00
36.	2 Mark (S) 1898. Type of #35	87.50

SCHWARZBURG-SONDERSHAUSEN

GUNTHER FRIEDRICH CARL II, 1835–80

Born September 24, 1801, son of Prince Gunther Friedrich Carl I and his consort, Caroline of Schwarzburg-Rudolstadt. He abdicated his throne in favor of his son July 17, 1880. Gunther Friedrich Carl II died September 15, 1889.

#37

37.   1 Double taler—3½ gulden (S) 1841, 45, 54. Head left. Rev. Helmeted arms with double eagle, flanked by wild male and female figures. Edge: GOTT MIT UNS   115.00

38. 1 Taler (S) 1859, 65, 70. Head left. Rev. Crowned double eagle with prince's crown on breast shield, holding scepter and orb. Edge: GOTT MIT UNS 30.00

39. 1 Silbergroschen (B) 1846–70. Crowned arms. Rev. Value 3.50

40. ½ Silbergroschen (B) 1846, 51, 58. Type of #39 2.00

41. 3 Pfennige (C) 1846, 58, 70. Type of #39 1.50

42. 1 Pfennig (C) 1846, 58. Type of #39 1.25

KARL GUNTHER, 1880–1909

Born August 7, 1830, son of Prince Gunther Friedrich Carl II and his consort, Caroline Irene Marie of Schwarzburg-Rudolstadt. Karl Gunther died March 28, 1909.

43. 20 Mark (G) 1896. Head right. Rev. Type 3 eagle. Edge: GOTT MIT UNS 450.00

44. 2 Mark (S) 1896. As #43, but reeded edge 92.50

COMMEMORATIVE ISSUES

45. 2 Mark (S) 1905. Head right, laurel branch and 1880 1905 below. Rev. Type 3 eagle 31.25

Commemorates the 25th year of the reign.

46. 3 Mark 1909. Head right, 1830 + 1909 below. Rev. Type of #45 30.00

Commemorates the death of the Prince.

Schwarzburg-Sondershausen • 263

STOLBERG-WERNIGERODE

Capital:Wernigerode

Stolberg, a county in the Harz mountains of central Germany, possessed rich silver mines. A division of the lands occurred in 1645 but only the Wernigerode branch issued coins after 1800. Although military and financial matters were administered by Prussia from 1714, the country retained a certain amount of sovereignty until 1876.

Capital: Arolsen

CHRISTIAN FRIEDRICH, 1778–1824

Born January 8, 1746, son of Count Henrich Ernst and his consort, Anna Agnes of Anhalt-Kothen. He abdicated his throne in favor of his son Henrich on June 15, 1809. Christian Friedrich died May 26, 1824.

COMMEMORATIVE ISSUE

1.   1 Ducat (G) 1818. Stag left. Rev. Value,
     D.XI.NOV. 1818 within ivy wreath   450.00

     Commemorates the golden wedding
     anniversary of the Count.

HENRICH XII, 1824–54

Born December 25, 1772, son of Count Christian Friedrich and his consort, Auguste of Stolberg-Stolberg. Henrich XII died February 16, 1854.

2.   1 Ducat (G) 1824. Uniformed bust left.
     Rev. Value, stag left   375.00

WALDECK-PYRMONT

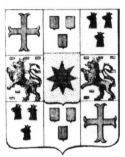

For centuries dependent upon Hesse, the county of Waldeck was made a principality of the Empire. Pyrmont was first united to Waldeck in 1625 but was ruled separately for a while early in the 19th century. The lands were reunited in 1812. Although the administration of the principality was turned over to Prussia in 1867, the princes retained a certain amount of sovereignty until 1918.

Coins for Waldeck-Pyrmont were struck in:
Arolsen (until 1840)
Berlin (1842–67, 1903)   Mintmark A
Hannover (1867)   B

CARL AUGUST FRIEDRICH, 1763–1812

Born October 25, 1743, son of Prince Carl. He never married and died on September 24, 1812. In 1805, he gave his younger brother, Georg, the earldom of Pyrmont. Georg ruled Pyrmont as Prince from 1807, and, upon the death of Carl August Friedrich in 1812, Georg inherited Waldeck.

3.	¼ Taler (S) 1810. As #1. Rev. STUCK		15.00

1. 1 Convention taler (S) 1810. Crowned arms within two bound laurel branches, FRIDERICUS PR. Rev. Value within pearl circle   175.00

2. 1 Convention taler (S) 1810. As #1, but FRIDERICUS D.G. PR.   225.00

4. ¼ Taler (S) 1810. As #3   15.00

5.   ½ Groschen (C) 1809. Crowned arms.
     Rev. Value   4.75

6.   3 Pfennig (C) 1809, 10. Crowned F,
     inscription. Rev. Value   3.00

7.   3 Pfennig (C) 1809. Type of #5   3.00

8.   3 Pfennig (C) 1810. Crowned arms
     within pearl circle. Rev. Value   3.00

9.   1 Pfennig (C) 1809, 10. As #6, but no
     inscription   2.50

10. 1 Pfennig (C) 1809, 10. Type of #5   2.50

266 • Waldeck-Pyrmont

GEORG, 1805–12

(See: Carl August Friedrich)
Born May 6, 1747, younger brother of Prince Friedrich.
Georg died September 9, 1813.

11. 1 Convention taler (S) 1811. Head
     right, L at truncation. Rev. Crowned,
     draped arms   95.00

12. 1/24 Taler—1 groschen—12 pfennige (S)
     1806, 07. Crowned arms. Rev. Value   43.75

AS PRINCE OF WALDECK AND PYRMONT

13. 1 Convention taler (S) 1813. Head left.
     Rev. Crowned arms, date below
     dividing F.W. Edge: X EINE FEINE
     MARK   300.00

14. 1 Kronentaler (S) 1813. Type of #13.
     Edge: KRONEN THALER with different
     types of decorations   300.00

15.   ¼ Taler (S) 1812. Crowned, draped arms, PYRMONT. &. Rev. Value   400.00

16.   ¼ Taler (S) 1813. As #15, but EC instead of &.   400.00

GEORG HEINRICH, 1813–45

Born September 20, 1789, son of Prince Georg and his consort, Auguste, Princess of Schwarzburg-Sondershausen. Georg Heinrich died May 15, 1845.

17.   1 Double taler—3½ gulden (S) 1842, 45. Crowned, draped arms, A below. Rev. Value within two bound oak branches. Edge: MUNZCONVENTION VOM 30 IULY 1838   375.00

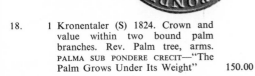

18.   1 Kronentaler (S) 1824. Crown and value within two bound palm branches. Rev. Palm tree, arms. PALMA SUB PONDERE CRECIT—"The Palm Grows Under Its Weight"   150.00

19.   1/3 Taler (S) 1824. Crowned, draped arms. Rev. Value   21.50

20.   1/3 Taler (S) 1824. Crowned, draped arms. Rev. Value   20.00

21.   1/3 Taler (S) 1824. As #20, but inscription on reverse   18.75

22.   1/6 Taler (S) 1837. Crowned, draped arms, inscription ends U.P. Rev. Value   11.25

23.   1/6 Taler (S) 1843, 45. Type of #22   4.00

24.   1 Silbergroschen (S) 1836, 39. Type of #22   5.00

25.   1 Silbergroschen (B) 1842, 43, 45. As #22, but inscription ends U. PYR-MONT   2.50

26.   2 Mariengroschen (S) 1820–25. Crowned, draped arms. Rev. Value, F.W. below   7.50

27.   2 Mariengroschen (S) 1827, 28. As #26, but A.W. below on reverse   8.00

28.   1/24 Taler—groschen (S) 1818, 19. Type of #26   —

29.   1 Mariengroschen (S) 1814, 20. Crowned arms. Rev. Value   4.50

30.   1 Mariengroschen (S) 1820. Star arms of Waldeck. Rev. Type of #29   4.00

31.   1 Mariengroschen (S) 1820, 23. Crowned, draped arms. Rev. Value   4.00

32.   ½ Mariengroschen—4 pfennig (C) 1825. Crowned, draped arms, inscription ends LAND MUNZE. Rev. Value   8.00

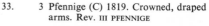

33.   3 Pfennige (C) 1819. Crowned, draped arms. Rev. III PFENNIGE   3.00

34.   3 Pfennige (C) 1819. As #33. Rev. III PFENNIGE SCHEIDE MUNZE   3.00

35.   3 Pfennig (C) 1819. As #33, but Rev. PFENNIG   2.75

36.   3 Pfennige (C) 1824, 25. As #34, but Rev. 3   2.50

37.   3 Pfennige (C) 1842, 43, 45. Crowned
        arms. Rev. Value   1.25

38.   1 Pfennig (C) 1816, 17. Crowned GH
        monogram. Rev. Value   4.50

39.   1 Pfennig (C) 1816, 17. Crowned star
        arms. Rev. Value   5.50

40.   1 Pfennig (C) 1821. Crowned arms.
        Rev. Value   1.25

41.   1 Pfennig (C) 1825. Crowned, draped
        arms. Rev. Value   1.25

42.   1 Pfennig (C) 1842, 43, 45. Type of #37   1.00

GEORG VICTOR, 1852–93

Born January 14, 1831, son of Prince Georg Heinrich
and his consort, Emma, Princess of Anhalt-Bernberg-
Schaumburg-Hoym. Georg Victor died May 12, 1893.

UNDER THE GUARDIANSHIP OF HIS MOTHER
FROM 1845 TO 1852

43.   1 Double taler—3½ gulden (S) 1847.
        Crowned, draped arms, A below.
        Rev. Value within two bound oak
        branches. Edge: MUNZCONVENTION
        VOM 30 IULY 1838   650.00

AS INDEPENDENT PRINCE

44.   1 Double taler—3½ gulden (S) 1856.
        Head left, A below. Rev. Arms—type
        of #43. Edge: Type of #43   400.00

50. 1 Pfennig (C) 1855. Type of #48   3.00

51. 1 Pfennig (C) 1867. Type of #49   1.00

45. 1 Vereinstaler (S) 1859, 67. As #44,
     but edge: MUNZVERTRAG VOM 24
     JANUAR 1857   75.00

FRIEDRICH, 1893–1918

Born January 20, 1865, son of Prince Georg Victor
and his consort, Helene, Princess of Nassau. Friedrich
abdicated his throne in 1918.

46. 1 Silbergroschen (B) 1855. Crowned,
     draped arms. Rev. Value, A below   3.75

47. 1 Silbergroschen (B) 1867. As #46,
     but Rev. B below   3.00

52. 20 Mark (G) 1903. Head left, A below.
     Rev. Type 3 eagle. Edge: GOTT MIT
     UNS   650.00

48. 3 Pfennige (C) 1855. Crowned arms.
     Rev. Value, A below   3.00

49. 3 Pfennige (C) 1867. As #48, but Rev.
     B below   2.50

53. 5 Mark (S) 1903. Type of #52   875.00

WALLMODEN-GIMBORN

By the late 17th century, the Wallmoden line was extinct except for Count Johann Ludwig who purchased the town and lordship of Gimborn from Schwarzenberg in 1782. The district was raised to a county and in 1806 was annexed to the Grand Duchy of Berg. In 1815, the land went to Prussia.

Coins for Wallmoden-Gimborn were struck in Hannover.

JOHANN LUDWIG, 1782–1806

Born April 24, 1736, natural son of King George II of England and Amalie Sophie Marianne of Wendt, Countess of Yarmouth, consort of Freiherrn Adam Gottlob of Wallmoden. Field Marshal Count Johann Ludwig died October 10, 1811.

2.	½ Taler (S) 1802. Crowned arms with garlands. Rev. Value	100.00

1.	1 Ducat (G) 1802. Crowned LW monogram. Rev. Value	375.00
3.	1/24 Taler (B) 1802. Type of #1	27.50

WESTPHALIA

Capital: Cassel

Napoleon created the Kingdom of Westphalia in 1807 for his brother Jerome who ruled until 1813. The new kingdom was made up of the former Brunswick-Wolfenbuttel, Hesse-Cassel, Hannover and others. The Congress of Vienna returned most of the lands to their former owners with the smaller parts going to Prussia.

Coins for Westphalia were struck in:

Cassel	Mintmark C with eagle's head
Clausthal	C
Brunswick	B

JEROME (HIERONYMUS) NAPOLEON, 1807–13

Born November 15, 1784, son of Karl Bonaparte and his consort, Maria Laetitia (nee Ramolino) of Ajaccio. After the collapse of the Napoleonic monarchies, he lived as Prince of Montfort until 1847. In 1852, after his return to France, he considered himself a royal prince and in line for the throne of France. Jerome Napoleon died June 24, 1860.

STRUCK IN GERMAN VALUES

1. 10 Taler (G) 1810. Chain of the Order of the Legion of Honor on crowned arms, HIERONYMUS NAPOLEON. Rev. Value between two rosettes   550.00

2. 10 Taler (G) 1811, 12, 13. Bust left with laurel wreath. Rev. Value   550.00

3. 10 Taler (G) 1811. As #2, but no laurel wreath   1,125.00

4. 5 Taler (G) 1810. Type of #1   300.00

5. 5 Taler (G) 1811, 12, 13. Type of #2   225.00

6. 5 Taler (G) 1811. Type of #3   875.00

7. 1 Convention taler (S) 1810. Crowned arms with chains of the Order of the Westphalian Crown and the Legion of Honor, in the background are crossed scepters of Grace and Justice. Rev. Value between two diamonds   —

8.   1 Convention taler (S) 1810, 11, 12.
Bust right with laurel wreath. Rev.
Type of #7   —

11.   2/3 Taler (S) 1809, 10. As #10, but inscription starts from the left   50.00

9.   1 Convention taler (S) 1811, 12, 13. As
#8, but different bust   112.50

12.   2/3 Taler—24 mariengroschen (S) 1810.
Crowned arms with chain of the
Order of the Legion of Honor. Rev.
Value   50.00

13.   1/6 Taler (S) 1808, 09, 10. As #12. Rev.
Value between two rosettes, F. below,
period after date   11.50

10.   2/3 Taler (S) 1808, 10. Bust left, C below,
HIERONYMUS NAPOLEON. Rev. Value   50.00

14.   1/6 Taler (S) 1808, 10, 12. Type of #13   10.00

Westphalia • 273

15.　1/6 Taler (S) 1808–13. As #13, but B
　　below and no period after date　　7.50

16.　1/6 Taler (S) 1809, 10, 13. As #13, but
　　c below on reverse　　10.00

17.　1/12 Taler (S) 1808, 09, 10. Crowned HN
　　monogram, c below. Rev. Value　　13.75

24.　1 Convention taler (S) 1811. Bust right
　　with laurel wreath. Rev. SEEGEN DES
　　MANSFELDER BERGBAUES—"Blessings
　　of the Mansfeld Mines"　　150.00

18.　1/24 Taler (B) 1807, 08, 09. Crowned HN
　　monogram with ribbons. Rev. Value　　6.50

19.　1/24 Taler (S) 1809. As #18, but without
　　ribbons. Rev. As #18, but mint mark
　　c　　5.00

20.　1 Mariengroschen (S) 1808, 10. Type of
　　#17　　4.00

25.　2/3 Taler (S) 1811, 12, 13. As #24, but c
　　below. Rev. Value　　50.00

26.　1 Convention gulden—2/3 taler (S)
　　1811. As #25. Rev. GLUCK AUF
　　CLAUSTHAL IM AUGUST 1811 within
　　two bound laurel branches　　125.00

21.　4 Pfennige (S) 1808, 09. Type of #17　　3.75

22.　2 Pfennige (C) 1808, 10. Type of #17　　3.75

STRUCK IN FRENCH VALUES

27.　40 Franken (G) 1813. Bust left with
　　laurel wreath, TIOLIER below. Rev.
　　Value within two bound laurel
　　branches, eagle's head and c around
　　date, WESTPHALEN. Edge: GOTT
　　ERHALTE DEN KOENIG—"God Save
　　the King"　　550.00

23.　1 Pfennig (C) 1808. Type of #17　　2.50

28. 20 Franken (G) 1808, 09, 11. As #27, but WESTPH. on reverse 115.00

37. 20 Centimes (B) 1808, 10, 12. Crowned HN monogram with ribbons, within two crossed laurel branches. Rev. Value, eagle's head, C and TIOLIER below, HIERONYMUS 4.50

29. 20 Franken (G) 1808, 09. As #28, but horse's head instead of eagle's head on reverse 125.00

38. 10 Centimes (B) 1808–12. As #37, but HIERON. in reverse inscription 3.75

30. 20 Franken (G) 1809. Type of #29 150.00

39. 10 Centimes (B) 1808. Type of #37 4.50

31. 10 Franken (G) 1813. Bust left with laurel wreath, TIOLIER below. Rev. Value, eagle's head and C below. Smooth edge 200.00

40. 5 Centimes (C) 1808, 09, 12. As #39, but without crown. Rev. Value, eagle's head and C below 2.50

32. 5 Franken (G) 1813. Type of #31 150.00

33. 5 Franken (S) 1808, 09. As #31. Rev. Value within two bound laurel branches, horse's head and J below, WESTPHALEN. Edge: GOTT ERHALTE DEN KONIG 250.00

41. 3 Centimes (C) 1808–12. Type of #40 1.50

34. 2 Franken (S) 1808. Type of #33 45.00

35. 1 Franken (S) 1808. As #33, but with eagle's head, C and WESTPH. on reverse 112.50

42. 2 Centimes (C) 1808–12. Type of #40 2.00

36. ½ Franken (S) 1808. Type of #33. Smooth edge 75.00

43. 1 Centime (C) 1809, 12. Type of #40 1.00

WURTTEMBERG

Capital: Stuttgart

The duchy of Wurttemberg was altered drastically in 1802 when Friedrich II ceded all of his possessions on the west bank of the Rhine to France in exchange for some important cities and territories nearer to Stuttgart, his capital city. Napoleon elevated Friedrich to the status of elector in 1803, and made him a king in 1806. The Congress of Vienna confirmed both possession of the lands and the regal title. Wurttemberg supported the losing Austrian side in the Austro-Prussian War of 1866 and was forced to pay an indemnity of eight million gulden. The kingdom joined the German Empire in 1871 and endured until the abdication of Wilhelm II in 1918.

Coins for Wurttemberg were struck in Stuttgart: Mintmark F (since 1872)

FRIEDRICH II (Duke, 1797–1805; Elector, 1803–05; King, 1806–16)

Born November 6, 1754, son of Duke Friedrich Eugen and his consort, Sophie Dorothea, Princess of Brandenburg-Schwedt. Friedrich died October 30, 1816.

FRIEDRICH II AS DUKE, 1797–1805

1. 1 Double convention taler (S) 1798. Bust left, inscription reads D.G.DUX. Rev. Crowned arms with the chain of Hubertus Order, CUM.DEO.ET.IURE 375.00

2. 1 Convention taler (S) 1798. As #1, but D:G.DUX and CUM DEO ET IURE on reverse 162.50

3. 1 Convention taler (S) 1798. As #2, but w under bust 162.50

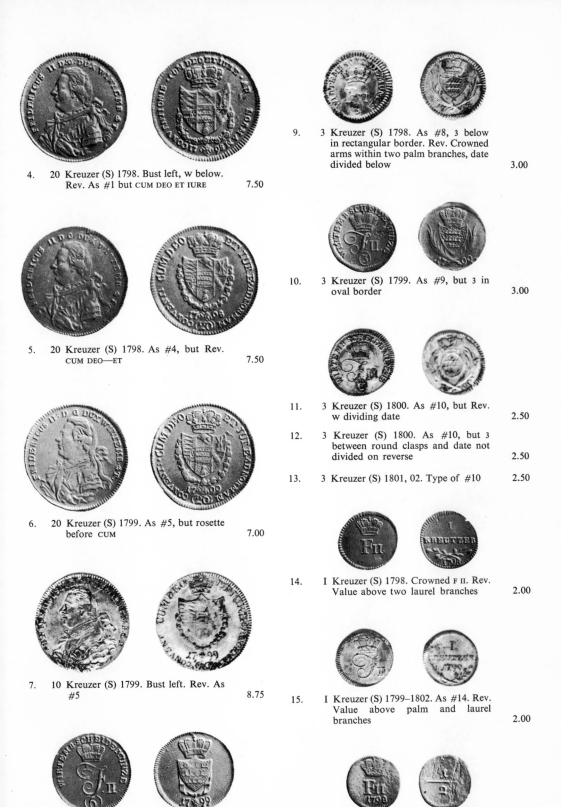

4. 20 Kreuzer (S) 1798. Bust left, w below. Rev. As #1 but CUM DEO ET IURE   7.50

5. 20 Kreuzer (S) 1798. As #4, but Rev. CUM DEO—ET   7.50

6. 20 Kreuzer (S) 1799. As #5, but rosette before CUM   7.00

7. 10 Kreuzer (S) 1799. Bust left. Rev. As #5   8.75

8. 6 Kreuzer (S) 1799. Crowned F-II monogram. Rev. Crowned arms   4.00

9. 3 Kreuzer (S) 1798. As #8, 3 below in rectangular border. Rev. Crowned arms within two palm branches, date divided below   3.00

10. 3 Kreuzer (S) 1799. As #9, but 3 in oval border   3.00

11. 3 Kreuzer (S) 1800. As #10, but Rev. w dividing date   2.50

12. 3 Kreuzer (S) 1800. As #10, but 3 between round clasps and date not divided on reverse   2.50

13. 3 Kreuzer (S) 1801, 02. Type of #10   2.50

14. I Kreuzer (S) 1798. Crowned F II. Rev. Value above two laurel branches   2.00

15. I Kreuzer (S) 1799–1802. As #14. Rev. Value above palm and laurel branches   2.00

16. ½ Kreuzer (S) 1798. Crowned F II, date below. Rev. Value   3.00

17. 1 Ducat (G) 1804. Bust right, I.L.W. below. Rev. Crowned arms within two palm branches ... 500.00

21. 10 Kreuzer (S) 1805. Type of #19 ... 6.25

18. 1 Convention taler (S) 1803. Bust left. Rev. Type of #17 ... 75.00

22. 6 Kreuzer (S) 1803. F.II. monogram, w below, inscription. Rev. Crowned arms ... 3.00

23. 6 Kreuzer (S) 1804, 05. As #22, but no w ... 3.00

24. 3 Kreuzer (S) 1803. Type of #22 ... 2.50

25. 3 Kreuzer (S) 1804, 05, 06. Type of #22 ... 2.00

19. ½ Convention taler (S) 1805. Bust left, I.L.W. below, inscription ends ELECT. Rev. Type of #17 ... 25.00

26. 1 Kreuzer (S) 1803, 04. Type of #23 ... 2.50

27. 1 Kreuzer (S) 1805. Crowned F.II monogram, no inscription. Rev. Value above palm and laurel branches ... 2.50

20. 20 Kreuzer (S) 1805. As #19, but inscription ends ELECTOR ... 10.00

278 • **Wurttemberg**

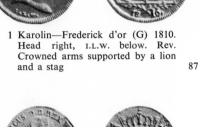

28.   1 Karolin—Frederick d'or (G) 1810. Head right, I.L.W. below. Rev. Crowned arms supported by a lion and a stag   875.00

29.   1 Ducat (G) 1808. Bust left. Rev. Type of #28   550.00

30.   1 Ducat (G) 1813. Type of #28   550.00

32.   1 Kronentaler (S) 1810. Head left, I.L.W. below. Rev. and edge: Type of #31   90.00

33.   1 Kronentaler (S) 1810. Type of #32   90.00

31.   1 Kronentaler (S) 1810. Bust left, I.L.W. below. Rev. Crowned arms supported by a lion and a stag. Edge: KOENIGL: WURTTEMB: KRONENTHALER   112.50

34.   1 Kronentaler (S) 1810. As #32. Rev. As #31 but slight difference. Edge: Type of #31   90.00

35.   1 Kronentaler (S) 1810. Type of #34   90.00

38.   1 Convention taler (S) 1806. Bust left, with D:G.REX. Rev. Crowned oval arms within two palm branches   250.00

39.   1 Convention taler (S) 1806. As #38, but D.G.REX   87.50

40.   1 Convention taler (S) 1806. Bust left, I.L.WAGNER F. below. Rev. As #38 but larger letters   112.50

37.   1 Kronentaler (S) 1812. Head right, with I.L.W. below. Rev. and edge: Type of #36   250.00

41.   1 Convention taler (S) 1809. Type of #40. Rev. Type of #38   112.50

36.   1 Kronentaler (S) 1811. As #32, but Rev. Crowned arms supported by a lion and a stag over crossed branches   95.00

42.   1 Convention taler (S) 1809. Bust left, I.L.W. below, WURTTEMBERGIAE. Rev. Type of #38   112.50

280   •   **Wurttemberg**

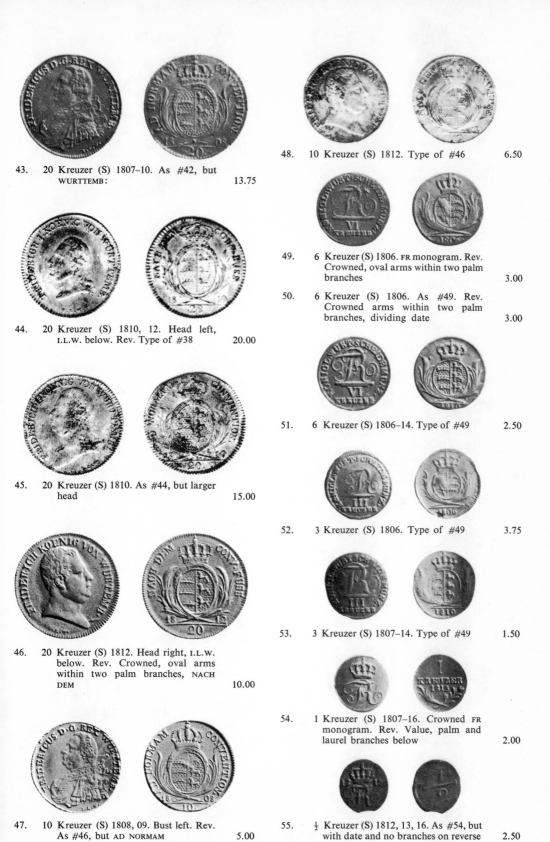

43. 20 Kreuzer (S) 1807–10. As #42, but
     WURTTEMB: 13.75

44. 20 Kreuzer (S) 1810, 12. Head left,
     I.L.W. below. Rev. Type of #38   20.00

45. 20 Kreuzer (S) 1810. As #44, but larger
     head   15.00

46. 20 Kreuzer (S) 1812. Head right, I.L.W.
     below. Rev. Crowned, oval arms
     within two palm branches, NACH
     DEM   10.00

47. 10 Kreuzer (S) 1808, 09. Bust left. Rev.
     As #46, but AD NORMAM   5.00

48. 10 Kreuzer (S) 1812. Type of #46   6.50

49. 6 Kreuzer (S) 1806. FR monogram. Rev.
     Crowned, oval arms within two palm
     branches   3.00

50. 6 Kreuzer (S) 1806. As #49. Rev.
     Crowned arms within two palm
     branches, dividing date   3.00

51. 6 Kreuzer (S) 1806–14. Type of #49   2.50

52. 3 Kreuzer (S) 1806. Type of #49   3.75

53. 3 Kreuzer (S) 1807–14. Type of #49   1.50

54. 1 Kreuzer (S) 1807–16. Crowned FR
     monogram. Rev. Value, palm and
     laurel branches below   2.00

55. ½ Kreuzer (S) 1812, 13, 16. As #54, but
     with date and no branches on reverse   2.50

56.   1 Ducat (G) 1803. Bust right, I.L.W.
      below. Rev. IN HOCHST within laurel
      wreath   650.00

57.   1 Ducat (G) 1804. Type of #56   650.00

      The above two coins mark the visit of
      the Duke to the mint.

WILHELM I, 1816–64

Born September 27, 1781, son of King Friedrich I
and his consort, Auguste of Braunschweig-Wolfenbuttel. Wilhelm I died June 25, 1864.

58.   10 Gulden (G) 1824, 25. Head right, w
      below. Rev. Crowned arms within
      oak and laurel branches. Edge:
      FURCHTLOS UND TREU—"Fearless and
      True"   550.00

59.   1 Ducat (G) 1818. As #58, but larger
      head. Rev. Crowned arms supported
      by a lion and a stag   550.00

60.   1 Ducat (G) 1840–48. Head left, AD
      below. Rev. Crowned arms sup-
      ported by a lion and a stag on scroll 120.00

61.   5 Gulden (G) 1824–39. Type of #58   250.00

62.   3½ Gulden—2 taler (S) 1840–55. Head
      left, VOIGT below. Rev. Value within
      oak wreath. Edge: CONVENTION VOM
      30 JULY 1838   100.00

63.   1 Kronentaler (S) 1817. Head left,
      WAGNER.F. below. Rev. Crown and
      value within laurel wreath   80.00

64.   1 Kronentaler (S) 1818. Head right.
      Rev. Type of #63   250.00

68. 1 Kronentaler (S) 1833. Head right, w in foliage decoration. Rev. As #67, but inscription ends BEWIRKT (Essay) —

69. 1 Kronentaler (S) 1834, 35, 37. Type of #67. Rev. Type of #65   37.50

65. 1 Kronentaler (S) 1825. Head right, WAGNER F at truncation. Rev. Crowned arms within oak and laurel branches. Edge: FURCHTLOS UND TREU   35.00

70. 1 Convention taler (S) 1817. Head left, WAGNER F below. Rev. Value within laurel and oak branches   95.00

66. 1 Kronentaler (S) 1826–33. Head right. Rev. As #65, but w below branches and above date   35.00

71. 1 Convention taler (S) 1818. Head right. Rev. Type of #70   80.00

72. 2 Gulden (S) 1823. Head right. Rev. Crowned arms within oak wreath, FURCHTLOS UND TREU—"Fearless and True" (Essay)   —

67. 1 Kronentaler (S) 1833. As #65, but w at truncation. Rev. Standing female with caduceus and charter between river god and cornucopia, HANDELS-FREHEIT DURCH EINTRACHT—"Free Trade Through Agreement." Edge: KRONENTHALER   75.00

73. 2 Gulden (S) 1824. Small head right, P.B. at truncation. Rev. Crowned, round arms within oak wreath. Edge: FURCHTLOS UND TREU   87.50

74.   2 Gulden (S) 1824. Larger head right, I.L.W. at truncation. Rev. and edge: As #73, but with w below on reverse   150.00

77.   1 Vereinstaler (S) 1857–64. Head left. Rev. Type of #76. Edge: MUNZVER-TRAG VOM 24 JANUAR 1857   20.00

78.   1 Gulden (S) 1823. Head right, PB below. Rev. Crowned arms within oak wreath (Essay)   —

79.   1 Gulden (S) 1824. Head right, w below. Rev. and edge: Type of #73   22.50

75.   2 Gulden (S) 1825. Head right, WAG-NER F at truncation. Rev. Crowned arms within oak and laurel branches. Edge: Type of #73   90.00

80.   1 Gulden (S) 1825. As #79, but Rev. Crowned, tapered arms   12.50

81.   1 Gulden (S) 1837. Head left, A. DIETELB: below, WILHELM KOENIG VON WURTTEMBERG. Rev. Value, EIN GULDEN 1837 (Essay)   —

82.   1 Gulden (S) 1837. Head right, w below. Inscription and Rev. Type of #81 (Essay)   —

83.   1 Gulden (S) 1837. As #82. Rev. Value within oak wreath (Essay)   —

76.   2 Gulden (S) 1845–56. Head left, C.VOIGT below. Rev. Crowned arms supported by a lion and a stag on scroll   35.00

84.   1 Gulden (S) 1837, 38. Head left, A.
       DTLBCH. below. Rev. Type of #83   17.50

85.   1 Gulden (S) 1838–56. Head left,
       VOIGT below. Rev. Type of #83   16.00

86.   ½ Gulden (S) 1838–64. Type of #85   25.00

87.   24 Kreuzer (S) 1824, 25. Head right, w
       and date below. Rev. Crowned,
       round arms within oak wreath   30.00

88.   20 Kreuzer (S) 1818. Head right, w be-
       low. Rev. Value within laurel wreath   7.50

89.   20 Kreuzer (S) 1823. As #87, but Rev.
       FURCHTLOS UND TREU   8.75

90.   12 Kreuzer (S) 1824. Type of #87   5.00

91.   12 Kreuzer (S) 1825. Head right, 1825
       below. Rev. Type of #87   11.25

92.   10 Kreuzer (S) 1818. Type of #88   5.00

93.   10 Kreuzer (S) 1823. Head right, 1823
       below. Rev. Type of #89   6.25

94.   6 Kreuzer (S) 1817–21. Crowned w
       within laurel wreath. Rev. Value   5.00

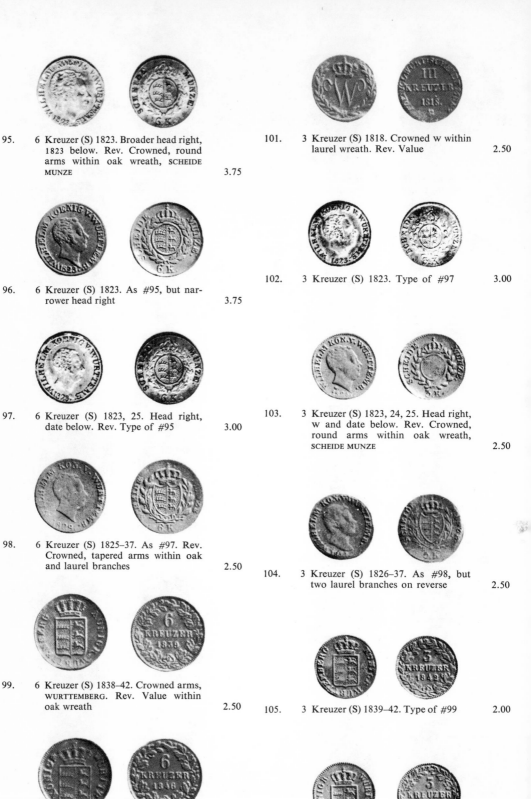

95.   6 Kreuzer (S) 1823. Broader head right, 1823 below. Rev. Crowned, round arms within oak wreath, SCHEIDE MUNZE   3.75

101.   3 Kreuzer (S) 1818. Crowned w within laurel wreath. Rev. Value   2.50

96.   6 Kreuzer (S) 1823. As #95, but narrower head right   3.75

102.   3 Kreuzer (S) 1823. Type of #97   3.00

97.   6 Kreuzer (S) 1823, 25. Head right, date below. Rev. Type of #95   3.00

103.   3 Kreuzer (S) 1823, 24, 25. Head right, w and date below. Rev. Crowned, round arms within oak wreath, SCHEIDE MUNZE   2.50

98.   6 Kreuzer (S) 1825–37. As #97. Rev. Crowned, tapered arms within oak and laurel branches   2.50

104.   3 Kreuzer (S) 1826–37. As #98, but two laurel branches on reverse   2.50

99.   6 Kreuzer (S) 1838–42. Crowned arms, WURTTEMBERG. Rev. Value within oak wreath   2.50

105.   3 Kreuzer (S) 1839–42. Type of #99   2.00

100.   6 Kreuzer (S) 1842–56. As #99, but WURTTB.   3.75

106.   3 Kreuzer (S) 1842–56. Type of #100   2.00

107.   1 Kreuzer (S) 1818. Type of #101   3.75

108.   1 Kreuzer (S) 1826–38. Type of #103   2.00

109.   1 Kreuzer (S) 1839–42. Type of #105   1.50

110.   1 Kreuzer (S) 1842–57. Type of #106   1.25

111.   1 Kreuzer (S) 1857–64. As #106, but inscription ends SCHEIDEMUNZE   2.00

112.   ½ Kreuzer (S) N.D. Crowned w. Rev. Value   2.50

113.   ½ Kreuzer (S) 1818. Crowned w dividing date. Rev. Value   2.50

114.   ½ Kreuzer (S) 1824–37. Crowned, round arms within oak wreath. Rev. Value   3.00

115.   ½ Kreuzer (C) 1840–56. Crowned, rectangular arms within two oak branches. Rev. Value   2.50

116.   ½ Kreuzer (C) 1858–64. As #115, but Rev. SCHEIDEMUNZE   2.50

117.   ¼ Kreuzer (C) 1842–56. Type of #115   1.25

118.   ¼ Kreuzer (S) 1858–64. Type of #116   1.00

COMMEMORATIVE ISSUES

119.   4 Ducats (G) 1841. Head left with laurel wreath, VOIGT below. Rev. Wurttembergia seated between two children, ZUR FEYER 25. Edge: VIER DUCATEN   312.50

Commemorates the 25th anniversary of the reign.

120.   4 Ducats (G) 1844. Head left, VOIGT
below. Rev. View of mint in Stuttgart,
KONIG WILHELM BESUCHT. Edge:
Type of #119   1,750.00

123.   1 Gulden (S) 1841. Type of #119.
Edge: EIN GULDEN   25.00

Commemorates the 25th anniversary
of the reign.

124.   1 Gulden (S) 1844. Type of #120.
Edge: EIN GULDEN   250.00

Marks the visit of the King to the
new mint.

121.   10 Gulden (G) 1825. Head right, W
below. Rev. IN DES KONIGS. Edge:
FURCHTLOS UND TREU   3,000.00

The above two coins mark the visit of
the King to the mint.

125.   1 Gulden (medal) (S) 1845. As #122.
Rev. DIE KOENIGIN U.D. KOENIGL:
within oak wreath   —

Marks the visit of the royal family to
the mint.

KARL, 1864–91

Born March 6, 1823, son of King Wilhelm I and his
consort, Pauline. Karl died October 6, 1891.

122.   1 Double taler—3½ gulden—2 taler (S)
1846. Head left, VOIGT below. Rev.
Conjoined heads. CARL KRONPR. . . .
OLGA GROSSFURSTIN. Edge: VEREINS-
MUNZE VII EINE F. MARK   100.00

Commemorates the marriage of
Crown Prince Carl of Wurttemberg
to Olga, Grand Duchess of Russia.

126.   1 Vereinstaler (S) 1865–70. Head right,
C.SCHNITZPAHN at truncation. Rev.
Crowned arms supported by a lion
and a stag over scroll. Edge: MUNZ-
VERTRAG VOM 24 JANUAR 1857   17.50

127.   ½ Gulden (S) 1865–71. As #126, but
C.S. at truncation. Rev. Value within
oak wreath   12.50

128. 1 Kreuzer (S) 1865–73. Crowned arms.
      Rev. Type of #127   1.00

129. ½ Kreuzer (C) 1865–72. Crowned arms
      within two oak branches. Rev. Value   1.00

130. ¼ Kreuzer (C) 1865–72. Type of #129   1.25

COMMEMORATIVE ISSUES

131. 2 Taler (S) 1869, 71. Head right, C.
      SCHNITZSPAHN at truncation. Rev.
      View of Ulm Cathedral, ZUR ERIN-
      NERUNG. Edge: XV EIN PFUND FEIN   187.50

      Commemorates the restoration of the
      Ulm Cathedral.

132. 1 Taler (S) 1871. As #131. Rev. Angel
      with palm branch over war trophies,
      MIT GOTT DURCH. Edge: XXX EIN
      PFUND FEIN   18.75

      Commemorates the victorious con-
      clusion of the Franco-Prussian War.

AFTER INCORPORATION INTO THE EMPIRE

133. 20 Mark (G) 1872, 73. Head right, F
      below. Rev. Type 1 eagle. Edge:
      GOTT MIT UNS   45.00

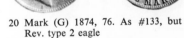

134. 20 Mark (G) 1874, 76. As #133, but
      Rev. type 2 eagle   45.00

135. 10 Mark (G) 1872, 73. Type of #133.
      Edge: Vines and stars   37.50

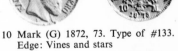

136. 10 Mark (G) 1874–88. Type of #134.
      Edge: Type of #135   32.50

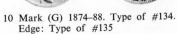

137.   10 Mark (G) 1890, 91. As #133, but
        Rev. type 3 eagle. Edge: Type of
        #135   50.00

138.   5 Mark (G) 1877, 78. Type of #134.
        Smooth edge   150.00

139.   5 Mark (S) 1874–88. Head right, F
        below. Rev. Type 2 eagle. Edge:
        GOTT MIT UNS   40.00

140.   2 Mark (S) 1876–88. Type of #139.
        Reeded edge   36.50

WILHELM II, 1891–1918

Born February 25, 1848, son of Prince Friedrich of
Wurttemberg and his consort, Katharina, Princess of
Wurttemberg. He abdicated his throne in 1918.
Wilhelm II died October 2, 1921.

141.   20 Mark (G) 1894–1914. Head right, F
        below. Rev. Type 3 eagle. Edge: GOTT
        MIT UNS   45.00

142.   10 Mark (G) 1893–1913. Type of #141.
        Edge: Vines and stars   40.00

143.   5 Mark (S) 1892–1913. Type of #141   12.50

144.   3 Mark (S) 1908–14. Type of #141   6.50

146.   3 Mark (S) 1911. Conjoined heads right, WILHELM II. UND. CHARLOTTE. Rev. and edge: Type of #141   10.00

Honors the silver wedding anniversary of the King and Queen.

145.   2 Mark (S) 1892–1914. Type of #141. Reeded edge   7.50

147.   3 Mark (S) 1916. Head right, laurel branch and 1891–1916 below. Rev. and edge: Type of #141   875.00

Honors the 25th anniversary of the reign.

WURZBURG
Grand Duchy

The bishopric of Wurzburg was founded in 741 and the bishops were granted the right to mint coins as early as the 11th century. In 1803 the territory was secularized and granted to Bavaria. In 1806 it was made a grand duchy for Ferdinand of Tuscany-Salzburg but the 1815 Congress of Vienna restored the district to Bavaria.

FERDINAND OF AUSTRIA, 1806–14
(Grand Duke of Tuscany, 1790–1801, 1814–24)

Born May 6, 1769, son of Leopold II of Austria and his consort, Maria Ludovica of Spain. Ferdinand died June 18, 1824.

4. 1 Kreuzer (S) 1808. Crowned arms. Rev. Value   10.00

1. 6 Kreuzer (S) 1807, 08, 09. Crowned arms over palm and laurel branches. Rev. Value   12.50

5. 1 Kreuzer (S) 1808. As #4. Rev. Value and G.W.L.M.   7.50

2. 3 Kreuzer (S) 1807, 08, 09. Type of #1   12.50

6. ½ Kreuzer (C) 1810, 11. Crowned arms, dividing date above. Rev. Value   10.00

3. 1 Kreuzer (S) 1808. Crowned arms, dividing G.W. L.M. above. Rev. Value   7.00

7. ¼ Kreuzer (C) 1811. Crowned arms dividing 18 11. Rev. Value   10.00

WURZBURG
City

From early times the city of Wurzburg followed the custom of presenting its ruler with a quantity of gold gulden as a New Year's gift. Coins were specially struck for this purpose and were not intended for actual circulation.

The Wurzburg gulden were struck in Darmstadt, Coburg and Saalfeld at the beginning of the 19th century, in Munich since 1815.

MAXIMILIAN IV, JOSEPH OF BAVARIA, 1803–05

BAVARIA AS ELECTORATE

8. 1 New Year's Goldgulden (G) 1803. Head right. Rev. Arms under palm tree, inscription reads SENATUS POPULUS. Reeded edge   212.50

9. 1 New Year's Goldgulden (G) 1803. As #8, but Rev. S.P. Q.W.   250.00

10. 1 New Year's Goldgulden (G) 1807, 09. Bust right. Rev. Value, palm tree dividing S.P.Q.W. Reeded edge   425.00

11. 1 New Year's Goldgulden (G) 1812. Head right, R at truncation. Rev. Arms within two branches dividing 1812, SENATUS POPULUSQUE   425.00

12. 1 New Year's Goldgulden (G) 1813. As #9, but Rev. S.P.Q.W.   650.00

13. 1 New Year's Goldgulden (C) 1814. As #9. Rev. Altar with three flaming hearts with arms, PATRI PATRIAE   650.00

MAXIMILIAN I, JOSEPH OF BAVARIA, 1814–25

BAVARIA AS KINGDOM

14.   1 New Year's Goldgulden (G) 1815.
Head left. Rev. City view, s.p.q.w.
above, flags below dividing 1815   325.00

15.   1 New Year's Goldgulden (G) 1817.
As #14. Rev. Arms within two laurel
branches, dividing s.p.q.w.   300.00

16.   1 New Year's Goldgulden (G) N.D.
Type of #15   375.00

LUDWIG I OF BAVARIA, 1825–48

17.   1 New Year's Goldgulden (G) 1826.
Head left, LUDOVICUS. Rev. LVDOVICO
CAROLO   500.00

18.   1 New Year's Goldgulden (G) N.D.
Head left, LUDWIG. Rev. City view,
s.p.q.w. below (minted in 1827)   275.00

19.   1 New Year's Goldgulden (G) N.D.
Type of #18 (minted in 1843)   237.50

20.   1 New Year's Goldgulden (G) N.D. As
#18. Rev. Arms within two laurel
branches dividing s.p.q.w. (minted
about 1843)   225.00

21.   1 New Year's Goldgulden (G) N.D. As
#18, but LUDWIG I   875.00

MAXIMILIAN II OF BAVARIA, 1848–64

22.   1 New Year's Goldgulden (G) N.D.
Head right, c.v. below, MAXIMILIAN
II. Rev. City view, s.p.q.w.   275.00

23.   1 New Year's Goldgulden (G) N.D. As
#22. Rev. Arms dividing s.p.q.w.,
two laurel branches below   275.00

LUDWIG II OF BAVARIA, 1864–86

24.   1 New Year's Goldgulden (G) N.D.
Head right, LUDWIG II. Rev. City
view, s.p.q.w.   375.00

25.   1 New Year's Goldgulden (G) N.D. As
#24. Rev. Arms dividing s.p.q.w.   375.00

LUDWIG III OF BAVARIA, 1912–18

26.   1 New Year's Goldgulden (G) N.D.
Head left, LUDWIG III. Rev. St. Kilian,
ORE ET CORDE s.p.q.w., city *view in
background   —

GERMANY (Empire)

Many of the German states united themselves economically and politically in the 1834 Customs Union (*Zollverein*) and the 1866 North German Confederation (*Norddeutscher Bund*). The southern states signed treaties with the Confederation in 1870 and the German Empire (*Deutsches Reich*) came into being. King Wilhelm I of Prussia was proclaimed emperor on January 18, 1871. The newly federated state received a constitution on April 16, 1871, which defined rights, boundaries and established a monetary system. The 25 member states—the kingdoms of Prussia, Bavaria, Saxony and Wurttemberg; the grand duchies of Baden, Hesse, Mecklenburg-Schwerin, Saxe-Weimar, Mecklenburg-Strelitz and Oldenburg; the duchies of Brunswick, Saxe-Meiningen, Saxe-Altenburg, Saxe-Coburg-Gotha and Anhalt; the principalities of Schwarzburg-Rudolstadt, Schwarzburg-Sonderhausen, Waldeck-Pyrmont, Reuss-Elder Line; Reuss-Younger Line; Schaumburg-Lippe and Lippe; the free cities of Lubeck, Bremen and Hamburg—were granted the right to issue their own 2, 3 and 5-mark silver coins and 5, 10 and 20-mark gold pieces, all with a common reverse design featuring an imperial eagle (see individual listings). A general issue of minor values from 1 mark to 1 pfennig circulated throughout the states.

World War I (1914–18) ended for Germany with the abolition of the monarchies and the establishment of a republic. The old constitution was abandoned in favor of a new one written in Weimar in 1919. World War II led to the country's partition into West Germany—the German Federal Republic (*Bundesrepublik Deutschland*) and East Germany—the German Democratic Republic (*Deutsche Demokratische Republik*).

Coins for the German Empire and republics have been struck in:

Berlin	Mintmark A
Hannover (until 1878)	B
Vienna (1938–44)	B
Frankfurt (until 1879)	C
Munich	D
Dresden (until 1887)	E
Muldenhutten (1887–1953)	E
Stuttgart	F
Karlsruhe	G
Darmstadt (until 1882)	H
Hamburg	J

Imperial eagles types:
Type 1: 1871–1873; Small eagle, date below, small inscription, value *M*.
Type 2: 1874–1889; Small eagle, date at right edge, larger inscription, value *MARK*
Type 3: 1890–1915; Large eagle and inscription, date at right, value *MARK*

SMALL DENOMINATION COINS FOR CIRCULATION THROUGHOUT THE EMPIRE
(For coins of 2, 3, 5, 10 and 20 mark denomination, see the individual state or city)

1. 1 Mark (S) 1873–87. Type 2 eagle. Rev.
    Value within oak wreath   5.00

1.

2. 1 Mark (S) 1891–1916. Type 3 eagle.
   Rev. Type of #1   1.50

3. 50 Pfennig (S) 1875, 76, 77. Type 2 eagle.
   Rev. Value   13.75

4. 50 Pfennig (S) 1877, 78. Type 2 eagle.
   within oak wreath. Rev. Value within
   oak wreath   22.50

5. 50 Pfennig (S) 1896–1903. Type 2 eagle
   within oak wreath. Rev. Type of #4   100.00

6. ½ Mark (S) 1905–19. Type of #5   .75

7. 25 Pfennig (N) 1909–12. Type 3 eagle.
   Rev. Value within wheat wreath   3.75

8. 20 Pfennig (S) 1873–77. Type 2 eagle.
   Rev. Value   5.00

9. 20 Pfennig (C–N) 1887, 88. Type 2 eagle
   within oak wreath. Rev. Value   7.50

10. 20 Pfennig (C–N) 1890, 92. Type 3 eagle
    within oak wreath. Rev. Type of #9   20.00

11. 10 Pfennig (C–N) 1873–89. Type of #8   1.75

12. 10 Pfennig (C–N) 1890–1916. Type 3
    eagle. Rev. Value   .25

13. 10 Pfennig (I) 1916–22. Type 3 eagle
    within pearl circle. Rev. Value   .50

14. 10 Pfennig (Z) 1917–22. Type of #12   .25

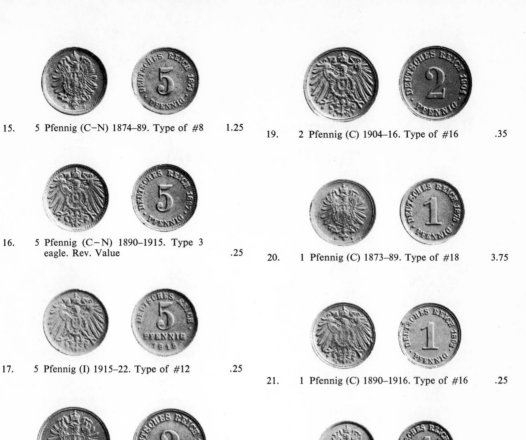

15. 5 Pfennig (C–N) 1874–89. Type of #8   1.25

19. 2 Pfennig (C) 1904–16. Type of #16   .35

16. 5 Pfennig (C–N) 1890–1915. Type 3
     eagle. Rev. Value   .25

20. 1 Pfennig (C) 1873–89. Type of #18   3.75

17. 5 Pfennig (I) 1915–22. Type of #12   .25

21. 1 Pfennig (C) 1890–1916. Type of #16   .25

18. 2 Pfennig (C) 1873–77. Type 2 eagle.
     Rev. Value   3.00

22. 1 Pfennig (Al) 1916, 17, 18. Type of
     #16   .25

GERMANY (Weimar Republic and Totalitarian State)

23. 500 Mark (Al) 1923. Eagle, EINIGKEIT
    UND RECHT UND FREIHEIT—"Unity
    and Right and Freedom." Rev. Value   1.00

26.   5 Reichsmark (S) 1934, 35. Eagle. Rev.
    Garrison church in Potsdam. Edge:
    GEMEINNUTZ GEHT VOR EIGENNUTZ—
    "Group Interest Comes Before Self
    Interest"   3.00

24.   200 Mark (Al) 1923. Type of #23   .75

27.   5 Reichsmark (S) 1935, 36. Head right,
    PAUL VON HINDENBURG. Rev. Eagle
    dividing date. Edge: Type of #26   3.00

25.   5 Reichsmark (S) 1927–33. Eagle.
    Rev. Oak tree, EINIGKEIT UND   50.00

28.   5 Reichsmark (S) 1936–39. As #27.
    Rev. Eagle perched on wreathed
    swastika, dividing value. Edge: Type
    of #26   4.00

29.   3 Mark (Al) 1922. Eagle. Rev. Value   10.00

30.   3 Mark (S) 1924, 25. Type of #29.
Edge: EINIGKEIT UND RECHT UND
FREIHEIT—"Unity and Right and
Freedom"   25.00

35.   1 Reichsmark (S) 1925, 26, 27. Type of
#31   12.50

31.   3 Reichsmark (S) 1931, 32, 33. Eagle.
Rev. Value within oak wreath. Edge:
Type of #30   25.00

36.   1 Reichsmark (N) 1933–39. Value
within oak leaves. Rev. Eagle,
GEMEINNUTZ   2.00

32.   2 Reichsmark (S) 1925–31. Type of
#31. Reeded edge   13.75

37.   50 Pfennig (Al) 1919–22. Value. Rev.
Wheat sheaf with inscription: SICH
REGEN BRINGT SEGEN   .25

33.   2 Reichsmark (S) 1936–39. Type of
#28   2.00

38.   50 Rentenpfennig (C) 1923, 24. 50 in
diamond shape with oak leaves, value
below. Rev. Stylized wheat stalks   12.50

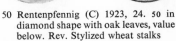

39. 50 Reichspfennig (C) 1924, 25. Type of
#38 275.00

40. 50 Reichspfennig (N) 1927–38. Eagle in
circle, two oak branches and date
below. Rev. Oak leaves above, 50 in
circle 2.50

41. 50 Reichspfennig (Al) 1935. Eagle. Rev.
Value above two oak leaves 2.00

42. 50 Reichspfennig (N) 1938, 39. Eagle
perched on circle with swastika,
DEUTSCHES REICH. above, oak leaves
below. Rev. Oak leaves below value
in circle 25.00

43. 50 Reichspfennig (Al) 1939–44. As #42,
but inscription above, no leaves. Rev.
Type of #41 .75

44. 10 Rentenpfennig (C) 1923–25. Type of
#38 1.00

45. 10 Reichspfennig (C) 1924–36. Type of
#38 .50

46. 10 Reichspfennig (C) 1936–39. Eagle
perched on wreath with swastika.
Rev. Value above two oak leaves .75

47. 10 Reichspfennig (Z) 1940–45. Type of
#43 .50

48. 5 Rentenpfennig (C) 1923, 24, 25. 5 in
diamond shape with oak leaves, value
below. Rev. Stylized wheat stalks .75

49. 5 Reichspfennig (C) 1924–36. Type of
#48 .50

300 • Germany (Weimar Republic and Totalitarian State)

50. 5 Reichspfennig (C) 1936–39. Type of
    #43 .65

51. 5 Reichspfennig (Z) 1940–44. Type of
    #43 .50

52. 4 Reichspfennig (C) 1932. Eagle. Rev.
    Value 5.00

53. 2 Rentenpfennig (C) 1923, 24. Value
    within circle. Rev. Sheaf of wheat
    dividing date 1.25

54. 2 Reichspfennig (C) 1923–36. Type of
    #53 .75

55. 2 Reichspfennig (C) 1936–40. Type of
    #46 .50

56. 1 Rentenpfennig (C) 1924, 25, 29. Type
    of #53 1.50

57. 1 Reichspfennig (C) 1924–36. Type of
    #53 .50

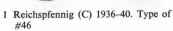

58. 1 Reichspfennig (C) 1936–40. Type of
    #46 .35

59. 1 Reichspfennig (Z) 1940–45. Eagle.
    Rev. Value with two oak leaves below .50

Germany (Weimar Republic and Totalitarian State) • **301**

60.   5 Reichsmark (S) 1925. Standing knight with eagle shield dividing date, JAHRTAUSEND FEIER. Rev. Value within oak wreath. Edge: EINIGKEIT UND RECHT UND FREIHEIT   70.00

Commemorates the 1000th anniversary of the Rhineland.
(See also #73.)

63.   5 Reichsmark (S) 1929. Head left dividing 1729 1929, GOTTH. EPHRAIM LESSING. Rev. Eagle   75.00

Commemorates the 200th anniversary of the birth of Lessing.
(See also #82.)

61.   5 Reichsmark (S) 1927. Three-masted ship, Bremer arms dividing date, HUNDERT JAHRE BREMERHAVEN. Rev. Eagle shield, eight-sided scrollwork in background. Edge: NAVIGARE NECESSE EST—"It is Necessary to Navigate"   137.50

Commemorates the 100th anniversary of Bremerhaven.
(See also #75.)

64.   5 Reichsmark (S) 1929. Man holding shields of Burg and Meissen dividing date, TAUSEND JAHRE BURG. Rev. Eagle   187.50

Commemorates the 1000th anniversary of Meissen.
(See also #84.)

62.   5 Reichsmark (S) 1927. Bust left, 450 JAHRE UNIVERSITAT. Rev. Eagle, DEUTSCHES REICH 1927. Edge: Type of #60   300.00

Commemorates the 450th anniversary of the University of Tubingen.
(See also #77.)

65.   5 Reichsmark (S) 1929. Head left, HINDENBURG REICHS-PRASIDENT. Rev. Hand in oath, TREU DER VERFASSUNG —"Loyal to the Constitution"   67.50

Commemorates the 10th anniversary of the Weimar Constitution.
(See also #85.)

66. 5 Reichsmark (S) 1930. Graf Zeppelin
over globe, GRAF ZEPPELIN WELTFLUG
1929. Rev. Eagle   100.00

Commemorates the world flight of
the Graf Zeppelin.
(See also #86.)

69. 5 Reichsmark (S) 1933. Head left,
1483–1933 below, MARTIN LUTHER.
Rev. Eagle. Edge: EIN FESTE BURG IST
UNSERER GOTT—"A Firm Mountain
is Our God"   67.50

Commemorates the 450th anniversary of the birth of Luther.
(See also #92.)

67. 5 Reichsmark (S) 1930. Eagle standing
on bridge, separating date, DER
RHEIN. Rev. Eagle shield, three half-
circles in background   95.00

Commemorates the evacuation of
the Rhineland.
(See also #88.)

70. 5 Reichsmark (S) 1934. Garrison
church in Potsdam dividing 21. MARZ
1933. Rev. Eagle dividing 19 34.
Edge: GEMEINNUTZ GEHT VOR EIGEN-
NUTZ—"Group Interest Comes Be-
fore Self Interest"   10.00

Marks the first anniversary of Nazi
rule.
(See also #93.)

68. 5 Reichsmark (S) 1932. Head left,
GOETHE below. Rev. Eagle dividing
1832 1932. Edge: ALLEN GEWALTEN
ZUM TRUTZ SICH ERHALTEN—"All
Power of Authority Should be Kept
for Maintaining Defense"   700.00

Commemorates the 100th anniversary of the death of Goethe.
(See also #91.)

71. 5 Reichsmark (S) 1934. Head left,
FRIEDRICH SCHILLER. Rev. Eagle.
Edge: ANS VATERLAND ANS TEURE
SCHLIESS DICH AN—"Adhere to the
Fatherland, the Dear One"   70.00

Commemorates the 175th anniversary of the birth of Schiller.
(See also #94.)

72.　3 Mark (Al) 1922, 23. Eagle, VER-
FASSUNGSTAG. Rev. Value　　　　1.00

Marks the third anniversary of the
Weimar Constitution.

76.　3 Reichsmark (S) 1927. Enthroned
royal couple, eagle shield dividing
19 27, NORDHAUSEN. Rev. Value on
six-sided scrolled background. Edge:
Type of #74　　　　　　　　87.50

Commemorates the 1000th anniversary of Nordhausen.

73.　3 Reichsmark (S) 1925. Type of #60　35.00

77.　3 Reichsmark (S) 1927. Type of #62　125.00

74.　3 Reichsmark (S) 1926. Eagle on
shield, LVEBECK. Rev. Value, two oak
branches below. Edge: EINIGKEIT UND
RECHT UND FREIHEIT　　　　75.00

Commemorates the 700th anniversary of Lubeck.

78.　3 Reichsmark (S) 1927. Hessian arms,
inscription: PHILIPPS UNIVERSITAET
MARBURG 1527–1927. Rev. Eagle.
Edge: Type of #74　　　　　75.00

Commemorates the 400th anniversary of the University of Marburg.

79.　3 Reichsmark (S) 1928. Bust left,
ALBRECHT DVRER GEDENKJAHR. Rev.
Eagle. Edge: EHRT EURE DEUTSCHEN
MEISTER—"Honor Your German
Master"　　　　　　　　137.50

Commemorates the 400th anniversary of the death of Durer.

75.　3 Reichsmark (S) 1927. Type of #61　75.00

 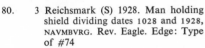   

80.   3 Reichsmark (S) 1928. Man holding shield dividing dates 1028 and 1928, NAVMBVRG. Rev. Eagle. Edge: Type of #74   75.00

Commemorates the 900th anniversary of Naumburg.

84.   3 Reichsmark (S) 1929. Type of #64   50.00

81.   3 Reichsmark (S) 1928. Reaper with scythe, two battlement towers, sheaf of wheat, DINKELSBUHL. Rev. Eagle. Edge: Type of #74   150.00

Commemorates the 1000th anniversary of Dinkelsbuhl.

85.   3 Reichsmark (S) 1929. Type of #65   21.50

86.   3 Reichsmark (S) 1929. Type of #66   42.50

82.   3 Reichsmark (S) 1929. Type of #63   32.50

83.   3 Reichsmark (S) 1929. Eagle with shield, WALDECKS MIT PREUSSEN. Rev. Eagle. Edge: Type of #74   75.00

Commemorates the union of Waldeck and Prussia.

87.   3 Reichsmark (S) 1930. Lyric poet seated with harp, WALTHER VON DER VOGELWEIDE. Rev. Eagle shield on three-sided scrolled background. Edge: EINIGKEIT UND RECHT UND FREIHEIT   50.00

Commemorates the 700th anniversary of the death of Vogelweide.

Germany (Weimar Republic and Totalitarian State) • **305**

| 88. | 3 Reichsmark (S) 1930. Type of #67 | 25.00 |
| 91. | 3 Reichsmark (S) 1932. Type of #68 | 67.50 |

92.   2 Reichsmark (S) 1933. Type of #69   12.50

89.   3 Reichsmark (S) 1931. City view, arms dividing 1631 and 1931, MAGDEBURG. Rev. Eagle shield on eight-sided scrolled background. Edge: Type of #87   90.00

Commemorates the 300th anniversary of the rebuilding of Magdeburg.

93.   2 Reichsmark (S) 1934. Type of #70   6.25

90.   3 Reichsmark (S) 1931. Head left, STEIN. Rev. Eagle dividing 1831 1931. Edge: Type of #87   67.50

Commemorates the 100th anniversary of the death of vom Stein.

94.   2 Reichsmark (S) 1934. Type of #71   25.00

GERMANY (Allied Occupation)

95.   10 Reichspfennig (Z) 1945–48. Eagle. Rev. Value, two oak leaves below   6.25

99.   50 Pfennig (C–N) 1949, 50. Value, BANK DEUTSCHER LANDER. Rev. Kneeling maiden planting oak tree   3.00

96.   5 Reichspfennig (Z) 1947, 48. Type of #95   6.25

100.   10 Pfennig (I, brass clad) 1949. Five-leafed oak branch, BANK DEUTSCHER LANDER. Rev. Value, wheat stalks   .50

97.   1 Reichspfennig (Z) 1944. After the occupation, a small quantity of pfennig pieces were minted (in Munich, 1945) with the die of 1944 after removing the swastika   500.00

101.   5 Pfennig (I, brass clad) 1949. Type of #100   .50

98.   1 Reichspfennig (Z) 1945, 46. Type of #95   12.50

102.   1 Pfennig (I, copper clad) 1948, 49. Type of #100   .90

GERMAN FEDERAL REPUBLIC
(West Germany)

103.   5 Deutsche Mark (S) 1951–date. Value.
       Rev. Eagle. Edge: EINIGKEIT UND
       RECHT UND FREIHEIT   1.35

110.   2 Deutsche Mark (C–N) 1951. Eagle.
       Rev. Value between wheat stalks,
       grapes and leaves. Edge: Type of
       #103   12.50

111.   2 Deutsche Mark (C–N) 1957–date.
       Eagle. Rev. Head left, MAX PLANCK
       1858–1947. Edge: Type of #103   .65

120.   1 Deutsche Mark (C–N) 1950–date.
       Eagle. Rev. Value within two oak
       leaves. Reeded edge   .30

130.   50 Pfennig (C–N) 1950–date. As #99,
       but BUNDESREPUBLIK   .15

140.   10 Pfennig (I, brass clad) 1950–date. As
       #100, but BUNDESREPUBLIK   .05

150.   5 Pfennig (I, brass clad) 1950–date.
       Type of #140   .05

160.   2 Pfennig (C) 1950–date. Type of #140   .05

170.   1 Pfennig (I, copper clad) 1950–date.
       Type of #140   .05

200. 10 Deutsche Mark (S) 1969. Spiraling beams, SPIELE DER XX OLYMPIADE. Rev. Eagle. Edge: ALTIUS FORTIUS CITIUS 8.75

Honors the 20th Olympic Games to be held in Germany in 1972.

210. 5 Deutsche Mark (S) 1952. Stylized eagle dividing 1852 and 1952, GERMANISCHES MUSEUM. Rev. Eagle. Edge: Type of #103 150.00

Commemorates the 100th anniversary of the Nurnberg Museum.

211. 5 Deutsche Mark (S) 1955. Head right, FRIEDRICH VON SCHILLER. Rev. Eagle. Edge: SEID EINIG EINIG EINIG—"Be United, United, United" 112.50

Commemorates the 150th anniversary of the death of Schiller.

212. 5 Deutsche Mark (S) 1955. Bust right, VON BADEN. Rev. Eagle, castle in background. Edge: SCHILD DES REICHES—"Shield of the Empire" 125.00

Commemorates the 300th anniversary of the birth of von Baden.

213. 5 Deutsche Mark (S) 1957. Head left, VON EICHENDORFF. Rev. Eagle. Edge: GRUSS DICH DEUTSCHLAND AUS HERZENSGRUND 100.00

Commemorates the 100th anniversary of the death of von Eichendorff.

214. 5 Deutsche Mark (S) 1964. Head left, FICHTE. Rev. Eagle. Edge: NUR DAS MACHT GLUECKSELIG WAS GUT IST— "Only that Which is Good Makes One Radiant" 45.00

Commemorates the 150th anniversary of the death of Fichte.

215. 5 Deutsche Mark (S) 1966. Head front, LEIBNIZ. Rev. Eagle. Edge: MAGNUM TOTIUS GERMANIAE DECUS 15.00

Commemorates the 250th anniversary of the death of Leibniz.

German Federal Republic (West Germany) • **309**

216. 5 Deutsche Mark (S) 1967. Conjoined heads left, WILHELM UND ALEXANDER. Rev. Eagle. Edge: FREIHEIT ERHOEHT ZWANG ERSTICKT UNSERE KRAFT— "Liberty Lifts Up Force, Suffocates our Strength"   12.50

Commemorates the Humboldt brothers on the 200th anniversary of the birth of Wilhelm von Humboldt.

219. 5 Deutsche Mark (S) 1968. Bust right, GUTENBERG. Rev. Eagle. Edge: GESEGNET SEI WER DIE SCHRIFT ERFAND— "Blessed Be He Who Invented the Movable Type"   6.25

Commemorates the 500th anniversary of the death of Gutenberg.

217. 5 Deutsche Mark (S) 1968. Bust front, RAIFFEISEN. Rev. Eagle. Edge: EINER FUR ALLE ALLE FUR EINEN—"One for All, All for One"   6.25

Commemorates the 150th anniversary of the birth of Raiffeisen.

220. 5 Deutsche Mark (S) 1969. Head left, FONTANE. Rev. Eagle. Edge: DER FREIE NUR IST TREU—"Only the Truth Is Faithful"   5.50

Commemorates the 150th anniversary of the birth of Fontane.

218. 5 Deutsche Mark (S) 1968. Head right, PETTENKOFER. Rev. Eagle. Edge: HYGIENE STREBT, DER UBEL WURZEL AUSZUROTTEN—"Hygiene Endeavors to Destroy the Roots of Evil"   6.25

Commemorates the 150th anniversary of the birth of Pettenkofer.

221. 5 Deutsche Mark (S) 1969. Head right, GERHARD MERCATOR, with Mercator map projection in background. Rev. Eagle. Edge: TERRAE DESCRIPTIO AD USUM NAVIGANTIUM   3.75

GERMAN DEMOCRATIC REPUBLIC
(East Germany)

The German Democratic Republic was created in 1949 out of the Russian zone of occupation.

240. 2 Mark (Al) 1957. Value between two oak leaves. Rev. Arms .50

241. 1 Mark (Al) 1956, 62. Type of #240 .25

242. 50 Pfennig (C) 1950. Value. Rev. Plow in front of industrial plant 2.00

243. 50 Pfennig (Al) 1958. Oak leaf over value. Rev. Type of #240 .20

244. 20 Pfennig (Al, Br) 1969. Value. Rev. Type of #240 .15

245. 10 Pfennig (Al) 1948, 49, 50. Value, DEUTSCHLAND. Rev. Corn in front of cog wheel .75

246. 10 Pfennig (Al) 1952, 53. As #245. Rev. Hammer within two corn stalks .40

247. 10 Pfennig (Al) 1963–68. Type of #243 .15

248. 5 Pfennig (Al) 1948, 49, 50. Type of #245 .50

249. 5 Pfennig (Al) 1952, 53. Type of #246 .50

250. 5 Pfennig (Al) 1968. Type of #240 .15

251. 1 Pfennig (Al) 1948, 49, 50. Type of #245 .75

252. 1 Pfennig (Al) 1952, 53. Type of #246 .50

253. 1 Pfennig (Al) 1960–68. Type of #241 .15

260. 20 MDN (S) 1966. Bust right, LEIBNIZ, artist's signature behind bust: RD. Rev. Arms. Edge: 20 MARK DER DEUTSCHEN NOTENBANK 17.50

Commemorates the 250th anniversary of the death of Leibniz.

261. 20 MDN (S) 1967. Bust left, HUMBOLDT, artist's signature at truncation, R4. Rev. Type of #260 17.50

Commemorates the 200th anniversary of the birth of Humboldt.

262. 20 Mark (S) 1968. Head left, KARL MARX, artist's signature below, R4. Rev. Type of #260. Edge: 20 MARK three times 17.50

Commemorates the 150th anniversary of the birth of Marx.

German Democratic Republic (East Germany) • **313**

263.   20 Mark (S) 1969. Bust left, VON GOETHE, artist's signature behind bust, F4. Rev. Type of #260. Edge: As #262   15.00

Commemorates the 220th anniversary of the birth of Goethe.

272.   10 Mark (S) 1968. G dividing 1468, JOHANN GUTENBERG and inverted G below. Rev. Type of #260. Edge: Type of #262, but value 10   8.75

Commemorates the 500th anniversary of the death of Gutenberg.

270.   10 MDN (S) 1966. Head right, SCHINKEL, artist's signature in front of throat, R4. Rev. Type of #260. Edge: As #260, but value 10   10.00

Commemorates the 125th anniversary of the death of Schinkel.

273.   10 Mark (S) 1969. Pitcher made of Boettger porcelain with hallmark of two crossed swords dividing 1682 and 1719. Rev. Type of #260. Edge: Type of #272   7.50

Commemorates the 250th anniversary of the death of Bottger.

271.   10 MDN (S) 1967. Head left, KATHE KOLLWITZ, artist's signature below hair, R4. Rev. Type of #260. Edge: As #270 with rosette before value   10.00

Commemorates the 100th anniversary of the birth of Kollwitz.

280.   5 Mark (N–S) 1968. Bust left, ROBERT KOCH, artist's signature behind bust, R4. Rev. Type of #262   4.50

Commemorates the 125th anniversary of the birth of Koch.

281.   5 Mark (N–S) 1969. Head right, HEIN-
        RICH HERTZ. Rev. Type of #260.
        Edge: Type of #262 but value 5   3.75
        Commemorates the 75th anniversary
        of the death of Hertz.

282.   5 Mark (C–N) 1969. XX JAHRE DDR
        1969. Rev. Arms. Edge: Type of
        #281   3.00
        Commemorates the 20th anniversary
        of the German Peoples Republic.

GERMAN OCCUPATION ISSUES

WORLD WAR I, 1914–18
(Latvia, Estonia, Lithuania)

300.   3 Kopecks (I) 1916. Four oak branches
around GEBIET DES OBERBEFEHLS-
HABERS OST—"District of the Eastern
Military Command." Rev. Iron cross
inscribed with Russian letters 3
KOPEIKI 1916   2.00

301.   2 Kopecks (I) 1916. Type of #300   1.50

302.   1 Kopeck (I) 1916. Type of #300   1.00

WORLD WAR II, 1939–45

303.   10 Reichspfennig (Z) 1940, 41. Swastika,
date. Rev. Eagle over oak leaves,
holed planchet   10.00

304.   5 Reichspfennig (Z) 1940, 41. Type of
#303   11.25

GERMAN COLONIES

GERMAN NEW GUINEA (Protectorate)

In 1884, the German New Guinea Company, through treaties with the natives, acquired Kaiser Wilhelm Land on the island of New Guinea and the Bismarck archipelago. The empire itself took over administration as a protectorate in 1889 and in the following years expanded the territory by acquiring Palau, the Carolines, the Marianas and the Marshall Islands. After World War I the territories were given as League of Nations mandates to Japan, Britain and Australia. The land is now the Territory of New Guinea, a United Nations Trusteeship.

Coins for German New Guinea were struck in Berlin: Mintmark A

305.   20 New Guinea Mark (G) 1895. 20 NEU GUINEA MARK 1895 within palm wreath. Rev. Bird of Paradise   1,050.00

306.   10 New Guinea Mark (G) 1895. Type of #305   1,150.00

307.   5 New Guinea Mark (S) 1894. Type of #305   237.50

308.   2 New Guinea Mark (S) 1894. Type of #305   75.00

309.   1 New Guinea Mark (S) 1894. Type of #305   52.50

310.   ½ New Guinea Mark (S) 1894. Type of #305   60.00

311.   10 New Guinea Pfennig (C) 1894. Type of #305   25.00

312.   2 New Guinea Pfennig (C) 1894. Two
       crossed palm leaves below NEU-
       GUINEA COMPAGNIE. Rev. Value   25.00

313.   1 New Guinea Pfennig (C) 1894. Type
       of #312   21.25

GERMAN EAST AFRICA COMPANY (Protectorate)

Through treaties made with native chiefs in 1885, the German East Africa Company obtained control over large territories. The borders were defined in 1890 by a treaty with England. Administration of the territory was taken over by the empire in 1891. After World War I, the area passed as a mandate to England and Belgium.

Coins for German East Africa were struck in:
Berlin	Mintmark A
Hamburg	J
Tabora (1916)	T

317.   ¼ Rupie (S) 1891, 98, 1901. Type of
       #314   20.00

314.   2 Rupien (S) 1893, 94. Uniformed,
       helmeted bust of Kaiser Wilhelm II,
       left. Rev. Shield with lion, palms,
       date, DEUTSCH OSTAFRIKANISCHE GE-
       SELLSCHAFT   150.00

318.   1 Pesa (C) 1890, 91, 92. Type 2 eagle.
       Rev. Swahili inscription within laurel
       wreath   3.75

315.   1 Rupie (S) 1890–1902. Type of #314   17.50

319.   1 Rupie (S) 1904–14. As #314. Rev.
       Value and date within two palm
       branches   12.50

316.   ½ Rupie (S) 1891, 97, 1901. Type of
       #314   21.25

320.   ½ Rupie (S) 1904–14. Type of #319   30.00

325.   1 Heller (C) 1904–13. Type of #323   2.50

321.   ¼ Rupie (S) 1904–14. Type of #319   12.50

326.   ½ Heller (C) 1904, 05, 06. Type of #323   5.00

EMERGENCY MONEY

322.   10 Heller (C–N) 1908–14. Crowned divided date, DEUTSCH OST-AFRIKA. Rev. Value, two laurel branches, holed planchet   10.00

327.   15 Rupien (G) 1916. Type 3 eagle. Rev. Landscape with elephant, date below   162.50

328.   20 Heller (C, Bra) 1916. Broad crown, date and DOA. Rev. Value within two crossed branches with three leaves on lower stem   9.00

329.   20 Heller (C–Bra) 1916. As #328, but one leaf on stem on reverse   3.00

330.   20 Heller (C–Bra) 1916. As #328, but narrow crown   11.25

323.   5 Heller (C) 1908, 09. Crowned, undivided date, DEUTSCH OSTAFRIKA. Rev. Value within laurel wreath   18.75

331.   20 Heller (C–Bra) 1916. Type of #330. Rev. Type of #329   2.50

324.   5 Heller (C–N) 1913, 14. Type of #322   11.25

332.   5 Heller (Bra) 1916. Type of #328   7.50

KIAUTSCHOU (Leased Territory)

When two German missionaries were assassinated in 1897, German troops occupied this area on the Shantung peninsula of eastern China. In 1898, a 99-year lease was negotiated but the territory was turned over to Japan after World War I. The Japanese returned control to China in 1922.

Coins for Kiautschou were struck in Berlin.

333. 10 Cent (C–N) 1909. Eagle on anchor, Value, DEUTSCH KIATSCHOU GEBIET. Rev. Chinese inscription 25.00

334. 5 Cent (C–N) 1909. Type of #333 25.00

SAARLAND

After the Second World War, the Saar district (Saarland since 1947) was put under French administration. Voting against becoming autonomous in 1956, the district was rejoined to Germany (*Bundesrepublik Deutschland*) in 1957.

Coins for Saarland were struck in Paris.

335. 100 Franken (C–N) 1955. Arms within circle, SAARLAND around rim. Rev. Value 3.75

337. 20 Franken (Al–C) 1954. Type of #336 2.50

336. 50 Franken (Al–C) 1954. Stylized mining area, arms, SAARLAND. Rev. Value 7.00

338. 10 Franken (Al–C) 1954. Type of #336 2.00